CAPE CONFLICT

CAPE CONFLICT

Protests and political alliances in a Dutch settlement

TEUN BAARTMAN

LEIDEN UNIVERSITY PRESS

This version of *Cape Conflict: protests and political alliances in a Dutch settlement* is published by arrangement with UCT Press, and is for sale outside Southern Africa only

Project manager: Mmakasa Ramoshaba
Editor: Martin Rollo
Proofreader: Renee Moodie
Cover designer: Genevieve Simpson
Typesetter: CBT Typesetting & Design
Indexer: Michel Cozien
Lay-out: CBT Typesetting & Design
Cover illustration: VOC ships at the Table Bay

ISBN 978 90 8728 334 6
e-ISBN 978 94 0060 364 6 (e-PDF)
e-ISBN 978 94 0060 365 3 (e-PUB)
NUR 680

This book is distributed in North America by the University of Chicago Press (www.press.uchicago.edu).

CONTENTS

INTRODUCTION

The Dutch presence on the African continent during most of the seventeenth and eighteenth centuries can hardly be called impressive. It consisted of nothing more than a string of strongholds along the West African coast (and a few on islands to the east of the continent). The length of stay of the Dutch varied greatly from place to place. Sometimes the forts outlived their usefulness and were abandoned. At other times they were taken over (by force or by trade) by other European seafaring nations. In some posts, the Dutch stayed for years (as in Elmina in Ghana from 1637 to 1872), but in others just a few months.[1]

The Dutch (and their European counterparts in Africa) were kept in check by surrounding African rulers and residents, who jealously guarded the supply of export goods like ivory, pepper and gold. This trade was soon surpassed by the one in human cargo, as the demand for slaves in the Americas grew. But Dutch power never extended beyond the walls of their forts. The Dutch had to be careful not to do anything to upset their African neighbours. The threat that they could be cut off from inland provisions was ever-present, and if that happened, they would become dependent on a meagre and sporadic supply of food from passing ships. Furthermore, because Europeans at the time had little resistance to tropical diseases, many of them perished — a further incentive to stay within the fort walls.[2] Thus almost none of the Dutch bases in Africa could be described as a settlement, let alone a colony.

This book is about the one exception: The Cape of Good Hope, which could make a plausible claim to be called Dutch Africa. At the Cape, in the southwestern corner of Africa, the Dutch East India Company or *Verenigde Oost-Indische Compagnie* (VOC) managed to build a proper settlement, which it governed from 1652 to 1795. The indigenous population was no match for the military might of the Company, and the temperate climate suited the Dutch residents well and was ideal for cultivation. The VOC authorities decided to release some of their men from their contracts as employees and settle them as *burghers*. These settlers pushed further and further inland, despite reservations from the authorities in the Netherlands

---

1 See a list of Dutch bases in Africa here: Ramerini, M. (n.d.) Africa. List of Dutch colonial forts and possessions. https://www.colonialvoyage.com/africa-list-dutch-colonial-forts-possessions (Accessed 12 April 2019).
2 Emmer, P & Gommans, J. 2012. *Rijk aan de Rand van de Wereld. De Geschiedenis van Nederland Overzee 1600–1800*. Amsterdam: Bert Bakker, 251–264.

about expanding the territory beyond the immediate environs of the central stronghold on the coast of Table Bay.

Cape society was shaped not only by people from the Netherlands (VOC personnel and the burghers) but also by other populations and social groups (like free blacks, the descendants of slaves). Many (if not most) of the VOC personnel came from other European countries. Slaves and political convicts were forcibly brought in from various parts of Africa and from India and Asia. All these nationalities, ethnicities and cultures left their mark.

Was Dutch Africa, therefore, really as Dutch as it seemed? Because of the diversity of its communities, there will always be a disclaimer when referring to Dutch settlements. But there were enough connections and organisational aspects to support the claim that the Cape was essentially a Dutch settlement. It is an important observation, and one that has not been sufficiently recognised in South African historiography about the VOC period.

It is now widely acknowledged that the Cape did not exist in isolation, but that it was actively engaged in a multitude of different networks, one of which was the Dutch world. Yet the 'Dutch connection' remains underexposed. South African historians are generally unfamiliar with Dutch historical studies, which is unfortunate because so much about the Cape can be explained better once put in the context of its Dutch character. The expansion of the settlement and the increasing size of the population created a need for more administrative organisation and rules, for which the institutions of the Netherlands served as examples. The Netherlands and the Cape had the same judicial system, the same administrative bodies, some of the same economic mechanisms, and many of the same social and political customs. Being Dutch had a profound effect on the way in which Cape residents experienced life in their settlement. In the first five chapters, I will elaborate on the Dutch-ness of the Cape settlement.

The Dutch character of the Cape had far-reaching consequences for the local political dynamics, which is what I will show in the remainder of the book. This was certainly true for the members of the two groups around whom this book is centred: Company officials and burghers, especially those operating in the middle and higher layers of Cape society. This is a story about the elite of the Cape. The Cape residents who dwelt in the higher social and political circles were undoubtedly closer to the Dutch experience than other inhabitants of the settlement. Both VOC officials and burghers had many kinds of connections with the Netherlands. Because of that, Cape burghers, as they developed their sense of belonging, saw themselves as equal to the burghers of Dutch towns and cities and felt that they should be afforded the same rights and privileges. This was not the view of the powerful Company, which took the position that everyone in its territories was always subject to its supreme power. This disagreement was a constant cause of tension between the VOC government and burghers.

But the burghers were not powerless in their battle against Company constraints. They used the means provided by Dutch traditions of protest to influence policies in their favour and were often quite successful. One of the main tools available to burghers was the petition, which was extensively used in the Netherlands by anybody who wanted to make a change in existing regulations or create new ones. Over time, the practice surrounding the construction, submission and acceptance or rejection of petitions had become broadly accepted in the Dutch political arena. Similarly, throughout the VOC period, Cape burghers used the petition to make their point. The best-known example of this was when they applied for Governor Willem Adriaan van der Stel to be removed from his post at the beginning of the eighteenth century, and were successful.

Another major political conflict erupted in the Cape settlement in the late 1770s. The argument of this book is that this conflict was a natural continuation and outcome of the political dynamics as they had developed at the Cape. Set on the cusp of the dying days of Company rule, it was the last eruption of the ongoing tensions between burghers and Company, but more importantly, of the tensions between leading members of the political establishment.

It is here that I fundamentally disagree with Coenraad Beyers, who wrote an extensive study about the conflict, which has since become known as the uprising of the Cape Patriots.[3] His argument is that the Cape protest movement was an awakening of Afrikaner nationalism in that the burghers who stood against oppression by an unjust ruler became Afrikaners. He then links the event to the Afrikaner uprising against British rule in the nineteenth and early twentieth centuries. This view fitted perfectly with the prevalent political narrative during the apartheid era, but one cannot escape the impression that it was specifically made to fit there. This is, in fact, a perfect example of how history has been abused to further the ideas and agendas of an authoritarian regime.

---

3 Beyers, C. 1967. *Die Kaapse Patriotte gedurende die Laaste Kwart van die Agtiende Eeu en die Voortlewing van hul Denkbeelde.* 2nd ed. Pretoria: Van Schaik.

This book will show that the protestors in the Cape political conflict of the 1770s and 1780s followed in the footsteps of their burgher and Dutch forerunners. I argue that the events of the conflict show that the protests were carried out in the best tradition of Dutch urban politics and revolt. I develop this argument further by examining the social origins of the supporters of the Cape protest movement, who were the middle and upper layers of burgher society. This was the same support base as for protests in Dutch towns and cities.

This is not the end of the story though. In my view, it is too simple to see the conflict as one purely between discontented burghers and an arrogant Company regime. Possible motives for the outbreak of the protests, such as adverse economic conditions or concerns about burgher status, are not enough to explain the scope and impact of the movement. This is not only my opinion, but also that of contemporary observers who had a good understanding of the situation. Joachim van Plettenberg, who was the governor of the Cape of Good Hope from 1771 to 1785 described the group of burghers involved in the protest, who by then were wealthy and powerful farmers and entrepreneurs, as 'matadors'. By this he meant that they were influential and powerful men who worked behind the scenes to whip up emotions among the burghers and mobilise them into action. These men had their own reasons to stir the pot, and none of these had anything to do with a general feeling of discontent or wanting to serve the common good of the community. They were seeking access to the centre of economic and political power for their personal benefit. The striking aspect of this group of men was that they were part of a closely related network of burghers and Company officials. The conflict as it occurred around 1780 was in fact an ordinary fight for the spoils between members of the ruling elite; and this was nothing unusual in the Dutch political world.

The view of Coenraad Beyers that the burgher protesters were Afrikaner Patriots fighting to liberate themselves from an oppressor is still held. But it is outdated. What happened at the Cape must be placed in the context of Dutch history and then the pieces fit together much more comfortably.

CHAPTER 1

From refreshment to settlement

The publication of the *Itinerario* by Jan Huygen van Linschoten in 1596 was a watershed in Dutch history and, by extension, in South African history. The book was an account of Van Linschoten's travels to East Asia with the Portuguese, describing the people and countries he had visited and providing information on merchandise and trade. It came at a time when Dutch merchants were finding that the trading and cargo shipping markets in the North Sea and Baltic areas were saturated. They were looking for new business opportunities. The *Itinerario* opened the lucrative world of East Asia to the merchants in the most tangible way possible.[1] They pounced on the second part of the document, the *Reys-gheschrift*, the actual itinerary, which contained detailed sailing instructions for all the routes from Europe around Africa to the Indian Ocean and Asia. Once fiercely guarded by the Portuguese, the secrets of these routes were now finally revealed. A preview of the *Reys-gheschrift* was given to Cornelis de Houtman in 1595 as he was about to embark on a voyage to Asia with a small fleet.

This first expedition was somewhat disastrous and not nearly as profitable as expected, but its major achievement was that it demonstrated that Dutch seafarers could do what so far only the Portuguese had done. Van Linschoten's *Itinerario* and De Houtman's journey together opened a new frontier and contributed greatly to the start of the Dutch Golden Age.[2]

The number of Dutch shipping companies and fleets going to the East and coming back with spices for the European markets increased tremendously. In the seven years between 1595 and 1602, no fewer than 65 Dutch ships (in 14 fleets) were sent to the East, whereas the former maritime giant Portugal managed to send only 59 ships in a decade (1591–1601). But while the Dutch dealt a decisive blow to their Portuguese competitors, a new threat emerged in the form of the British East India Company, which was established in 1600. At the same time, the many small Dutch trading companies were becoming victims of their own success,

---

1 Huygen van Linschoten, J. 1596. *Itinerario, Voyage ofte Schipvaert van Jan Huygen van Linschoten naar Oost ofte Portugaeis Indien.* Amsterdam: Cornelis Claesz.
2 Saldanha, A. 2010. The itineraries of geography: Jan Huygen van Linschoten's *Itinerario* and Dutch expeditions to the Indian Ocean, 1594–1602. *Annals of the Association of American Geographers* 101(1): 149–177.

because the supply of spices had increased to such an extent that prices and profits were rapidly decreasing. To survive economically, and to be able to continue to dominate the Asian spice trade, it now became vital for the Netherlands to bring internal competition under control. The political leadership of the United Netherlands recognised the potential of bringing rival Dutch trading companies together as a formidable weapon against competitor European nations like Spain, Portugal and England. The Dutch merchants were forced to accept the formation of the United Dutch East India Company or *Verenigde Oost-Indische Compagnie* (VOC) in March 1602. This Company, the world's first public company formally listed on a stock exchange, became enormously successful and it sent more ships to the East than its British, French, Portuguese and Scandinavian competitors combined. Soon more than half of the total number of European ships rounding the Cape of Good Hope were Dutch.[3]

The ships brought the wonderful mysteries of the East and untold prosperity to the Netherlands, which in turn inspired great achievements in arts and science. The Dutch Golden Age of the seventeenth century has become etched in collective memory as a period of triumph. But beneath the glittering surface of profit and success was a decidedly foul world of exploitation and misery.[4] For the sailors and soldiers in the service of the VOC life was harsh and unbearable. Their quarters on the ships were before the mast, cramped and overcrowded, without any form of privacy. There was a constant overpowering stench of sweaty, unwashed bodies and dirty clothes, intensified by human waste, because most men relieved themselves wherever they could. Their daily diet consisted of rock-hard biscuits, beans, stock-fish and heavily salted meat, and lacked any fresh fruit or vegetables. It did not take long for the food to rot and to become infested with insects. Weevils had to be knocked out of the biscuits before they could be eaten. Water and beer turned green with algae, and after a while swam with worms. The men had to put up with all kinds of pests, like fleas, bed lice, cockroaches and rats. It is not surprising that many became sick in these circumstances, especially because a considerable number of them

---

3 Gaastra, FS. 1991. *De Geschiedenis van de VOC*. Zutphen: Walburg Pers, 13–20; Gaastra, FS & Bruijn, JR. 1993. The Dutch East India Company's shipping, 1602–1795, in a comparative perspective. In FS Gaastra & JR Bruijn (eds). *Ships, Sailors and Spices. East India Companies and Their Shipping in the 16th, 17th and 18th Centuries*. Amsterdam: NEHA, 177–182.

4 This section is about the men employed by the VOC in the lowest positions, their life on board Company ships and the health reasons for the establishment of a refreshment post. This does not mean to exclude or deny the many other negative aspects of the Dutch seaborne empire: colonial oppression, raids, violence and, above all, slavery.

were poor and malnourished to start with and thus had weak immune systems. Common illnesses were colds, pneumonia, typhus, dysentery and venereal diseases. Since the sick could not be isolated, infections spread rapidly in the confined conditions. Nutritional deficiencies particularly of Vitamin C, led to scurvy, which resulted in bleeding gums, sores, internal bleeding and fever, and if left untreated, in death. The mortality rate on the VOC ships bound for Asia averaged 6.7 per cent in the seventeenth century and 7.3 per cent in the eighteenth (with outliers of 20 per cent between 1690 and 1695, and 23 per cent in the years 1770–1775). The men had to endure the awful conditions for about eight months, which was the typical duration of a voyage from the Netherlands to Batavia, the VOC headquarters in Asia. Behind the mast were the more comfortable quarters of the officers, passengers and VOC officials. While looking down on the human misery of the sailors one of them wondered why they did not drown themselves rather than live as they did.[5]

Medical knowledge and treatment of the various diseases that VOC personnel succumbed to were limited, but experience had taught that a varied and proper diet could work wonders.[6] In 1647 the Dutch ship *Haerlem* was stranded in Table Bay. Several men and cargo were left behind to be picked up by the next fleet on its way to the Netherlands eight months later. Once back in the Netherlands two of the men were asked to submit a report about the possibilities and benefits of creating a permanent settlement, to the Heeren XVII, the central managing board of directors of the VOC. The two men, Leendert Jansz and Matthijs Proot, handed in their *Remonstrantie* (Memorandum) on 26 July 1649.[7] They claimed that a large variety of vegetables and fruit could be grown in the Cape, and stated: 'Just consider, honourable Gentlemen, when all the aforementioned fruits are obtained in abundance, how many sick, through God's merciful blessings,

---

5 Boxer, CR. 1973. *The Dutch Seaborne Empire, 1600–1800.* Harmondsworth: Penguin Books, 82–87; Dash, M. 2002. *De Ondergang van de Batavia. Het Ware Verhaal.* Amsterdam/Antwerpen: de Arbeiderspers, 104–117; Schoeman, K. 2004. *'n Duitser aan die Kaap, 1724–1765. Die Lewe en Loopbaan van Hendrik Schoeman.* Pretoria: Protea, 116–128; Van Gelder, R. 1997. *Het Oost-Indisch Avontuur. Duitsers in Dienst van de VOC (1600–1800).* Nijmegen: SUN, 157–172.

6 For medical care by the VOC read: Bruijn, I. 2009. *Ship's Surgeons of the Dutch East India Company. Commerce and the Progress of Medicine in the Eighteenth Century.* Leiden: Leiden University Press. It was only by the late eighteenth century that it became generally accepted that a steady supply of Vitamin C and other healthy foods prevented the occurrence of scurvy among sailors.

7 Council of Policy. *Incoming Correspondence C 274*, Cape Town: Western Cape Archives and Record Service (WCARS), 1649.07.26, 14–27.

could be restored to their former health.'[8] Even more so, they added, when the fruit was supplemented with meat, butter, milk and cheese.

To be able to offer fresh produce and water to the crews of the Company ships it was essential to have a stable and consistent supply. Each of the European trading companies had their stations along the route to the East where they could repair and replenish. The French used part of the island of Mauritius, and the Portuguese stopped over in Angola and Mozambique. In the first half of the seventeenth century VOC ships sometimes anchored at Madeira, the Cape Verde Islands, St Helena or the Cape of Good Hope. But before long the small islands in the Atlantic Ocean were unable to supply the growing number of ships and their large crews with sufficient fresh food and drinking water. According to Jansz and Proot, resources at St Helena had been spoiled and ruined through the negligence of ship captains and inconsiderate sailors, whose attitude was: 'Why would I care? There is no chance I will ever come here again.'[9]

The Heeren XVII recognised that it was necessary for the sustainability of VOC shipping to Asia, and for the benefit of the ship crews, to have a halfway stop along the route to refresh resources. The Cape of Good Hope was certainly not unknown to the directors, and suggestions had been made in the past to establish a more permanent post there. The *Remonstrantie* now firmly focused their attention on this remote part of Africa. Jansz and Proot were undeniably enthusiastic about all the Cape had to offer. They pointed out that the soil and climate were good, and that even in the dry season there was water for irrigation. It was possible to grow many kinds of vegetables and fruit there. There were ample fish, birds and game. The indigenous population was friendly and approachable, and, if treated properly, they were happy to barter their cattle and sheep.[10] In later times they might even be employed as servants. Above all, Jansz and Proot mentioned that the operation of a permanent station at the Cape was possible without much financial investment, and had the potential to be profitable. This last point may have clinched the deal for the profit-driven Heeren XVII, and in 1650 the decision was made to establish a provisional post and fort at the Cape.

---

8 Council of Policy. *Incoming Correspondence C 274*, Cape Town: WCARS, 1649.07.26, 15.
9 Council of Policy. *Incoming Correspondence C 274*, Cape Town: WCARS, 1649.07.26, 17.
10 It is remarkable that this opinion on the natural benefits of the Cape did not change during Dutch rule, and that this view of Jansz and Proot was often repeated in documents of reporting VOC officials and protesting burghers alike, right until the political conflict of the 1770s and 1780s. Then, it was not used as an argument for settlement, but to show that existing policies needed to change for all free residents to reap the rewards of this fundamental constitution.

For the Company this station was no more than a utility and therefore had to remain small and adequate. There was no intention of starting a potentially costly expansion into the surrounding territory.

The job of governing this new establishment was first offered to Matthijs Proot, but he declined. The second choice for the position was VOC merchant Jan van Riebeeck. He had worked previously for the Company in Asia but was recalled to the Netherlands after being accused of illegally enriching himself. He was eager to get back in the good graces of the directors and return to Asia, so he accepted his appointment as commander of the Cape, which he regarded as a stepping stone to future greatness and wealth. He left the Netherlands in December 1651 with a small fleet and arrived at the Cape in April 1652.[11]

Van Riebeeck had his work cut out for him. His instructions were clear: establish a fort and post at the Cape, from which it would be possible to supply passing ships with meat, vegetables, water and other necessities, which would restore to health the sick on board.[12] Van Riebeeck and his small contingent of men were immediately put under pressure. The masters of all VOC ships, both outgoing and homecoming, were ordered to call at the Cape to get their provisions.[13] During the years 1651 to 1701 on average 20,6 outgoing and 11,6 homebound Company ships visited the Cape to pick up fresh supplies. Every year, hundreds of men would spend about three weeks at a time there expecting to be fed and looked after properly.[14] The tiny settlement was far from ready to deal with this and it was not long before Van Riebeeck was criticised by captains who complained that there was not enough food for their men.

The optimistic view of Jansz and Proot on relations with the local Cape population, the Khoikhoi, turned out to be unrealistic. The Khoikhoi were used to European strangers visiting their shores, but these had always left once they had what they came for. The Dutch set out to treat the local population with kindness and goodwill, but the Khoikhoi realised that their visitors were overstaying their welcome and they became suspicious of their intentions. The Khoikhoi were not persuaded that an idyllic patron-client

---

11 Böeseken, AJ. 1981. The arrival of Van Riebeeck at the Cape. In CFJ Muller (ed.). *Five Hundred Years. A History of South Africa*. 3rd ed. Pretoria/Cape Town/Johannesburg: H&R Academica, 18–35, 18–21.
12 Council of Policy. *Incoming Correspondence C 274*, Cape Town: WCARS, 1651.03.25, 38.
13 Bruijn, JS, Gaastra, FS & Schöffer, I. 1987. *Dutch-Asiatic Shipping in the 17th and 18th Centuries*. Vol. I. The Hague: Rijks Geschiedkundige Publicatien, 111.
14 Biewenga, A. 1999. *De Kaap de Goede Hoop. Een Nederlandse Vestigingskolonie, 1680–1730*. Amsterdam: B Bakker, 19–20.

relationship, as the Dutch had envisaged, would serve their needs. They were furthermore not inclined to barter their best cattle for the copper and other trinkets on offer. Instead, they sold old and sick beasts, which was acceptable in the beginning, but once the demand for meat increased, the Dutch started to look for healthy livestock for breeding purposes.

The relationship between Dutch and Khoikhoi gradually soured and the descriptions of the Khoikhoi by Dutch observers became less guarded and more negative. From 'friendly natives' they turned into 'godless savages'. The use of this kind of terminology made it more acceptable to treat the Khoikhoi with contempt and subject them to violence.[15] The local VOC officials were not allowed to make slaves of the Khoikhoi, because the Company had strict instructions in place that an indigenous population was not to be enslaved. Instead, the Khoikhoi were to be regarded as trading nations. The original people of the Cape were, in Dutch eyes, a foreign nation, living outside the territory occupied by the Company and settlers. But with the continuous expansion of the settlement, Khoi independence became increasingly difficult to sustain, and many were forced to become labourers for the burghers, working on the farms alongside the slaves. There were no laws governing labour relations with the Khoikhoi and they were not recorded in tax and other official records. However, they appeared in criminal records, which has skewed the picture of them considerably, not only socially, but also in terms of numbers. Despite the lack of systematic records on the Khoikhoi, it has recently been estimated that by the 1780s there were many thousands of them living and working within the borders of the Cape settlement.[16] It is one of the great ironies of history that the first people of the Cape, the Khoikhoi were effectively kept out of the official resolutions and correspondence, inventories, estate accounts and tax rolls of the Company, while the outsiders who occupied their territory featured

---

15 Trotter, HM. 2001. Sailors as scribes: Travel discourse and the (con)textualization of the Khoikhoi at the Cape of Good Hope, 1649–90. *The Journal of African Travel-Writing* Vols 8 & 9: 30–44; Elphick, R. 1985. *Khoikhoi and the Founding of White South Africa.* 2nd ed. Johannesburg: Ravan Press, 95–103.

16 Ulrich, N. 2016. Rethinking citizenship and subjecthood in Southern Africa: Khoesan, labor relations, and the colonial state in the Cape of Good Hope (c. 1652–1815). In E Hunter (ed.). *Citizenship, Belonging and Political Community in Africa: Dialogues between Past and Present.* Athens, Ohio: Ohio University Press, 43–73; Fourie, J & Green, E. March 2013. The missing people: Accounting for indigenous populations in Cape colonial history. *Economic Research Foundation Southern Africa (ERSA) Working Paper 425.*

prominently. The Khoikhoi were literally and figuratively erased from the historical narrative of South Africa.[17]

As a semi-nomadic people, the Khoikhoi were stock farmers who did not engage in any form of agriculture, so to acquire crops Van Riebeeck had to start from nothing. He planned to adopt an intensive form of cultivation, as used in the Netherlands, which involved crop rotation, thorough weeding, and careful manuring. The available manpower could not cope with these demands as well as the extra work of building a fort, stores and other buildings, getting firewood, fishing, looking after cattle, and all the tasks related to the primary refreshment function of the Cape. It was evident that to deliver enough fresh produce, meat and wine, a larger outlay of labour and capital was needed, both of which the Company was hesitant to invest because it wanted the Cape to become self-sufficient.[18] The directors did not want the new settlement to become a costly affair, especially since it did not have anything else of profitable interest to offer.

To solve the labour problem, Van Riebeeck asked that Chinese men be permitted to come to the Cape as free settlers. He had seen the agricultural development of Formosa by Chinese migrants first-hand and was impressed. But the VOC administration in Batavia had shut down this possibility a few years earlier, in 1657, stating that the Chinese would not go voluntarily and that they were unwilling to force Chinese to go to the Cape because it would surely mean an exodus of Chinese from the Dutch Asian territories which the Company could not afford.[19] Another option available to Van Riebeeck was slave labour. Slavery was an accepted practice and widespread in the Dutch Asian territories. But as the local population could not be enslaved, slaves had to be imported, mainly from East Africa, India and Indonesia. And even though slaves were brought to the Cape right from the beginning, these were initially just a handful. It was only later in the seventeenth century

---

17 For a concise investigation into the fate of the Khoikhoi and Khoisan people under Dutch and British colonial administrations see: Adhikari, M. 2010. *The Anatomy of a South African Genocide: The Extermination of the Cape San Peoples.* Cape Town: UCT Press.

18 Guelke, L. 1989. Freehold farmers and frontier settlers, 1657–1780. In R Elphick & H Giliomee (eds). *The Shaping of South African Society, 1652–1840.* 2nd ed. Cape Town: Maskew Miller Longman, 66–108, 69–73; Ross, R. 1989. The Cape of Good Hope and the world economy, 1652–1835. In R Elphick & H Giliomee (eds). *The Shaping of South African Society, 1652–1840.* 2nd ed. Cape Town: Maskew Miller Longman, 243–280, 244.

19 Ward, K. 2009. *Networks of Empire: Forced Migration in the Dutch East India Company.* Cambridge: Cambridge University Press, 142–143.

that the Cape became a more established part of the slave-trading network and larger numbers of slaves became available.[20]

Without the prospect of Chinese immigration and the supply of slaves still at a trickle, Van Riebeeck had to look for yet another solution to his labour shortage. He proposed that agricultural production would be done by men who would be released from Company service and settled as farmers. Through his experience in other VOC settlements in Asia, Van Riebeeck knew about these groups of so-called 'free-burghers'. The Company had allowed some of their employees to settle in the Moluccas, Batavia and Ceylon. The thinking was that these men would form a stable core of settlers in the mix of transient Company employees and indigenous populations. They could supply products that the Company needed, although strict Company control prevented them from becoming competitors. As it turned out, the burghers in Asia hardly fulfilled the Company's vision. Many of them just wanted to gather enough wealth to be able to return to the Netherlands and live there in comfort. They engaged in enterprises that were of no benefit to the Company and often were unlawful so that the VOC administrators had to spend time and energy to try to keep them in check.[21]

Van Riebeeck wanted to carefully select settlers who had an interest in and aptitude for farming, because they would work harder for themselves than they did for the Company. It was cheaper for the VOC to have burghers who were financially independent than paying for the labour of employees and the keeping of slaves. The Company could also reduce the garrison and military expenses because the burghers were expected to contribute to the defence of the settlement. Of course, there were costs incurred in settling and governing the burghers, but these could be offset against the various taxes collected from them. This idea was immediately accepted by the Company leaders. For once, Van Riebeeck and the VOC directors agreed completely. In 1657 the first group of nine Company servants was released from their contracts and granted plots of land on the banks of the Liesbeek River.[22]

Despite the decision to settle a group of burghers, the Company was still against the expansion and large-scale colonisation of the Cape territory.

---

20 Armstrong, JC & Worden, NA. 1989. The slaves, 1652–1834. In R Elphick & H Giliomee (eds). *The Shaping of South African Society, 1652–1840*. 2nd ed. Cape Town: Maskew Miller Longman, 109–183, 110–112.

21 Boxer 1973:242–244; Schutte, GJ. 1989. Company and colonists at the Cape, 1652–1795. In R Elphick & H Giliomee (eds). *The Shaping of South African Society, 1652–1840*. 2nd ed. Cape Town: Maskew Miller Longman, 283–323, 288–290.

22 De Wet, GC. 1981. *Die Vryliede en Vryswartes in die Kaapse Nedersetting, 1657–1707*. Kaapstad: Historiese Publikasie-Vereniging, 5–6.

The directors wanted to stick to the plan of having a small refreshment post and to keep the number of burghers small and contained. There were various ways in which the VOC administration aimed to keep the burghers under control. There were strict terms and conditions to their freedom. They could not engage in any form of private or free trade, and their products could be sold only to the VOC even though the prices the Company paid were pre-determined and often rather low. If a burgher broke the law, he could be re-enlisted in Company service and transferred to another VOC settlement.

Van Riebeeck's successor as commander of the Cape, Zacharias Wagenaer, was decidedly negative towards the burghers. According to him, most of them were lazy and unreliable. He was not inclined to promote their interests and did not hesitate to force several of them back into Company service and banish them from the Cape.[23] The initial difficulties experienced by the burghers and their struggle to make a good living convinced some of them that it was better to leave or go back to Company employ. The number of burghers did not increase significantly during the first two decades after 1657.

But by 1679 there was a shift. In that year, the ultimate symbol of the Dutch permanent settlement, the Castle, was completed, and Simon van der Stel took up his position as the new commander of the Cape. He energetically set out to make the Cape what it was meant to be: a place which provided a constant and sufficient supply of wine, wheat and meat for the Company's ships. In doing so, he also set the first firm steps towards an expansion of the original settlement. During his administration burghers could settle in newly established towns like Stellenbosch, Drakenstein and Franschhoek. Initially, the size of new farmlands was not limited, on condition that the granted land would be cultivated within three years or be lost. The farmers also used large tracts of unallocated land to graze their cattle and sheep, because good grazing was hard to find in the dry Cape area. The Dutch expansion pushed the Khoikhoi further and further out. Van der Stel's policies were successful. Wheat production steadily increased, and so did the output and quality of the wine. In 1685 the VOC directors finally had enough confidence in the sustainability of the Cape and decided to make it a permanent settlement officially and allow more burghers to make it their home. This new policy was demonstrated a few years later when almost

---

23 Böeseken, AJ. 1981. The settlement under the Van der Stels. In CFJ Muller (ed.). *Five Hundred Years. A History of South Africa*. 3rd ed. Pretoria/Cape Town/Johannesburg: H&R Academica, 35–50, 35.

200 French Huguenot refugees were given permission to emigrate from the Netherlands to the Cape. By 1700 there were well over 1 300 burghers.[24]

By that time the Cape's governing bodies had been set up. The position of the burgher group was one step below the ruling VOC officials, but because they were closely related (often literally, through kinship), the Company thought it best to give the burghers a place in the administration.[25] All Dutch posts under VOC rule copied the administrative institutions of the VOC headquarters in Batavia. The Cape government was formed by the Council of Policy, which consisted of the commander (later governor), the *secunde* (second highest official), the cellar master, cashier, warehouse master and the captain of the garrison. Another member of the Council was the independent fiscal (prosecutor). He was directly accountable to the Heeren XVII and did not fall under the command of the governor. The Council of Policy reflected all four civil departments: policy, commerce, human resources and justice. When the Council dealt with crime and transgressions against the law, it acted as the Council of Justice.

Initially, burghers were not represented on the Council of Policy. But after the burgher group was established in 1657 one burgher sat on the Council of Justice in an advisory capacity and only when matters involving burghers were heard. After the first year the number of burgher councillors (*burgerraaden*) was doubled, and in 1676 it was increased to three. They soon developed into a separate body, the Burgher Council, and were gradually given more tasks. They supervised the *ratelwag* (night watch), controlled the burgher butchers and bakers, and took care of the financing of the maintenance of roads and bridges in the town and Cape District. They raised taxes from the burghers in the Cape District to be able to perform these functions.

The burgher councillors served in terms of two years, and when they were not part of the Burgher Council, they served on other administrative boards. They were also often the highest officers in the burgher militia, and elders or deacons of the Church Council of the Dutch Reformed Church. Even though these prominent burghers became part of the administration,

---

24 De Wet 1981:10–23; Böeseken 1981 (Settlement under the Van der Stels):39–43; Guelke 1989:73–75.

25 The sections on Cape administration are based on: Böeseken, AJ. 1981. The Company and its subjects. In CFJ Muller (ed.). *Five Hundred Years. A History of South Africa.* 3rd ed. Pretoria/Cape Town/Johannesburg: H&R Academica, 63–65; Ross, R & Schrikker, A. 2012. The VOC official elite. In N Worden (ed). *Cape Town between East and West. Social Identities in a Dutch Colonial Town.* Cape Town: Jacana, 26–44, 28–29.

the VOC officials remained in control. On all the administrative bodies VOC officials either formed a majority, or the presiding officer, who was always a Company man, had a deciding vote. And above all, the governor had the final say on the appointment of burghers as burgher councillors or members of other governing bodies, which usually meant that the appointees were burghers with a favourable attitude towards the Company government.

The position of burgher councillor at the Cape derived from an institution in towns and cities in the Dutch Republic, where the ruling elite co-opted members of the middle layer of the burgher population into the administrative structures of the cities to obtain their political and economic support.[26] In the Cape settlement, the size of the burgher group grew rapidly, along with their economic influence. It was a group that could not be ignored, and the VOC directors followed the Dutch example by incorporating burghers into the governing structures of the settlement. Without co-operation from the burghers, there was potential for conflict and that was something the Company could do without.

The burgher councillors were awarded a high status in Cape society. The Cape sumptuary laws of 1755 determined that they were equal in rank to a junior merchant in the VOC, which was the third highest rank in the VOC hierarchy.[27] They were therefore allowed to wear gold or silver shoe buckles and their wives could own jewellery up to a certain value and wear clothes made of expensive material. Enormous importance was placed on being recognised with the proper rank and status in Dutch (and thus Cape) society. Arrivals of high officials, inaugurations of governors, funerals of dignitaries, and other such high-profile occasions were very public events and the perfect opportunity to show one's standing to the general populace. Accordingly, the place one was awarded during the proceedings was precisely circumscribed. In the 1760 funeral procession of *secunde* Sergius Swellengrebel, the incumbent burgher councillors were in the 11th position (out of 31) immediately behind various VOC officials, but grouped together with the members of the Council of Justice. Former burgher councillors were placed 17th and came before the captains of the burgher militia and members of the Orphan Chamber and Commission of Civil and Marriage

---

26 Leupen, P. 2002. Burger, stad en zegel: Een verkenning door de Noordelijke Nederlanden. In J Kloek & K Tilmans (eds). *Burger. Een Geschiedenis van het Begrip 'Burger' in de Nederlanden van de Middeleeuwen tot de 21ste Eeuw*. Amsterdam: Amsterdam University Press, 19–31, 27–29; De Jong, J. 1987. *Een Deftig Bestaan. Het Dagelijks Leven van Regenten in de 17de en 18de Eeuw*. Utrecht/Antwerpen: Kosmos, 16.
27 Council of Policy. *Placaat Books C 2283*, Cape Town: WCARS, 1755.07.15.

ffairs.[28] Burgher councillors were also given an honourable position at the table of government and were seated between the *secunde* and the captain of the garrison.

It is hardly surprising then that having deep pockets was one of the prerequisites and criteria for becoming a burgher councillor. These men were, without exception, major entrepreneurs, frequently owned several houses and farms, and descended from influential families. Their careers in government often spanned several decades, and they were replaced only when they were too old or when they died, which made them an exclusive group among the burgher population. Everything pointed to the fact that these gentlemen of rank and position belonged to the ruling elite in the Cape settlement. By accepting their position on the administrative colleges of the Cape they became regents (*regenten*) just like their VOC counterparts.

After 1700 the Company moved to slow down immigration at the Cape from Europe. During 1716 and 1717 there was an exchange between the Company directors and the Cape administration about European immigration versus slave arrivals. Six of the seven members of the Cape government argued that slave labour was cheaper than employing immigrants. The farmers could then be paid less for their produce, and the VOC could earn a good profit when this produce was resold to the passing ships. The minority opinion of the single dissenting member, Dominique Marius Pasques de Chavonnes, held that immigration of free people should be encouraged because free men would constantly innovate and look for ways to improve production.[29] Naturally, the economy could only benefit. But the Company directors were focused on short-term financial gratification and resolved to promote the importing of slaves rather than immigration from European countries. It was not a wise decision, because as the century progressed much-needed capital became locked up in slave ownership. Some farmers ended up without enough cash-flow to cover their financial commitments or grow their enterprises.[30]

---

28 *Miscellaneous Documents, M 41*, Funeral Notices, Cape Town: WCARS, 1760.12.
29 See for De Chavonnes' full report: The Van Riebeeck Society. 1918. *The Reports of Chavonnes and his Council, and of Van Imhoff, on the Cape*. Cape Town, 25–32. De Chavonnes also pleaded to allow the burghers a measure of free trade, which was completely against VOC policy, and was therefore quite enlightened for a Company official.
30 Giliomee, H. 2003. *The Afrikaners. Biography of a People*. Charlottesville/Cape Town: University of Virginia Press/Tafelberg, 90; Fourie, J. 4 April 2016. *Three hundred years of firm myopia*. https://johanfourie.com/2016/04/12/three-hundred-years-of-firm-myopia-2/ (Accessed 13 April 2019).

However, though immigration was not actively pursued, it never completely stopped during the VOC period. Yet the increasing size of the burgher population during the eighteenth century was mainly a result of natural growth. Women married at an early age and had a long fertile period during which they had many children. The size of burgher families therefore was relatively large: it has been estimated that men fathered nine children on average.[31] Consequently, at the end of the VOC period in 1795 there were almost 15 000 burghers at the Cape. This group did not consist solely of white Europeans, as was and is often stated. All children of free blacks, the descendants of slaves, were automatically classified as burghers, which I will discuss in Chapter 4.

As the Cape gradually took the shape of a permanent Dutch settlement, with a large contingent of burghers, it came to hold a unique position within the VOC seaborne empire. It operated on the fringes of two major networks, namely the Dutch Atlantic and the Indian Ocean worlds, but it was never fully part of either of them. It was nothing more than a transit point for Asian luxury goods transported via the Republic to other parts of the Dutch Atlantic world. But this function was of only minor economic importance to the Atlantic world and, according to some historians, the Cape Colony should therefore not be included when discussing the Dutch Atlantic.[32] The Cape also was not a source of the lucrative spices and other trade goods that Asian settlements offered, and that were so essential to the financial prosperity of the VOC. However, the shipping network between Europe and Dutch Asia, which connected at the Cape, was exclusively European and VOC, and it was this that separated the Cape settlement from other existing Asian and African shipping networks.[33] So for the 143 years of Dutch rule, the Cape of Good Hope kept its function as a refreshment station, where the

---

31 Ross, R. 1993. The 'white' population of South Africa in the eighteenth century. In R Ross. *Beyond the Pale. Essays on the History of Colonial South Africa*. Hanover and London: Wesleyan University Press, 125–137. This study by Robert Ross was first published in 1975. Recent research has taken another look at demographic trends in South Africa. Although they are built on a much larger database and therefore more reliable, it is remarkable that the outcomes of this research are close to what was originally published by Ross. See for this recent research: Cilliers, J & Fourie, J. November 2012. New estimates of settler life span and other demographic trends in South Africa, 1652–1948. *Stellenbosch Economic Working Papers: 20/12*; Fourie, J & Cilliers, J. 2014. Die huwelikspatrone van Europese setlaars aan die Kaap, 1652–1910. *New Contree* 69: 45–70.

32 Oostindie, G. & Roitman, JV. 2014. Introduction. In G Oostindie & JV Roitman (eds.). *Dutch Atlantic Connections, 1680–1800: Linking Empires, Bridging Borders*. Leiden: Brill, 1–21, 5–6.

33 Ward 2009:170.

crews of VOC ships could take a breather on the long and gruelling journey between Europe and Asia. At the junction between two continents, it was of essential importance to the ongoing maritime power of the Company, and was certainly part of a large and vibrant complex of interactions between goods, people, information and ideas.[34]

The Cape post was one of many settlements established by the VOC in its territories during the seventeenth century. In fact, between 1600 and 1800 there were 93 VOC posts.[35] The only places the Dutch colonised and settled permanently were Ceylon, Indonesia and the Cape of Good Hope. But it was only the Cape settlement that developed into a full-scale settler colony. This was certainly made possible by a moderate climate and an environment that was relatively healthy for residents in comparison to Dutch Asian settlements. Furthermore, there was no serious threat from a large or hostile indigenous population or from other European nations.[36] But above all, the reason for the development of the new settlement was that economic conditions were favoured by a steady and increasing flow of ship traffic, which created a demand and stimulated agricultural activity (wheat and wine production), as well as a vibrant hospitality industry.[37]

Not all burghers were making a living as farmers, nor were some of them keen on that kind of career. Before they entered Company service many of them had worked in all kinds of trades and occupations, and it was natural for them to want to continue with that same work at the Cape once they became burghers. There was support for this among Company authorities because, they argued, it would stimulate the development of the Cape and its economy. Besides that, there was an obvious need for skilled artisans. Soon the burghers were occupied in a wide range of trades and enterprises.[38]

Otto Friedrich Mentzel, a visitor who spent eight years at the Cape during the 1730s and later published a detailed description of the settlement, wrote:

---

34 It is generally accepted that the loss of the Cape to the British in 1795 was the final nail in the coffin for the already struggling Company, which subsequently went bankrupt in 1799.

35 Van Oers, R. 2000. *Dutch Town Planning Overseas during VOC and WIC Rule (1600–1880)*. Zutphen: Walburg Pers, 25–26.

36 Oostindie, G. 2008. Migration and its legacies in the Dutch colonial world. In G Oostindie (ed). *Dutch Colonialism, Migration and Cultural Heritage*. Leiden: Brill, 1–22, 2–3; Ward 2009:10–11.

37 See Chapter 8: pp. 121-124 for more detail on this.

38 De Wet 1981:24–105.

The farmer requires wagons and ploughs; the wheelwright and the wagonmaker cannot do without the blacksmith; the locksmith follows up the joiner and gives the finishing touches to doors, window-frames, chests and drawers. No one can do without shoemakers and tailors, and I doubt whether there is another town in the whole world which has so many tailors in proportion to its population as the town at the Cape. All human needs are inter-dependent, and there is probably no trade that is not, in one way or another, assisted by some other craft. Nothing is more essential for each artisan in this country than the possession of his own home and hearth. Hence the number of house-builders is ever on the increase.[39]

The burgher families of the Cape thrived. For them, the Cape truly became a home. They worked the land and set up their businesses. They passed on their experience, knowledge and possessions to the next generation. And with every generation, a greater sense of belonging developed. By about 1770 the traveller and seafarer Johan Splinter Stavorinus made this observation about the Cape residents:

Although the first colonists here were composed of various nations, they are, by the operation of time, now so thoroughly blended together, that they are not to be distinguished from each other; even most of such as have been born in Europe, and who have resided here for some years, have, in a manner, changed their national character, for that of this country.[40]

But even though the Cape was the place where the burghers belonged, it did not belong to them. They were at the Cape of their own accord, yet their freedom was prescribed by the greater structure of which they were part: the world of the VOC and the policies of its directors. For the Company and its employees, the Cape was and remained a refreshment post established for a specific reason to which everything and everybody was subject. Local VOC officials had the backing of the authority of the powerful Company and often acted with the arrogance of rulers. They were the ones who made the laws and regulations to which the burghers had to adhere. Yet the administrators

---

39 Mentzel, OF. 1921. *A Geographical-Topographical Description of the Cape of Good Hope.* Vol. I. Cape Town: The Van Riebeeck Society, 65.
40 Stavorinus, JS. 1798. *Voyages to the East Indies.* Trans. S.H. Wilcocke. Vol. III. London: GG & J Robinson, 435.

were at the Cape for only a limited period. For the burghers, the Cape had become a place of permanent settlement where they had chosen to settle permanently. It was their home and they sometimes found it hard to accept that they did not have more say over how it was run.

CHAPTER 2

Dutch Africa

In the eighteenth century, the population of the Cape consisted mostly of immigrants and their descendants, originating from both West and East, and all these different people shaped Cape society.[1] Because of this, even contemporary visitors 'would have difficulty in deciding to which of the two worlds Cape Town belonged'.[2] One result of historical research since the 1980s and 1990s is that it is no longer necessary to agonise about that choice.[3] The very nature of the Cape as a refreshment post, at which ships stopped constantly, and its position as a connection point between two oceans and three continents, meant that the settlement 'was shaped by forces beyond its immediate geographical confines, as a port which was part of a much wider network of interchanges of people, material goods and ideas'.[4]

The nodes of empire

Historian Kerry Ward elaborates on this concept in her study *Networks of Empire*.[5] Colonial empires were traditionally described as consisting of a centre and its peripheries, whereby overseas territories were governed and influenced from a central point in Europe. The colonies were nothing more than places from where goods were extracted for the sole benefit of the colonising power. In opposition to this view of trading empires as simple two-way streets, Ward supports the notion that empires consisted of a collection of nodes. These nodes are not only places of residence, but also groups of people, corporate institutions or even influential individuals. Each node could be part of one or more networks and they were often centres with their own peripheries. It was via these networks of nodes that goods, information, institutions and people were exchanged. The 'webbed

---

1 Parts of this chapter were published in: Baartman, T. 2015. Dutch contexts of Cape burgher protests. *New Contree* 73: 40–60.
2 Ross, R. 1985. Cape Town (1750–1850): Synthesis in the dialectic of continents. In RF Betts, R Ross & GJ Telkamp (eds). *Colonial Cities. Essays on Urbanism in a Colonial Context*. Dordrecht: Martinus Nijhoff Publishers, 105–121, 107.
3 Worden, N. 2007. New approaches to VOC history in South Africa. *South African Historical Journal* 59(1): 3–18; Worden, N. 2012. Introduction. In N Worden (ed). *Cape Town between East and West. Social Identities in a Dutch Colonial Town*. Cape Town: Jacana, ix–xxii, xi–xiii.
4 Worden 2012:xiii (Introduction).
5 Ward 2009. See especially pages 6–14.

character of colonial spaces' is also described by Remco Raben.[6] He states that the enquiry into the various ways in which places and people were connected in the VOC world will 'widen our understanding of the workings of the Dutch trade empire'. Such an enquiry will, among other things, demonstrate that non-European populations contributed significantly to Dutch colonisation. For instance, the Dutch settlements in Java and Taiwan would have been hardly possible without numerous Chinese immigrants. Several authors have commented on the impact of non-Europeans on the shaping of overseas societies.[7]

In Kerry Ward's study the Cape appears as an important node in a web of networks. She uses this model to explain that the forced migration of slaves and political exiles between the Dutch territories made the Cape part of the Indian Ocean network and, as such, influenced the spread of Islam at the Cape and challenged existing hierarchies. Other historians have given the interaction of Cape slaves across continents a human face. Susan Newton-King has written about the personal letters sent to a freed slave named Arnoldus Koevoet and his wife Anna Rebecca of Bengal during the period 1728 to 1733.[8] The letters demonstrate that this couple had cultivated and maintained their own support network of family, friends and patrons reaching from Batavia to Amsterdam. Even though this kind of material is rare in the Cape archives, it is very possible that there were more networks of communication of Cape slaves and free blacks with people in their place of origin than we may think.[9]

The attempts to bring colonial centres and settlements together in a framework of connectedness help to integrate colonial history. They also create a better understanding of the experiences of non-European people during this time. But we should not forget that the direct link between motherland and settlement remained strong and especially so in the case of the Cape. After all, the Cape was the only VOC post which became a settler colony. It was here that the Company authorities implemented a 'Dutch-ness', which was not seen in other settlements. This shaped the social, cultural, political, judicial and economic structures of the Cape to

---

6   Raben, R. 2013. A new Dutch imperial history? Perambulations in a prospective field. *BMGN — Low Countries Historical Review* 128(1): 5–30.

7   See works by Leonard Blussé, Jean Gelman Taylor, Remco Raben and Ulbe Bosma, and Kerry Ward.

8   Newton-King, S. 2012. Family, friendship and survival among freed slaves. In N Worden (ed.). *Cape Town between East and West. Social Identities in a Dutch Colonial Town.* Cape Town: Jacana, 153–175.

9   See also: Worden, N. November 2014. Cape slaves in the paper empire of the VOC. *Kronos* 40: 23–44.

a large extent. Dutch historian Gerrit Schutte writes: 'The settlement at the Cape was, after all, only one of the territories of the VOC, and the VOC formed part of the Republic of the United Netherlands. This means that Cape structures and events should be seen in the context of the Netherlands and of common Dutch colonial patterns.'[10] His observation is the basis of this chapter. Before we embark on a journey through Cape politics, I will sketch the contours of Dutch influence at the Cape because this enhances our understanding of the political conflicts that occurred during the time of VOC rule. This Dutch influence also contributed to the perspective of burghers on Cape society as a place where they belonged, and which in turn belonged to the Dutch world.

The chambers of administration

The foremost link between the Netherlands and its overseas territories was forged by the VOC. The Company's organisation reflected the organisation of the Dutch Republic, in which administration was organised in six chambers, each of which was based in a Dutch town or area: Amsterdam, Zeeland, Delft, Rotterdam, Hoorn and Enkhuizen. Of these, Amsterdam and Zeeland were the most important. They were the chambers where the central administrative apparatus of the VOC was based. Even though the *bewindhebbers*, or directors of these chambers, mostly came from the name-giving cities, other towns were represented. For instance, in the Amsterdam chamber the cities of Haarlem and Leiden, which had significant interests in the overseas trade, managed to acquire a seat on the board after 1645. It was the original intention of the founders of the VOC that the appointment of new directors in the chambers would be the responsibility of the respective provincial governments, the Provincial States. But almost immediately, the province of Holland delegated this authority to the cities; the same thing happened in Zeeland in 1646 after a fierce battle between the Provincial States and the cities.

The close connection between the cities and the large trading companies was strengthened further by the fact that many Company directors had one or more functions in the administration of the participating cities. Just 20 years after the formation of the VOC a widespread grievance was: '[I]f we complain to the regents and the magistrates of the towns, there sit the directors … if to the admiralties, there are the directors again. If to the States-General, we find that they and the directors are sitting there together

---

10 Schutte, G. 1989:317.

at the same time.'[11] This did not change as time went on. Throughout the period of activity of the VOC most of the directors were recruited from *regenten*, the Dutch ruling elite. Only two of the 29 men who were directors of the VOC Delft chamber after 1750 did not have a position in the city government. And the directors of the Rotterdam chamber each had on average about 10 functions in the city administration in the second half of the eighteenth century.

The incestuous relationship between Dutch patricians and VOC administrators resulted in a high level of patronage with regards to the appointments of Company officials overseas. In the case of the Cape settlement, it was established that the 'top three employees — Governor, *secunde* and fiscal — were generally appointed from the Netherlands'.[12] From the middle of the eighteenth century the highest Company employees in the Cape were all appointed by the VOC directors in the Republic and not by Batavia, the VOC headquarters in Asia. More importantly, the men appointed to these high positions were born and educated in the Republic and were not from the Cape. By appointing men from their own circles, the VOC directors wanted to strengthen their control over the Cape. The Cape Company elite in turn made sure that lower positions were given to men belonging to their clientele.[13] Patronage and the cultivation of clientele, which was deeply entrenched in Dutch society, extended its reach to overseas settlements via the Company.

VOC employees made use of social and familial networks, which stretched from the Netherlands to as far as Japan, to advance their rise through the ranks. The careers of various VOC officials who were rooted in Cape families suggest that there was a fair amount of mobility within the Dutch seaborne empire. And not only men moved around. There were many Cape women who married officials from elsewhere and then moved to other settlements. Without doubt they became a vital part of the networks of patronage that existed within the VOC hierarchy.[14]

As Dutch colonial societies became more settled, more women moved from the Netherlands to overseas settlements or were born there to settler parents. These women became 'agents of imperial culture in their

---

11 Boxer 1973:50. The original Dutch quote is found in Gaastra 1991:34. Both Boxer and Gaastra discuss the close links between regents and directors. This has been well set out in: Den Heijer, HJ. 2005. *De Geoctroieerde Compagnie: De VOC and de WIC als Voorlopers van de Naamloze Vennootschap*. Deventer: Kluwer.
12 Ross & Schrikker 2012:32.
13 Ibid 31–35.
14 Ibid 26–44.

own capacity.[15] They were the ones who were most preoccupied with the implementation of Dutch values with regards to social practices and status, and they expressed these through their material culture. The type and extravagance of clothing that was worn was a preferred way to demonstrate status. Cape women belonging to the social elite made sure that they were dressed according to the latest Dutch fashion.

Replicating Dutch social structure

The VOC was issued with a charter by the Dutch States-General that ensured the Company a monopoly of Dutch trade and navigation east of the Cape of Good Hope and west of the straits of Magellan. The Heeren XVII were given wide-ranging powers. They had the authority to conclude treaties of peace and alliance, to wage defensive wars against competitors as well as indigenous populations, and to approve the building of fortresses and strongholds in the overseas territories.[16] Besides these extensive powers, the VOC had the authority to exercise judicial and administrative functions in their settlements. It was no surprise then, that elements of Dutch social structure were exported, because 'the Dutch replicated all the well-developed municipal institutions of their burgher society in the home country, such as town halls, hospitals, courts of justice, churches, reformative institutions and alms houses'.[17]

One of those institutions was the Orphan Chamber, a body responsible for overseeing the administration of the estates of orphans, until the children became adults, and of people placed under guardianship. The *weesmeesters* or orphan masters not only administered the monies and possessions of orphans, but also invested the monies under their control by extending credit. Their position was considered to be of great importance in Dutch society. At the Cape, the Orphan Chamber was established in 1673 and functioned until the early nineteenth century. The board of orphan masters consisted of burghers and VOC employees, but the Company men held the majority vote. The archives of the Orphan Chamber are an invaluable

---

15 Coetzee, L-M. 2015. Fashion and the world of the women of the VOC official elite. *New Contree* 73: 61–87, 64.

16 There is a vast amount of literature on the VOC. See the following website for a good introduction to this literature: http://www.voc-kenniscentrum.nl/literatuur1. html#overzichtswerken (Accessed 20 July 2019).

17 Blussé, L. 2008. *Visible Cities. Canton, Nagasaki, and Batavia and the Coming of the Americans*. Cambridge, Massachusetts: Harvard University Press, 39.

source of information on family relationships, material culture and economic development.[18]

Another administrative body which made its way overseas was the Commission of Civil and Marriage Affairs. It dealt with minor judicial issues, like arguments between neighbours and matters that involved small amounts of money, and it regulated and registered marriages, making sure, for instance, that the intended spouses were not too closely related. At the Cape, this body consisted of an equal number of VOC employees and burghers.

The Burgher Council discussed in the previous chapter was also an institution borrowed from administrative structures in the Netherlands, although in the Cape it was invested with less power. The men on the Council often served on one of the above-mentioned boards, in between their appointments as burgher councillors.

None of the official institutions at the Cape — or in the Asian settlements for that matter — were unique. Anybody coming from the Netherlands would have been familiar with them. The policy of copying Dutch institutions overseas was well recognised and eventually used by protesting burghers at the Cape as an argument against the VOC in their struggle for greater freedom. In 1783 an interesting pamphlet appeared in the Netherlands. Originally it was written in French by François Bernard, a political refugee from France, who had ended up in Leiden, where he became one of the leading men of the Patriot protest movement against the rule of the Dutch *stadholder* of the House of Orange and his cronies. ('*Stadholder*' or '*stadhouder*' literally means 'place holder' or 'steward'.) The pamphlet was translated into Dutch by Barend Jacob Artoijs, who studied law at Leiden University, but was born at the Cape. In 1780 he had made his way to the Netherlands as one of the representatives of the Cape burghers, who by then were involved in a major conflict with the VOC and its officials against their oppressive and corrupt regime. The pamphlet was a political statement against the Company, its directors and employees. The title of the pamphlet is interesting: *Nederlandsch Afrika* (Dutch Africa).[19] It indicates that the writer considered the Cape to be an integral part of the Dutch

---

18 TEPC Transcription Team. 2007. The inventories of the Orphan Chamber of the Cape of Good Hope. In N Worden (ed.). *Contingent Lives. Social Identity and Material Culture in the VOC World.* Cape Town: UCT Press, 3–22.

19 Bernard, F. 1783. *Nederlandsch Afrika; of Historisch en Staatkundig Tafereel van den Oorsprongelyken Staat der Volkplantinge aan de Kaap de Goede Hoop, Vergeleeken met den Tegenwoordigen Staat dier Volkplantinge, In't licht Gegeeven naar het Handschrift van een wel onderricht Opmerker.*

Republic: '[T]he residents of this tip of Africa live under the rule of the High Government of the Commonwealth of the seven United Netherlands.'[20] In his view, the Cape was not some distant settlement without any Dutch identity. With the publication of this work in the Netherlands, Bernard and Artoijs brought a local conflict in a remote outpost of the Dutch empire to the attention of the Dutch public, and in doing so pointed to the direct links between the Cape and the Dutch Republic. Their action supports the argument that, even though the Cape was situated miles away, its society was not far removed from the Dutch and European experience at all.

The power of language

Language is arguably the prime vehicle for the expression of social and cultural values. The VOC had an official policy that decreed Dutch to be the lingua franca in its settlements, but the Company administrators took a pragmatic approach when they felt it was better for business. When the Dutch took over several Asian settlements from the Portuguese, their group of administrators was small in relation to the local population, so they thought it beneficial and more practical to allow the Portuguese language to remain in use. Yet when indigenous women wanted to marry Dutch men, they were obliged to become Christian and have a basic knowledge of the Dutch language. This was supposed to promote their integration in European society and act as a countermeasure against the advance of the Portuguese language. But it was only in territories that had not been formerly occupied by another European power, such as New Netherland on the east coast of North America, and the Cape of Good Hope, that the Dutch language could really take hold.

The Cape was again the exception to the rule among the VOC settlements, because here the directors urged the local government to make Dutch the official language. Visitors to the Cape commented that one could also hear Portuguese and Malay, which were prevalent among slaves and free blacks and a result of the connection between the Cape and the East Indies. Even so, Dutch was the language of the church, law and government, and therefore very much the language of the ruling elite. All official documents were recorded in Dutch. The sizeable group of French Huguenots who emigrated to the Cape at the end of the seventeenth century were prohibited by the authorities from using the French language and most had lost the ability to speak their language after one generation. It was the deliberate

---

20 Bernard, F. 26.

intention of the VOC directors that the French language would die a natural death at the Cape.[21] In 1709 the Dutch Reformed Church of Drakenstein was told that 'from now on no nominations or letters from the church council to the government could be written in French, but that this had to happen only in Dutch'.[22] Dutch was also the language of commerce. Otto Friedrich Mentzel observed: 'It is difficult for a foreigner to make a living at the Cape, since ignorance of Dutch is a great handicap'.[23] Foreigners simply had to stop using their own language if they wanted to make a successful living at the Cape.[24]

Recreating a Dutch town

Travellers from Europe often commented on how familiar overseas Dutch settlements seemed — their appearance was so like that of towns in the Netherlands. Dutch minister François Valentijn, who travelled in Asia around 1700, wrote about Fort Cochin in Kerala (India): '[B]ecause of high buildings, churches and towers, it resembles a European city'.[25] He also commented on the first grand houses built at the Cape, which were double-storied and 'very Amsterdam-like with spacious living quarters downstairs'.[26] A visitor described Zeelandia (a Dutch colonial city on the formerly Portuguese island of Formosa, now Taiwan) in 1670 '... as perfectly and beautifully built as any city in Holland ... The streets had been paved with square bricks'. The sugar cane and paddy mills around Zeelandia were situated in polders.[27] The town of Batavia was 'laid out as a Dutch [town], with houses in a row and manifold canals bordered by shady

21 Schoeman, K. 2013. *Twee Kaapse Lewens. Henricus & Aletta Beck en die Samelewing van hul Tyd, 1702-1755*. Pretoria: Protea Boekhuis, 70–71.
22 Council of Policy. *Resolutions C 27*, Cape Town: WCARS, 1709.12.10, 64.
23 Mentzel, OF. 1925. *A Geographical-Topographical Description of the Cape of Good Hope*. Vol. II. Cape Town: The Van Riebeeck Society, 100.
24 Groeneboer, K. 1998. *Gateway to the West. The Dutch Language in Colonial Indonesia 1600–1950. A History of Language Policy*. Amsterdam: Amsterdam University Press; G. Stell, 'Dutch and colonial expansion: Different contact settings, different linguistic outcomes. Introduction. In: *Revue belge de philologie et d'histoire*, tome 91, fasc. 3, (2013), 689–694; Stell, G. 2013. Cape Malay Dutch: The missing link between Cape Dutch pidgin and Afrikaans? *Revue Belge de Philologie et d'Histoire* 91(3): 763–786.
25 Singh, A. 2007. Fort Kochin in Kerala 1750–1830. The Social Condition of a Dutch Community in an Indian Milieu. PhD thesis, Leiden University, 17.
26 Schoeman 2013:136 (*Twee Kaapse Lewens*).
27 Polder is a Dutch word describing the farmland between dykes. Oosterhoff, JL. 1985. Zeelandia, a Dutch colonial city on Formosa (1624–1662). In J Ross & GJ Telkamp (eds). *Colonial Cities: Essays on Urbanism in a Colonial Context*. Dordrecht: Martinus Nijhoff Publishers, 51–63, 51, 54.

trees'.[28] The Dutch colonial picture was often completed with drawbridges, so well known in the cities in the Republic. Another common sight in Dutch overseas settlements was the fort, which housed the local government and trade centre of the Company. These structures were built with either four or five bastions and it was general practice to name the bastions after places or provinces in the United Netherlands.[29] The Castle of Good Hope in Cape Town is a prime example, with its five bastions named after titles of Willem III of Orange-Nassau: Leerdam, Buuren, Katzenellenbogen, Nassau and Orange.

The planning and building of Dutch overseas towns have been the subject of many studies. It has been argued that they were planned and laid out according to a strict grid pattern and that this was this concept of Dutch mathematician and engineer Simon Stevin in the early seventeenth century. His blueprint depicted a rectangular, walled and fortified place, divided into strict geometrical blocks where open spaces and public buildings were given a fixed position. The concept was taught at prestigious institutions, like Leiden University, as part of a course on fortification and town development. Many of the engineers and land surveyors who subsequently worked in overseas settlements were educated in the Republic and would therefore have been familiar with this blueprint. The chessboard pattern was also used in Cape Town and is still visible today in the city centre. The layout was surely recognisable to any attentive traveller who visited the VOC settlements in the East Indies and will have contributed to the observations quoted earlier.[30]

However, Charles van den Heuvel, the Dutch historian of architecture and urban planning, points out that Simon Stevin was in the first place the private tutor of *stadholder* Prince Maurits, and that Stevin's ideas must be seen in the light of his teaching function rather than as a desire to provide a blueprint for Dutch or overseas town planning. Furthermore, his thoughts and city plan appeared in print only in 1649, after many overseas settlements had been set up or too soon before their founding to have had a profound influence. And it is unlikely that all engineers working overseas had access

---

28 Blussé, L. 1985. An insane administration and insanitary town: The Dutch East India Company and Batavia (1619–1799). In R Ross & GJ Telkamp (eds). *Colonial Cities: Essays on Urbanism in a Colonial Context.* Dordrecht: Martinus Nijhoff Publishers, 65–85, 66.

29 Raben, R. 1993. Klein Holland in Azie. Ideologie en pragmatisme in de Nederlandse koloniale stedebouw, 1600–1800. *Leidschrift* 9(2): 45–63, 46; Singh 2007:23.

30 See especially R van Oers. 2000. *Dutch Town Planning Overseas during VOC and WIC Rule (1600–1880).* Zutphen: Walburg Pers. Furthermore: Raben 1993:54–55; Oosterhoff 1985:51–52.

to them.[31] The fact is that no official regulations on the shape and size of new overseas towns have been found in Dutch archives. Van den Heuvel concludes that surveyors and engineers overseas were not necessarily working with a fixed notion of an urban form. They were rather using various temporary and flexible grids, which had worked in Dutch cities and could be adapted to local circumstances.[32]

What gave Dutch urban planning a certain level of uniformity was the experience gained in the long-standing and constant struggle with flooding in the Netherlands. A significant characteristic of the colonial cities, and a circumstance that Dutch town planners were very familiar with, was that they were all situated on the coast and at the mouth of a river or on a bay, an estuary, or in some cases on an island.[33] This was not surprising, because these cities were the primary link between sea routes and the hinterland. The most important need of the VOC was to have a port from where colonial goods could be exported to the Republic, and to which wares from Europe or other parts of the empire could be imported. There also needed to be a supply of fresh water for city residents and visitors and for growing produce. The water could furthermore be used for defence purposes. In Cape Town, a stream coming down from Table Mountain was channelled into a moat around the Castle. Water leading from the mountain was canalised to run through and irrigate the Company Gardens; this channel was extended into the main axis in Cape Town running from the Gardens to the bay. This route eventually became the Heerengracht, where the most prestigious Company buildings (the Dutch Reformed Church, the hospital and the slave lodge) were constructed, and which became a favoured place of residence for prominent citizens (as the name implies).[34] The presence of a river or stream, which frequently was canalised, explains why most Dutch overseas settlements had an elongated shape and a main street running down the centre.

---

31 Van den Heuvel, C. 2011. Multi-layered grids and Dutch town planning. Flexibility and temporality in the design of settlements in the Low Countries and Overseas. In P Lombaerde & C van den Heuvel (eds). *Early Modern Urbanism and the Grid. Town Planning in the Low Countries in International Context. Exchanges in Theory and Practice 1550–1800, Architectura Moderna 10.* Turnhout: Brepols, 27–44, 29.
32 Ibid 44.
33 Raben 1993:46.
34 Worden, N. 1998/1999. Space and identity in VOC Cape Town. *Kronos* 25: 72–87, 75–78; Van Oers, R. 2012. *Landscape as guiding element in the design and planning of Dutch colonial settlements (1600–1800).* http://www.projetsdepaysage.fr/fr/landscape_as_guiding_element_ in_the_design_and_planning_of_dutch_colonial_settlements_1600_1800_ (Accessed 14 April 2019), 1–18, 11–12.

Military tradition had taught the Dutch that there needed to be a distance between the fort and the city around it. There was better visibility of the surrounding terrain from the castle bastions if there were no buildings obstructing the view. In Cape Town, once the construction of the Castle began, in the 1670s, the Company even removed and demolished some of the houses that were built near the site. The open space created in this manner was used as a drill and parade ground.[35]

In setting up overseas settlements Dutch engineers and town planners based their ideas on practical experience going back to the sixteenth and early seventeenth centuries. They worked according to a plan, but in executing it, they were pragmatic and flexible, considering the conditions and circumstances they were confronted with locally. This accounts for both the similarity as well as the differences between Dutch colonial towns. Yet it cannot be denied that the Dutch colonial cities in the Asian territories (like Batavia, Colombo, Zeelandia) and Cape Town, displayed a remarkable regularity, and one could be forgiven when describing this as a uniformity in overseas town planning. A tangible connection between the overseas settlements and the motherland was formed, and the Company was the instrument of that link. The Company wanted trading posts that were easily defensible against competitors or other aggressors. And, although it was not the preferred option, if it did become necessary to have larger settlements where residents of different backgrounds had to live together, then the Company needed these to be stable and well-organised. Most of all, the overseas posts had to be cost-effective and cheap to maintain. That is why there were no elaborate status buildings, like big cathedrals or government palaces, in Dutch settlements. The regular grid served the purposes of the Company perfectly. This design was 'symbolic of an ordered, well-managed society, hierarchical but democratic, it was emblematic for the hard working god-fearing Dutch Calvinists'.[36]

The Dutch Reformed Church

Another connection between the Netherlands and the VOC posts overseas was religion. After the northern Dutch provinces liberated themselves from Spanish rule and formed the United Netherlands through the *Unie van Utrecht* in 1579, the Dutch Reformed Church embarked on a mission

---

35 Worden 1998/1999:79. On the development of Cape Town see also: Malan, A. 2012. The cultural landscape. In N Worden (ed.). *Cape Town between East and West. Social Identities in a Dutch Colonial Town.* Cape Town: Jacana, 1–25.
36 Van Oers 2000:156.

to take over the privileged position of the Catholic Church. Over time the Dutch Reformed Church became the public and preferred denomination in the Netherlands, which meant, among other things, that its religious rituals were perfomed in public functions and it had a large say in issues of public morality. In many (but not all) Dutch towns only members of the Dutch Reformed Church were eligible to hold public office and be appointed to high positions.

But while the Dutch Reformed Church was dominant, it never held a religious monopoly or became the official state church. This was partly due to the nature of the Dutch Revolt against the Spanish rulers. This was not essentially a religious uprising of Protestant Calvinists against the Catholic Church or Catholic rulers, but a struggle for several liberties which ranged from political autonomy to freedom of conscience. These freedoms were clearly spelt out in the *Unie van Utrecht* constitution. Dutch regents were not keen to have the law prescribed to them by church ministers. Although the Dutch Reformed Church was the public church, the principle of freedom of conscience was not abandoned and religious convictions were not enforced. The regents sought social and cultural consensus rather than having to deal with religious disputes.

During most of the seventeenth and eighteenth centuries only about half of the Dutch population confessed to be Dutch Reformed. More than a third of the people were still Catholic, and the rest formed several other Christian religious communities, such as Huguenots, Mennonites, Baptists and Lutherans. Recent research has shown that there was an active interplay between the Dutch Reformed Church and these other denominations, which shaped the public morality that came to be known as 'Calvinism', and that left an imprint on Dutch society for a long time to come. It has furthermore become apparent that, even though other religious denominations may not have been allowed officially, they were not heavily or actively suppressed. This attitude of tolerance resulted in a public sphere that was not uniquely or predominantly Dutch Reformed.[37]

Like other institutions the Dutch Reformed Church was exported overseas by the VOC. The second charter of the VOC, issued in 1622, stated that one of the reasons for the continuation of the monopoly of the

---

37 On Calvinism and the Dutch Reformed Church see: Schutte, GJ. 2002. *Het Calvinistisch Nederland. Mythe en Werkelijkheid*. Hilversum: Verloren; and Frijhoff, W. 2008. Was the Dutch Republic a Calvinist community? The state, the confessions, and culture in the early modern Netherlands. In A Holenstein, T Maissen & M Prak (eds). *The Republican Alternative. The Netherlands and Switzerland Compared*. Amsterdam: Amsterdam University Press, 99–122.

Company was the preservation of the public Reformed faith.[38] It was assumed that the overseas settlements would be Christian and Protestant. And because the Dutch Reformed Church was the public church at home it followed that it would be the same elsewhere. The leaders of the church, with the backing of the Company directors, sent ministers, schoolmasters and sick comforters overseas, and they built their churches in territories controlled by the Dutch.[39] This must have contributed to a considerable transfer of Dutch religious values to overseas settlements.

Yet, the commercial motive of the Company remained paramount. The Dutch, and their Protestant religion, were a minority in most of their territories. For the VOC enterprise the spread of Christianity was certainly not a priority.[40] Little effort was made to convert the many Hindus and Muslims and only a minimal Christian legacy was left. In this narrative, it was yet again the Cape that was the exception, because it did have a large and growing European population and Christianity therefore had more impact. But even here the Dutch Reformed Church faced competition. The Cape happened to have a sizeable Lutheran population mainly due to the many German immigrants. Many of them achieved important positions in Cape society, and they pushed hard to be allowed to worship in their own church. In 1780 the VOC finally had to give in to the demand from the significant Lutheran congregation, despite the best efforts from Dutch Reformed ministers and governors to prevent this from happening. It is remarkable that, although the Lutherans were overwhelmingly German, all records of the church had to be written in Dutch. The VOC administration needed to know what was going on, but this was also a means to prevent a foreign subculture from gaining too much ground.

The Company kept a firm control on what happened in its settlements. It monitored virtually all major decisions taken by other institutions and

---

38 Schutte, GJ. 2002. De kerk onder de Compagnie. In GJ Schutte (ed.). *Het Indisch Sion. De Gereformeerde Kerk onder de Verenigde Oost-Indische Compagnie.* Hilversum: Verloren, 43–64, 47.

39 Weststeijn, A. 2019. Colonies of concord: Religious escapism and experimentation in Dutch overseas expansion, ca. 1650–1700. In J Spaans & J Touber (eds). *Enlightened Religion. From Confessional Churches to Polite Piety in the Dutch Republic.* Leiden: Brill, 104–130, 108.

40 It appears that the Company directors could be quite pragmatic in their approach to other religious denominations. Once the VOC had conquered Melaka from the Portuguese, it openly tolerated the Roman Catholic Church to ensure co-operation and loyalty from the sizeable Catholic population. See: Borschberg, P. 2010. Ethnicity, language and culture in Melaka after the transition from Portuguese to Dutch rule (seventeenth century). *Journal of the Malaysian Branch of the Royal Asiatic Society* 83(2): 93–117.

groups, including the church. Like the regents in Dutch towns, the Company officials in the overseas settlements controlled all appointments to church councils and in other church functions, and the ministers were Company employees. It must also be noted that, as in patria, not all overseas settlers were loyal Dutch Reformed churchgoers. The terms 'Christian', 'Reformed', and 'burgher' were certainly not synonymous.[41] The Dutch Reformed Church was therefore neither autonomous nor supreme in the Netherlands or overseas, but as the public church it held a strong (if dependent) position in colonial society, and it served as a conduit for the religious mores and traditions that prevailed in Dutch society to reach overseas settlements, where they were adopted especially in the circles of the ruling elite of VOC employees and burghers. Company and church worked closely together and they 'created a hybrid colonial conglomeration where gain and godliness constantly interacted in the creation of a global Dutch empire of trade and religiosity.[42]

The legal system and Roman-Dutch law

A further link between patria and overseas settlements was the justice system. The criminal and civil cases that were heard by the Court of Justice in Cape Town were judged according to Roman-Dutch law as used in the Netherlands.[43] Lawyers in the Cape referred to legal precedents set in the Republic and quoted Dutch legal scholars in their arguments. One of these was Hugo de Groot (Grotius) and his *Inleydinghe tot de Hollandsche Rechtsgeleerdheydt* (Introduction to Dutch Law published in 1631). Another was Simon van Leeuwen, who described Roman-Dutch law in the seventeenth century in *Het Rooms-Holland-Regt* (1665).[44] The procedure that the Cape civil court followed was virtually the same as that in the courts of many Dutch towns and regions.[45] Besides this, the administration

---

41 Schutte 2002:43–64 (De kerk onder de Compagnie); Biewenga, AW 2002. Kerk in een volksplanting: de Kaap de Goede Hoop. In GJ Schutte (ed). *Het Indisch Sion. De Gereformeerde Kerk onder de Verenigde Oost-Indische Compagnie*. Hilversum: Verloren, 201–218.

42 Weststeijn 2019:113.

43 Baartman, T. 2012. *The most precious possession: Honour, reputation and the Cape Council of Justice*. Unpublished paper, Cape Town.

44 An English translation was used by the British after they took over the Dutch settlements to assist their lawyers in overseas courts that still used Roman-Dutch law.

45 Broers, EJ. 1996. Vrij onbeschaamt en zeer oneerbiedig. De civiele rechtspraak in Brabantse beledigingszaken in de zeventiende en achttiende eeuw. *Leidschrift* 12(1): 55–72; Van der Heijden, M et al (eds). 2009. *Serving the Urban Community. The Rise of Public Facilities in the Low Countries*. Amsterdam: Amsterdam University Press;

of justice created a network of links between the overseas settlements and the motherland. Parties who were not satisfied with the outcome of a trial in Cape Town could lodge an appeal with the Council of Justice in Batavia. From there the case could be referred to the Dutch Republic. In his book *Bitters Bruid* Leonard Blussé describes the marital battle between Joan Bitter and his wife Cornelia van Nijenroode, which lasted two decades.[46] The judicial fight between the spouses took place in Batavia and the Netherlands, and the parties had to travel several times from one location to the other to submit themselves to the jurisdiction of the local courts.

Education at the Cape

Other regular travellers between the Cape and the Netherlands were the children of Cape families seeking higher education. Burghers at the Cape were not uneducated. About 60 per cent of the burghers could write; their literacy levels were comparable to those of burghers back home and were even higher in the more affluent social strata of Cape society.[47] But education at the Cape was basic and limited to reading, writing and some calculus. For advanced education Cape residents had to travel to the Dutch Republic.[48] There are several requests to the Council of Policy from fathers who asked permission to send their sons to the Republic to pursue a higher education. This was a costly exercise and the family concerned had to be financially well-off, which indicates that these families came from the upper layers of Cape society. Some of the boys left at a young age and spent several years in the Netherlands. During this time, family members and associates in the Republic and at the Cape corresponded, which ensured that the people at the Cape remained aware of events and ideas in the Netherlands. After finishing their education, many students returned, bringing with them Dutch values and new customs, fashion and literature, while they had also gained and maintained personal connections with friends and family in the Republic.

Van Meeteren, A. 2006. *Op Hoop van Akkoord. Instrumenteel Forumgebruik bij Geschilbeslechting in Leiden in de Zeventiende Eeuw.* Hilversum: Verloren.

46 Blussé, L. 1997. *Bitters Bruid. Een Koloniaal Huwelijksdrama in de Gouden Eeuw.* Amsterdam: Uitgeverij Balans.

47 Biewenga 1999:165–171; Worden, N, Van Heyningen, E & Bickford-Smith, V. 1998. *Cape Town. The Making of a City.* Cape Town: David Philip Publishers, 74.

48 Du Toit, PS. 1937. *Onderwys aan die Kaap onder die Kompanjie 1652–1795.* Cape Town and Johannesburg: Juta, 94–101; Schutte, G. 2008. What was Pieter Cloete doing in Utrecht? *Quarterly Bulletin of the National Library of South Africa* 62(1): 36–43.

Letters back home

In 2006, Dutch historian Roelof van Gelder discovered that the National Archives in Kew (UK) houses some 38 000 Dutch letters. These letters had been seized by the British Admiralty from captured Dutch ships. They confirm the existence of private networks. The writers were people from all social levels, based in Batavia, Colombo, Paramaribo and Cape Town, who corresponded with family members who had stayed behind in the Netherlands. The letters contained family news about births, deaths and marriages, and just plain gossip about friends and neighbours. There was correspondence about business matters and there were requests for assistance with careers. Overseas residents were informed about wars and important political events. Often newspaper clippings, political pamphlets, books and gifts were included with the letters.[49]

A wonderful example of correspondence flowing between the Cape and the Republic is the letters exchanged between Dutch regent Hendrik Swellengrebel junior, a son of Governor Hendrik Swellengrebel, and Hendrik Cloete, a wealthy Cape landowner and wine producer.[50] Both men also corresponded with several other Cape and Dutch notables. The letters give a vivid insight into the political trouble that rocked the Cape settlement during the 1780s (I use them extensively in this book). Although many cover the political situation, they are not an official correspondence, but reflect personal opinions.

The men had a wide knowledge of the world and were well versed in Dutch customs and mindsets. But they also discussed people and relationships, and Hendrik Cloete in particular delighted in relating, sometimes juicy, Cape gossip.

The letters illustrate that many people in the Dutch Republic and the rest of the empire had contact with each other outside of official channels and wrote letters about their daily lives and thoughts. It follows that people overseas were not at all isolated. There was a lively correspondence and a constant flow of news and ideas, all of which contributed to them staying in touch and maintaining a Dutch identity.

---

49 Van Gelder, R. 2012. *Zeepost. Nooit Bezorgde Brieven uit de 17de en 18de Eeuw*. Amsterdam: Olympus; Van Gelder, R. Letters, journals and seeds: Forgotten Dutch mail in the National Archives in London. In N Worden (ed). 2007. *Contingent Lives. Social Identity and Material Culture in the VOC World*. Cape Town: UCT Press, 538–545; Brouwer, J. 2014. *Levenstekens: Gekaapte Brieven uit het Rampjaar 1672*. Hilversum: Verloren. See also the website: http://www.gekaaptebrieven.nl (Accessed 17 September 2016).

50 Schutte, GJ. 1982. *Briefwisseling van Hendrik Swellengrebel jr oor Kaapse Sake 1778–1792*. Cape Town: Van Riebeeck-Vereniging.

There were many Cape residents who wanted to read or study, but there was no public library or printing press during the VOC period. Books were imported from Europe and many were held in private collections. Some of these collections were small, but there were some that contained several hundreds or even thousands of books. Of the 2 052 inventories assembled by the Orphan Chamber between 1673 and 1799, almost a third (603 to be precise) had books. And books were sold at 132 of the 351 auctions held between 1691 and 1748. Unfortunately, in most cases the titles of these books were not recorded, but there were works on all kinds of topics, like religion, philosophy, history, science and geography.[51] The Cape social and ruling elite remained aware of the latest philosophies and trends in the home country.

How Dutch was Dutch?

Even though the many different connections between the United Netherlands and the outposts of the empire resulted in the latter 'being Dutch', one needs to put this in perspective, because the obvious question is: how Dutch was Dutch? The term 'Dutch' is an anachronism when applied to the eighteenth century and before. Even though many of the settlers inhabiting the overseas territories came from an area known as the United Dutch Provinces, this common origin was still in its infancy. A Dutch nation came into being only in the nineteenth and twentieth centuries. Before that the residents of the Netherlands were subjects of local and regional authorities rather than an overarching national government. Laws differed from city to city. There were many different dialects, customs, kinds of dress, and systems of coinage and measure. Therefore, it is arguable that there was something like a unified Dutch culture. And furthermore, it was especially the regents from the provinces of Holland and Zeeland who drove the overseas expansion, while the other provinces invested far less in it and had less influence in colonial settlements. In that sense one should speak of a '*Hollands-Zeeuws*' empire rather than a Dutch one.[52] Also, Dutch colonialism depended heavily on people from other European nations, because there were not enough Dutch men and women willing to travel and settle overseas. Despite this, they shared a common background: most settlers were Protestant

---

51 Dick, AL. (n.d.) Gewone lesers aan die Kaap, c. 1680 tot 1850. *LitNet Akademies* 9(2): 21; Westra, PE. 2011. Boeke en boekversamelings tydens die Kompanjiesbewind aan die Kaap. *Quarterly Bulletin of the National Library of South Africa* 65(1&2): 42–50.
52 Cantwell, A-M. 2008. Landscapes and other objects: Creating Dutch New Netherland. *New York History* Fall: 315–345, 316; Emmer & Gommans 2012:14.

northern European and shared 'the same social system with the same norms and values'.[53]

The Cape of Good Hope was the exception among the VOC's possessions, because there the Dutch demographic, linguistic, religious and cultural legacy was substantial and persistent.[54] It is undeniable that many elements of Dutch social, economic and political life found their way to the Cape, and that this was particularly evident among members of the colonial elite who absorbed and exhibited a Dutch identity and character. The political and economic relations as well as the personal links of settlers with family and friends back home played a role in the way they experienced and set up their environment. They held on to their Dutch legacy, which influenced their identities as well as their views on society.[55]

---

53 Cantwell 2008:316.

54 Oostindie 2008:1–22.

55 I am not claiming that the Dutch simply transplanted their complete culture, values and beliefs to exotic territories, because there are many arguments to be made against this. One must think of the (in)famous Dutch tolerance and ideas of political freedom as opposed to the violent behaviour and attitudes of some Dutch colonialists towards slaves and indigenous people overseas. Frances Gouda makes this point concisely and clearly in her introduction to *Dutch Culture Overseas: Colonial Practice in the Netherlands Indies 1900–1942* (Singapore 2008), 1–9. Another interesting study on this topic and situated in a different part of the Dutch empire is: D Merwick *The Shame and the Sorrow. Dutch-Amerindian Encounters in New Netherland* (Philadelphia 2006).

CHAPTER 3

A big mistake

O n 21 February 1657 the Council of Policy of the Cape of Good Hope released nine men from their VOC contracts and resolved that they could, 'after careful consideration, ... settle here, under favourable conditions, as freemen'.[1] Initially they were meant to be just farmers, but soon they were issued with letters of freedom which permitted them to engage in other ways of making an income, like operating a small tavern, hunting, fishing or performing a skilled craft. The group of nine men eventually grew into a sizeable population of burghers, a title imported from the Netherlands. This book has many references to burgher rights and status, burgher identity, and the struggle of Cape burghers with Company authorities. So, what did the title 'burgher' encompass, and to what extent did the Dutch burgher find a place in Cape society?

The creation of the 'burgher'

The King of Spain, the head of state of the Netherlands, was officially deposed as monarch in 1581 by the seven northern Dutch provinces after years of uprising. Dutch political leaders tried to find another sovereign but could not settle on a satisfactory replacement. They then decided against monarchy, and at the end of 1587 the new political entity of the Republic of the United Netherlands was born, a federation of seven provinces in the Northern Netherlands.[2]

---

1 Council of Policy. *Resolutions C 1*, Cape Town: WCARS, 1657.02.21, 209.
2 The following section on the Dutch Republic is based on information contained in: Groenveld, S et al. 1979. *De Kogel door de Kerk? De Opstand in de Nederlanden en de Rol van de Unie van Utrecht 1559–1609*. Zutphen: Walburg Pers; Israel, JI. 1995. *The Dutch Republic. Its Rise, Greatness and Fall 1477–1806*. New York: Oxford University Press; 't Hart, M. 1995. The Dutch Republic: The Urban Impact upon Politics. In K Davids & JA Lucassen. *A Miracle Mirrored: The Dutch Republic in European Perspective*. Cambridge: Cambridge University Press, 57–98; Prak, M. 2005. *The Dutch Republic in the Seventeenth Century: The Golden Age*. Cambridge: Cambridge University Press; Van Deursen, AT. 2006. The Dutch Republic, 1588–1780. In JCH Blom & E Lamberts (eds). *History of the Low Countries*. Oxford, New York: Berghahn Books, 143–218; Prak, M. 2000. The Dutch Republic's city-state culture (17th–18th centuries). In MH Hansen (ed). *A Comparative Study of Thirty City-State Cultures*. An Investigation Conducted by the Copenhagen Polis Centre Copenhagen: Kongelige Danske Videnskabernes Selskab, 343–358.

Unlike its European neighbours, the Republic did not have a head of state. Its central governing body was the States-General, which concluded treaties, handled ambassadorial issues and dealt with concerns pertaining to the provinces. The States-General was further responsible for the defence of the Union and had oversight of the army and fleet. Some of its executive duties were delegated to a *stadholder*. During the preceding monarchy the *stadholder* was the representative of the Habsburg emperors. In the new political dispensation, he became a public servant of the provinces. Over time, however, his position evolved to become an informal head of state with royal undertones. He was always a member of the prestigious Orange family, held court and lived in a palace, and was often appointed to the position of Captain General of the standing army and Admiral General of the fleet, which further bolstered his powers.

What made the Dutch Republic even more of a 'political freak'[3] was that it had an extremely intricate governmental structure. Without a strong central government, all decisions were subject to constant political bartering between the States-General and the seven provincial governing structures, the Provincial States. In these provincial bodies several groups were represented, each with very different interests, which resulted in more negotiations, making governing even more complex. In the Provincial States the old landed nobility and ecclesiastical estates were represented. Newer entities were towns and cities. The Netherlands was highly urbanised in comparison to other European countries.[4] In many provinces the landed gentry managed to hold on to a 50 per cent share of the vote, but in the Provincial States of the two leading provinces, Holland and Zeeland, the nobility held just one vote against many individual cities. The cities became key political players in the Republic simply because of their considerable financial and economic power.

Any attempt to limit the powers of the cities was met with fierce resistance. Dutch cities did not want a state structure in which they would lose their autonomy. They acquiesced to the construction of the United Netherlands only because this offered the most stable environment for them to pursue their own interests. Of course, the cities were never politically

---

3 Prak 2000:4.
4 In 1500 about 15.8 per cent of the population of the Netherlands lived in towns with 2 500 residents or more. By 1800 this number had increased to 37 per cent. The province of Holland was the most populous area: almost half of the total Dutch population lived there and 60 per cent of these people lived in urban areas. In contrast, the number of city dwellers in France reached only 12 per cent of the population. The Republic was the most urbanised area in Europe. Prak 2000:343; Mijnhardt, WW. 1998. The Dutch Republic as a town. *Eighteenth-Century Studies* 31(3): 345–348, 345.

independent. But the complex interplay between the various political structures and layers within the Republic meant that the period between 1580 and 1800 was 'the period of the urban domination of the state which made the Dutch Republic so unique in Europe'.[5] The many different interests and local pride prompted a contemporary observer to describe the Republic as a federation of 'about fifty republics, all very different the one from the other'.[6]

The residents of these Dutch cities, and particularly those who were vital components of their political and economic life, were the burghers. They became the basic and central building block of Dutch society. As the power-players in cities, the burghers completely dominated public affairs in the Dutch Republic. 'At the center of the Dutch world was a burgher, not a bourgeois'.[7] This statement from British historian Simon Schama expresses that the typical Dutch city dweller was not primarily defined in economic terms, despite the Golden Age being the time that the Dutch Republic became famous for its commercial empire. These people were first and foremost *burgers*, privileged members of a political unit, the city. The development of the concept 'burgher' is closely linked to the formation of cities as political entities. Since early medieval times regional rulers started to award privileges to communities, such as the right to a certain measure of political and judicial autonomy, in exchange for the payment of taxes and tolls, which the rulers needed to finance their administration. Gradually, the need to highlight the difference between privileged and non-privileged people and to associate them with a circumscribed space, like a city, became stronger. It was at this time that the inhabitants of cities received their own designation. Initially they were called *poorters*, which came from the Middle Dutch word *port*, meaning city. Later the term *burger*, meaning a resident of a *burcht* or walled city, found its way into the Dutch language.[8] So not everybody could call themselves a burgher. *Burgerschap* (burgher-ship) was reserved for city dwellers, thereby excluding the rural population.[9]

The concept of *burgerschap* was transplanted to the overseas settlements by the Dutch trading companies to describe free residents who

---

5   Mijnhardt 1998:345.
6   Prak 2000:353.
7   Schama, S. 1987. *The Embarrassment of Riches: An Interpretation of Dutch Culture in the Golden Age*. New York: Vintage, 7.
8   Leupen 2002:19–31.
9   Mijnhardt 1998:347; Kuijpers, E & Prak, M. 2002. Burger, ingezetene, vreemdeling: Burgerschap in Amsterdam in de 17e en 18e Eeuw. In J Kloek & K Tilmans (eds). *Burger. Een Geschiedenis van het Begrip 'Burger' in de Nederlanden van de Middeleeuwen tot de 21ste Eeuw*. Amsterdam: Amsterdam University Press, 113–132, 113.

could not be placed into any other category. These people were no longer employees, but they were also not indigenous residents or slaves. For the Company directors the tried and tested answer was to use a concept they knew from Dutch society. And so, they named this new population group, with its special status, burghers.

Burghers in Dutch Asia

In Batavia and in other Dutch Asian settlements the establishment of a burgher group preceded the one at the Cape. The first burghers in Asia were given their freedom in 1616 in the eastern part of the Indonesian territories: the Moluccas, Ambon and Banda. Once Batavia was firmly in Dutch hands (after 1619) most burghers chose Batavia as their place of residence.[10] The city grew steadily and by the second half of the seventeenth century Batavia was a city with many different inhabitants: Company employees from various parts of Europe, free burghers, people of mixed descent, Chinese immigrants, and slaves. The city began to expand beyond its walls and officials had 'to devise laws and institutions that could control the city's inhabitants. Quite naturally, the model they chose was that of the Dutch municipality, just as in the design of the earliest buildings and layout of the city they strove to recreate the appearance of a Dutch town'.[11] However, the Dutch laws had to be changed and adapted to local circumstances and a mix of inhabitants for which there was no precedent in the Netherlands. This became apparent from the way the VOC administration dealt with the burghers.

The VOC held on firmly to its monopoly over trade. In the early years, the burghers enjoyed some freedom with regards to maritime trade, but from 1632 this became increasingly limited. Eventually, the VOC directors decided that they did not want to support the establishment of colonies of burghers in the East Indies, with whom they would have had to share the lucrative trade and who would become a threat to the VOC monopoly. Burghers were allowed to engage in only such business as the Company permitted. Consequently, the lucrative trade with the Moluccas, India, China and Japan was closed to burghers and goods such as textiles, diamonds and

---

10 For information on the burghers in Dutch East Asia and Batavia see: Blussé 1985; Taylor, JG. 1983. *The Social World of Batavia. European and Eurasian in Dutch Asia.* Madison: University of Wisconsin Press, 9–12; Nas, PJM. 1990. The origin and development of the urban municipality in Indonesia. *Sojourn* 5(1): 86–112; Bosma, U & Raben, R. 2008. *Being 'Dutch' in the Indies: A History of Creolisation and Empire, 1500–1920.* Singapore: NUS Press, 35–42; Boxer 1973:241–250.
11 Taylor 1983:20.

spices became the exclusive domain of the VOC. Simultaneously, many high Company employees set up their own trading businesses, which officially was not permitted, but was condoned by the VOC. It was an unequal struggle for the burghers. Some returned to the Netherlands while others decided to rejoin the service of the Company. The burghers who stayed in Batavia tried to eke out a living by supplying the Company headquarters and the town with fresh produce, which was difficult because most of the land around Batavia was owned by high-ranking VOC officials, who preferred to lease it to Chinese cultivators. For some, the only thing left to do was to enter the service sector as innkeepers, shopkeepers and artisans. In 1674 most Batavian burghers declared that they made their living in this way and only a minority group described themselves as free merchants.[12] Politically, the burghers of Batavia were not given any real power. All administrative bodies remained under the control of Company officials.

In the settlements of Galle and Colombo in Ceylon the economic opportunities for burghers were even more limited than in Batavia. The Company monopolised the most important trade with India and made sure that the burghers were excluded. The small amount of trade allowed to them — mainly in rice, textiles and saltpetre — was gradually lost to indigenous traders with whom burghers could not compete financially.[13]

As a result of the economic and political restrictions placed on burghers in Batavia and other Asian settlements, *burgerschap* was not very appealing. The burgher group in Batavia remained small throughout the seventeenth and eighteenth centuries — at about three hundred people.[14] They were too few and too economically and politically suppressed to develop a conscious identity. The Cape was the only settlement in the Dutch territories that boasted a large, growing and relatively self-sufficient burgher group which, over time developed its own view on its status and identity.

The Dutch burghers at the Cape

Although the Cape settlement was a far cry from being a city (like those in the Republic), its residents considered themselves to be part of a distinct political entity. As the settlement developed, its free inhabitants came to

---

12 Bosma & Raben 2008:36.
13 Bosma & Raben 2008:40.
14 In 1632 there were 229 burghers and 1 560 Company employees (Bosma & Raben 2008:29). In 1673 the burghers numbered 340 out of a total population of 7 286 (outside the walls of Batavia — Taylor 1983:10). The unhealthy living conditions in the East also proved to be a threat to the Europeans and may have contributed to their low numbers and their wish to repatriate instead of settling there. See for this Blussé 1985.

believe that their exclusive politico-legal status should be acknowledged by the authorities. One of the claims made during the Cape burgher protest movement of the 1770s and 1780s was that local burghers were on an equal footing, in terms of privileges and rights, with burghers in the United Netherlands. They argued that because the VOC received its mandate from the government of the United Netherlands, the Cape burghers were free burghers like those of the cities in the Republic. Part of their argument was that, when Dutch orphan girls were sent to the Cape to become wives of Cape burghers during the rule of Jan van Riebeeck, this was done with the explicit promise that they 'would not lose any of the undeniable rights of the Burghers of the Seven Provinces'. Their status as burghers would remain the same as in the land of their birth and would extend to their husbands and descendants. The Company would treat all burghers as members of a 'free Commonwealth'.[15] The burghers believed that these promises had not been kept and that over time their rights had been eroded by the VOC administration, so that finally they had been reduced to second-rate citizens.

Cape burghers could be forgiven for thinking that they were equal to Dutch city burghers, because the similarities seemed evident. One of significance was the oath that all Dutch burghers were expected to swear, pledging allegiance to the States-General and the *stadholder*, and promising to obey the local government and laws, preserve the peace and to support and protect the city and fellow burghers, if needed, by military means. The oath was a contract between the city and the burgher. The burgher became part of an exclusive and privileged community in exchange for financial, political and social support till 'death us do part' as the burghers of the city of 's Hertogenbosch promised. The burgher oath furthermore stressed the existence of local allegiance as opposed to national identity.[16]

The Cape burghers, too, promised allegiance and obedience to the States-General, the *stadholder*, the directors of the VOC and the governor, magistrates and other authorities of the settlement. They also swore to defend the United Netherlands and 'this city' (*deese Steede*) to the utmost, even if it cost them their lives.[17] The oath was taken once a year in October or November by burghers who had received their letters of grant in the

---

15 *Nederlandsch Afrika*, 15–18.
16 Prak, M. 1997. Burghers into citizens: Urban and national citizenship in the Netherlands during the revolutionary era (c. 1800). *Theory and Society* 26(4): 403–420, 405; Kuijpers & Prak 2002:118; Streng, JC. 1997. *Stemme in Staat: De bestuurlijke Elite in de Stadsrepubliek Zwolle 1579–1795*. Hilversum: Verloren, 94.
17 Council of Policy. *Oath Book C 2661*, Cape Town: WCARS, 1725.10.23, 69; *C 2663*, 1748.10.21, 67.

previous year and by residents who were born as burghers and had reached the age of 16, which was when they were expected to become members of the burgher militia.

The wording of the burgher oaths in Dutch cities and the oath taken at the Cape was strikingly similar, as was the promise that Cape burghers would be loyal to the government of the United Provinces. The Cape burgher oath also unmistakably referred to events in the Dutch Republic itself. The Dutch Republic did not have a *stadholder* between 1702 and 1748, a time known as the second 'stadholder-less' period. This political status was reflected in the difference between the oath taken before 1748 and the one after that year. The former did not contain a swearing of allegiance to the *stadholder*, whereas from 1748 onwards the burgher swore loyalty to 'his illustrious highness the Lord Prince of Orange and Nassau as *Stadholder*'. The swearing of an oath like this must have reinforced the perception among Cape burghers that they were an exclusive group with the same status as Dutch burghers.

However, the VOC officials denied that there was any similarity between Cape burghers and the burghers of towns in the Netherlands. Independent Fiscal Willem Cornelis Boers wrote that 'one makes a big mistake if one wants to compare the residents of a settlement like this with the privileged burghers of our great cities in the Republic'. He pointed out that the forefathers of the Dutch burghers had fought hard for their independence and that of the Republic. Their path to freedom, which they had achieved by their own hand, was glorious. In contrast, the decision by government to allow Cape burghers to settle as 'farmers, tailors, shoemakers and saddle makers' was a handout. Cape *burgerschap* was qualified, and the burghers there did not have unlimited freedom and rights. Ultimately, they had to abide by whatever decisions the Company government took concerning their fate.[18]

So what does a comparison between Dutch and Cape burghers show? Which view was closer to the truth? It needs to be looked at from two angles: first, comparing the tangible economic, political, legal and social benefits of *burgerschap*; second, determining if the ways in which *burgerschap* was obtained also applied to the Cape.

---

18 Boers, WC. 1779. *Verantwoording Gedaan Maken, ende aan de Wel-Edele Hoog Achtbare Heeren Bewindhebberen der Generale Geoctroyeerde Oost-Indische Compagnie der Vereenigde Nederlanden.* Cabo de Goede Hoop, 43–45.

The economic aspects of being a burgher

The biggest advantages of being a burgher of a Dutch town were probably economic in nature. At a basic level, there was the exemption from payment of certain tolls and taxes or the right to graze cattle on the city commons. By far the most important advantage was the exclusive right to practise a craft or trade in a city. Groups of artisans, and entrepreneurs involved in the same profession, were organised into guilds. The guilds made sure that their members were protected against interlopers and outsiders. Guild members had access to co-operation, credit and other forms of assistance. The collective offered protection to the individual. Without being a guild member, it was virtually impossible to set up a business, and one could not become a guild member if one did not have burgher rights first. Being a burgher was therefore crucial to economic survival.[19]

The many requests by Company employees to be released from the service show that economic imperatives were behind the desire to be a burgher — even if there is no evidence that there were guilds at the Cape.[20] Once a Company employee reached the end of his contract, he could decide if he wanted to settle at the Cape and work for himself. He then applied for permission to do so. These written requests had a fixed formula, which did not change much throughout the period of VOC rule. The Company employee introduced himself, named his place of birth and recorded when and in what capacity he had arrived at the Cape. He then declared that he now wanted to use his skill to make an honest living outside the Company service. The last sentence would be the humble request 'to release him from the service and favour him with the burgher rights of this place'. This wording is quite significant. The applicant did not ask for a general Dutch *burgerschap*, but for a specific local *burgerschap*. This was in line with the local nature of *burgerschap* in the Dutch Republic. Burghers were members of specific urban communities, not of a national collective. In this way, the new burgher became part of the *Caabsche burgerij*. In most cases the requests were granted, and an official letter of freedom (*vrijbrief*) was issued to the new burgher. These letters stated that the request 'to be appointed as Burgher' was approved and the applicant could now set himself up in a burgher trade accepted by the authorities.[21]

---

19 Prak, M. 1997. Burghers, citizens and popular politics in the Dutch Republic. *Eighteenth-Century Studies* 30(4): 443–448, 444; Prak 1997:405 (Burghers into citizens); Kuijpers & Prak 2002:116.

20 For an example of such a request for Cape burgher rights, see: Council of Policy. *Petitions and Nominations C 1172*, Cape Town: WCARS, 1778.10.01, 45–46.

21 For an example of such a letter of freedom, see: Master of the Supreme Court.

Political advantages

Only burghers were eligible for political office, such as being a member of the city council *(vroedschap)*, council of justice *(schepenbank)*, or a burgher councillor *(burgermeester)*.[22] The most prominent and wealthiest men among the burgher population were the regents, who were often major entrepreneurs. But even though power was in the hands of a ruling elite, the point is that city governors were still burghers, and there was essentially no difference in status between rulers and subjects. City residents were not afraid to remind their administrators of this and to caution them not to elevate themselves too much above the general population.

The burghers of the Cape settlement were also given the right to become members of the various administrative bodies, but it was more a matter of window-dressing than a sign of real power. The highest policy-making body, the Council of Policy, remained the exclusive domain of high-ranking Company officials. Together with the Company directors in the Netherlands and administrators in Batavia, these men determined all the rules and laws of the settlement without any form of burgher participation. François Bernard, in his *Nederlandsch Afrika,* was harsh in his judgment of the VOC government members: 'I would, without being far from the truth, say that the members of the Grand Council have always been personal enemies of the Settlers and Burghers, seeing that they make themselves guilty of many abuses of power towards them.'[23] He conveniently left out that, in essence, the Cape was not a Dutch city ruled by the burghers. It was a VOC refreshment post, which was governed by Company officials, who were given wide-ranging powers over their subjects. There was a small but significant difference in the burgher oaths sworn by the Dutch and Cape burghers. Cape burghers had to promise allegiance and obedience to VOC authorities, but Dutch burghers did not. It was a distinction that the Cape burgher protesters found hard to accept.

Judicial advantages

Burghers could be tried only by a local court consisting of their peers, ie burghers of their own city. This meant that even if a burgher committed a crime in a city he visited, he could escape justice by proving he was a

---

Liquidation and Distribution Account MOOC 14–62 (vol.13, 20), Cape Town: WCARS, 1772.02.06.

22 Prak 1997:444 (Burghers, citizens); Prak 1997:405–406 (Burghers into citizens).
23 *Nederlandsch Afrika,* 36.

registered burgher elsewhere, return there and then prevent extradition.[24] In Dutch cities justice over burghers was administered by fellow burghers.

No such situation existed in the Cape, because burghers were subject to the jurisdiction of the Company. There were no burgher courts and the Council of Justice was dominated by VOC employees. Even though the burgher councillors had a seat on the Council 'they were called to the meeting oftentimes only to be witnesses to the unjust sentences pronounced over the Settlers'.[25] In cases between a burgher and a Company employee, there could be no justice for a burgher, 'because wolves do not devour each other'.[26]

The control of the Company over the burghers was made clear in the letters of freedom issued by the VOC government, which stipulated conditions: the new burgher was not allowed to make any applications for land belonging to the Company, he was subject to all rules and laws pertaining to burghers, and the Company reserved 'the power and authority to re-enlist him in his former rank and pay, if that would become necessary or when his behaviour is not appropriate'.[27] His burgher status could be taken away from him if he did not behave himself. Once that happened the Company could do what it wanted with him including deporting him from the Cape, because he was now again in the employ of the VOC.[28] In Dutch cities, too, a burgher could be removed from the burgher register if he misbehaved or was found guilty of a crime. Subsequent banishment from the city or district could be added to the punishment.

There are several examples of instances when the Company enforced its rights as set out in the letters of freedom. Haije Jansz Swarsenburg lost his burgher rights in 1765 as punishment for repeated drunkenness and bad behaviour, which meant that he could no longer be tolerated as a member of the burgher community. He was conscripted into Company service for five years and banished to India.[29] Another case was that of Michiel Engelhard, who became a burgher in 1776, but was recruited back into Company

---

24 Prak 1997:406 (Burghers into citizens).
25 *Nederlandsch Afrika*, 38–39.
26 *Nederlandsch Afrika*, 38–39.
27 Master of the Supreme Court. *Liquidation and Distribution Account MOOC 14–62* (vol.13, 20), Cape Town: WCARS, 1772.02.06.
28 Kuijpers & Prak 2002:124; Streng 1997:94.
29 Council of Policy. *Petitions and Nominations C 1151*, Cape Town: WCARS, 1770.07.31, 86–88; Council of Policy. *Resolutions C 143*, Cape Town: WCARS, 1765.06.15, 438–440; *C 148*, 1770.07.31, 234–237.

service and banished from the Cape in 1778 for bad behaviour.[30] The VOC government upheld the law and followed a custom accepted throughout the Dutch empire: burgher rights were granted in return for duties and obligations.

Social advantages

Lastly, *burgerschap* had certain social advantages. Many Dutch towns had special orphanages for the children of burghers. The *Burgerweeshuis* (burgher orphanage) in Amsterdam provided a better diet for orphaned burgher children than other orphanages did, and trained the children in forms of craft. They were thus set up with a relatively good start in life. Social welfare for burghers also included caring for the elderly in old-age homes and almshouses.[31]

At the Cape, care for the poor was entrusted to the deacons of the Dutch Reformed Church and orphans were cared for by the Orphan Chamber. Although this care was not limited to burghers, they did have an advantage over other groups. At the beginning of the eighteenth century it was determined that the financial assistance given to free blacks should be half of that provided to burghers.[32] Cape burghers had access to social welfare.

Obtaining *burgerschap* in the Cape

In the United Netherlands, there were generally four ways to achieve *burgher status:* through birth, marriage, purchase and grant.

To get burgher status by birth was not straightforward, because different cities applied different rules. Until the end of the eighteenth century the city of 's Hertogenbosch applied quite broad criteria: all people born or even just baptised within the town automatically received *burgerschap* and could never lose it. Amsterdam and Deventer were more restrictive: only children born in wedlock to burgher parents were assured of automatic *burgerschap* in these cities. Either way, *burgerschap* acquired by birth had to be confirmed at a later age. The registration process involved being able to prove that one's

---

30 Council of Policy. *Petitions and Nominations C 1166*, Cape Town: WCARS, 1776.10.04, 26; Council of Policy. *Resolutions C 157*, Cape Town: WCARS, 1779.01.05, 46.
31 Prak 1997:444 (Burghers, citizens); Kuijpers & Prak 2002:117–118.
32 Iliffe, J. 1987. *The African Poor. A History*. Cambridge, NY: Cambridge University Press, 97–98.

father was indeed a burgher, which was then followed by the swearing of the burgher oath.[33]

The situation in Cape Town seemed to be the same as in Amsterdam, ie, children born to burghers automatically inherited burgher status. For example, the sons of burgher families who went to work for the Company and wanted to be restored as burghers after the end of their contract could request this. Pieter Laurens Cloete, son of burgher and landowner Hendrik Cloete, entered Company service in April 1781, but in March 1787 he asked to be restored to his 'previous burgher freedom', because he wanted to assist his father in his business.[34] Johan Meijndertz Cruijwagen junior, the son of a burgher councillor, went to work for the Company in 1777. In 1789 he left the service to attend to personal business affairs and asked to be restored to his 'inherited burgher right'.[35]

It is clear that at the Cape one could not be a VOC employee and a burgher at the same time. Even though one was born a burgher, one would lose this status on entering the Company service and had to officially request the administration to get it back. In most cases this was a formality.

Another way of acquiring burgher rights in most towns in the Republic was by marrying a daughter of a burgher. Many (immigrant) men sought to marry into a burgher family, and burgher girls and women were in high demand on the wedding market. The rules in Amsterdam stated that the newly wedded husband, if he wanted to become a burgher, had to register as such within two weeks after the nuptials. If he died unregistered within that two-week period, any child conceived beforehand and later born would not be recognised as a burgher. This implied that burgher rights were not transferable through the mother to the child, even if she was a burgher daughter.[36]

In the Cape settlement, there are numerous examples of Company employees who married into a burgher family and applied for burgher rights at about the same time. Willem Cornelis Arendsz became a burgher on 30 July 1774 and married his burgher bride Maria Maasdorp on 28 August 1774. Andries Willem Beck was granted burgher rights on 11 October 1779 and married Maria Cecilia van der Merwe on 31 October. However, in the Cape marrying a burgher daughter was not always a precursor to becoming a burgher. Once a Company employee was ready to settle down as

---

33 Prak 1997:405–406 (Burghers into citizens).
34 Council of Policy. *Resolutions C 174*, Cape Town: WCARS, 1787.03.19, 285; Schutte 1982:186.
35 Council of Policy. *Resolutions C 184*, Cape Town: WCARS, 1789.12.11, 306–308.
36 Kuijpers & Prak 2002:120.

a burgher, he applied to leave the service. Starting a family could be part of this process, but the one could be done without the other. There were many high-ranking VOC officials who married burgher women but remained in Company service. Their aim was to make a career in Company service and not to become burghers. However, in the case of lower-placed VOC employees without obvious career prospects in the Company, marrying into a well-off burgher family created the opportunity to improve their lives. For both higher- and lower-ranking VOC employees who were immigrants, marrying into an established burgher family had a financial motive. It gave them access to a potentially useful kinship network, and to capital and property.

The cost of *burgerschap*

In the Netherlands if one could not find a burgher bride, there was always the possibility of buying *burgerschap*. The purchase price varied from city to city and was often determined by the market. *Burgerschap* of Amsterdam was hugely desirable in the Golden Age and the city fathers could therefore ask the hefty sum of 50 guilders, part of which went to the city orphanage and to care for the poor.[37] Nijmegen was not far behind charging 48 guilders, but in most Dutch towns more modest amounts in the order of 10 to 20 guilders were paid for burgher rights. Most Dutch cities did not have restrictions on buying *burgerschap*, but there were a few cities, like Deventer and Nijmegen, where this was open only to members of the Dutch Reformed church.[38] In some cases the purchase price of *burgerschap* became an instrument of social regulation and exclusivity. Fees could be raised to a level that would make it difficult for poorer outsiders to become burghers and thus prevent a city from being flooded by poor people who would place a burden on welfare institutions.

At the Cape neither the requests for burgher rights nor the letters of grant issued by the administration mentioned anything about costs. François Bernard is the only source who has referred to burghers 'who had bought their burgher right there'.[39] However, he did not quote any amounts, and in the Cape VOC archives I have not been able to find any record of payments for *burgerschap*. It seems that purchasing burgher rights was not an option

---

37 Amsterdam introduced a *groot burgerschap* in 1652, which could be acquired for the small fortune of 450 guilders. However, this attempt to boost the city coffers ended in failure and was terminated in 1668. Only one person bought major *burgerschap*, and it was granted to or inherited by just 11 others. Kuijpers & Prak 2002:116–117.
38 Prak 1997:406 (Burghers into citizens).
39 *Nederlandsch Afrika*, 116.

at the Cape but there are some indications that there could have been administrative costs involved in the process. The Resolutions of the Council of Policy record that the earlier mentioned Haije Jansz Swarsenburg was restored to his former burgher rights in 1770, but that since he was too poor to be able to afford the costs of a new letter of freedom the Council decided that the original *vrijbrief* issued to him in 1762 would do.[40] Another mention of monies paid in the process of acquiring burgher rights was recorded in the Resolutions of the Council of Policy in 1780 when the procedure to be followed by people who obtained burgher freedom was outlined. The new burgher had to register himself with the burgher councillors. To do so he needed to present his letter of freedom and, as further proof, an extract of the minutes of the Council of Policy referring to their decision to release him from Company service. A copy of the resolution could be obtained against a payment of stamp duty of six *stuijvers*.[41]

The last option to get burgher rights was by way of a grant by the city government. This mostly happened in the case of immigrants, who were invited to become burghers. Groups of refugees, too, especially those with useful skills, were given burgher rights. Ministers of the Dutch Reformed Church on entering the service of a local parish were also granted *burgerschap*.[42] The Dutch were more pragmatic than principled with regards to their *burgerschap* admissions. If it was beneficial for the city community to welcome outsiders, they would do so. A well-known example of this practice in the Cape settlement was the granting of *burgerschap* to the French Huguenots, whose knowledge of wine farming and brandy distilling was in demand.

The granting of *burgerschap* to specific groups of outsiders sometimes met with opposition. The shopkeepers of 's Hertogenbosch complained in 1775 that they were disadvantaged by the illegal practices of aliens, particularly Jews, whom they accused of not paying taxes and selling stolen goods. The shopkeepers demanded that Jews be banned from *burgerschap* and in 1777 the city council gave in to this demand.[43] At the Cape it was the financial assistance and certain privileges (eg the right to have their own church gatherings) granted to the Huguenots that eventually led to resentment among other burghers, and in 1700 it was officially decided to stop the Huguenot immigration.[44]

---

40 Council of Policy. *Resolutions C 148*, Cape Town: WCARS, 1770.07.31, 234–237.
41 Council of Policy. *Resolutions C 158*, Cape Town: WCARS, 1780.07.25, 225–236.
42 Prak 1997:444 (Burghers, citizens).
43 Prak 1997:407–409 (Burghers into citizens).
44 Wijsenbeek, T. 2007. Identity lost: Huguenot refugees in the Dutch Republic and its

It is fair to say that at the Cape a curious mix of Dutch custom and local conditions developed around the implementation of *burgerschap*. At face value, this was not extraordinary. After all, Dutch cities and towns themselves varied in the customs and laws surrounding burghers. There seemed nothing unusual about the fact that Cape administrators and burghers appeared to pick and choose which rules would apply. In the end, there were enough similarities to the Dutch processes to contribute to the thinking among Cape burghers that their status was the same as those of burghers of Dutch towns.

In the Cape burgher protests of the 1770s and 1780s the issue of *burgerschap* was paramount. The protesters quoted Jan van Riebeeck in support of their claims that their burgher rights were inalienable. Yet Van Riebeeck had made it clear that the burgher group was created for the benefit of the Company and not to 'provide an island of liberty for some of its employees'.[45] The only reason for their presence at the Cape was to serve the needs of the Cape settlement and the VOC. By the 1780s this had not changed, as was stated by a VOC official in no uncertain terms: '[T]he Cape burghers are really nothing more than slaves of the Company employees. They are only there to cook the food for the Company employees and keep the fire burning underneath the pot.'[46] When Independent Fiscal Boers stated that it was a big mistake to compare the Cape and Dutch burghers, he was merely reiterating official VOC policy. As far as the VOC was concerned, the Dutch settlers at the Cape and the Asian settlements were never meant to be equal to the residents of towns in the Dutch Republic. The social differences between them were clear. Economically, the burghers were subject to restrictions imposed by the Company. Politically, they were pretty much toothless. Judicially, they were at a disadvantage.

The burgher problem

One could argue that the Company directors had made a big mistake themselves, and caused a lot of misunderstanding and ambivalence, by introducing the term 'burgher' to describe the free settlers. The combination of this designation with some of the same rights that free residents of Dutch cities enjoyed, almost inevitably created an expectation of freedom and

former colonies in North America and South Africa, 1650 to 1750: a comparison. In N Worden (ed.). *Contingent Lives. Social Identity and Material Culture in the VOC World.* Cape Town: UCT Press, 91–109, 98.
45 Giliomee 2003:6.
46 *Nederlandsch Afrika*, 51.

equal standing among the Cape burgher population. Even though they had a sense of belonging to Cape society, they believed they were equal to Dutch burghers 'back home'.

One high-level Company official had the astute insight that this could lead to trouble. In 1685 the VOC directors sent Commissioner-General Hendrik Adriaan Van Reede tot Drakenstein on a fact-finding mission to the Asian settlements and asked him to report on possible administrative improvements. His first stop was the Cape of Good Hope. One of his recommendations for this VOC post was to sift through the burgher population and get rid of all those who were lazy, unmotivated or misbehaving. The designation of the remaining ones should then change 'from free burghers to peasants and farmhands' to make it clear that farming and supplying the Company was their purpose. He further advised that these men should not be allowed to live in Cape Town.[47] It seems that Van Reede believed that by excluding the Cape settlers from the community of town dwellers, they could not view themselves as a group of privileged residents. His advice was ignored, and it is doubtful if it would even have been practical at that stage of the development of the settlement, because clearly skills other than farming were needed for its success. Nevertheless, the Cape burghers could argue as much as they wanted that they were a privileged group of residents equal to their counterparts in the United Netherlands, but they were not: the settlers at the Cape were not 'free' burghers, but Company burghers.

---

47 Hulshof, A. 1941. H.A. van Reede tot Drakenstein, journaal van zijn verblijf aan de Kaap. *Bijdragen en Mededeelingen van het Historisch Genootschap*. Utrecht, 62, 130–131.

CHAPTER 4

Status or race: Free blacks

Although predominant in Cape society, VOC personnel and burghers were not the only social groups at the settlement. Other groups, including slaves and free blacks, also contributed to the shaping of the Cape community.[1] And despite the small size of the Cape settlement before 1800 it was a complex society.

Robert Ross writes that 'in Cape Town, more than elsewhere in South Africa, social relations have never been a direct function of economic activity, but have been heavily influenced by all sorts of other considerations'.[2] Other than Company officials and free burghers, the population of the Cape consisted of soldiers, sailors, craftsmen, traders, farmers, free blacks, (political) convicts from Asia and slaves, all of whom tried to assert and maintain their status and position within and outside their respective groups. They classified each other in terms of gender, class, occupation, legal status, religion, ethnicity, clothing and language, and in many other ways. Different classifications led to different hierarchies, which were by no means coincident. The cause of conflicts at the Cape settlement cannot simply be reduced to binary opposites, such as insiders against outsiders, VOC employees against burghers, free against slaves, or even white against black.

The Company tried to create some order in the diversity. In official documents, Cape residents generally were grouped in the following categories ranked according to status: VOC employees, burghers, free blacks and slaves. The Cape administration collected data on these people in the *opgaaf* (annual tax census). Every year, VOC employees, burghers and free blacks were to account for the number of people in their household and for the number of cattle, horses, sheep, pigs, guns and slaves they owned. Based on this information an amount of tax was determined. One must assume that there was a fair measure of under-reporting, but still, the *opgaafrolle*

---

1 Parts of this chapter were published in: Baartman, T. 2012. Protest and Dutch burgher identity. In N Worden (ed.). *Cape Town between East and West. Social Identities in a Dutch Colonial Town.* Cape Town: Jacana, 65–83.

2 Ross, R. 1989. Structure and culture in pre-industrial Cape Town: A survey of knowledge and ignorance. In WG James & M Simons (eds). *The Angry Divide. Social & Economic History of the Western Cape.* Cape Town: David Philip, 40–46, 43.

made it possible to divide the Cape population, in all its diverse groupings, into a socio-economic hierarchy.

Gerrit Schutte divides the residents of Cape Town into 'a labouring class, a modest middle class, and a well-established "haute bourgeoisie"'.[3] In the first group were the slaves, but also some free blacks, lower-ranked VOC employees and poor burghers. The last group consisted of the higher-level Company officials and wealthy burghers (urban entrepreneurs as well as affluent landowners and farmers). In between were free blacks, white servants and overseers (*knechten*).

Most of the burghers and Company officials had a European background: they came from the Netherlands, German states, Scandinavia and France, among other countries in Europe. It would be safe to assume that they were white. Slaves were imported from many different countries and regions. At the beginning of VOC rule, some slaves were brought in from West Africa, but this route was not legally open, because that part of the continent fell under the Dutch West India Company. Towards the end of Dutch rule (after 1776) a significant number of slaves were brought in from Mozambique and East Africa. Most, however, were drawn from Asia: Bengal, Malabar, Coromandel (all in India), Ceylon and the Indonesian islands.[4] The Cape administrators did not go out of their way to distinguish between the various people they forcibly brought to the settlement. Slaves were called *slaven* or *lijfeigenen* (serfs). And whether of African or Asian origin they were all grouped together under the denomination *zwarten* (blacks).[5]

Cape society before 1800 could reasonably be described as one in which white people subjugated black people. After all, most people in the highest-status groups were white, and those in the lowest were almost all black. But leaving it at that would obscure the complexity of the social groups. In fact, the burgher group was not exclusively white at all. Robert Ross states that eighteenth-century Cape society 'did not see itself as divided along racial lines, but rather as containing a multitude of statuses'.[6] There was no race definition in the *opgaafrolle* or other official documents in which the VOC delineated the status groups. Ross also points out that 'many of the skilled

---

3 Schutte 1989:300.
4 Armstrong & Worden 1989:110–122; Shell, R. 1994. *Children of Bondage. A Social History of the Slave Society at the Cape of Good Hope, 1652–1838.* Johannesburg: Witwatersrand University Press, 40–43.
5 Armstrong & Worden 1989:122.
6 Ross, R. 1993. *Beyond the Pale. Essays on the History of Colonial South Africa.* Hanover and London: Wesleyan University Press. 72.

trades were performed by both slaves and free, and by both free blacks and whites'.[7] As a consequence, there was no clear racial hierarchy in the trades. Siegfried Huigen has studied the accounts of many travellers to the Cape and finds that, while they described the differences between population groups, they did not necessarily do so from a racist or racial perspective. Some of the accounts categorised the various groups by aspects like culture, language, physiognomic characteristics and the presence or absence of laws, and constructed a hierarchy of the population groups on this basis. Others used morality as an approach and found that, though European settlers were supposed to be more 'civilised', morally they were the most repulsive group; the Dutch settlers came off worst in the view of many visiting scientists.[8] In contrast, Xhosas and Khoikhoi were regarded as 'noble savages'. Obviously, drawing a rigid line between white ruler and black subject does not bring us closer to a greater understanding of the social dynamics in the Cape settlement.

Then there was the institution of slavery. The Cape settlement developed firmly into a slave society and especially so during the eighteenth century.[9] After the VOC government took the decision to support slavery as a source of labour in 1717 (see Chapter 1), there was a noticeable increase in the number of slaves, which was further spurred by the growing Cape economy. Slave ownership became widespread. Most of the slaves were privately owned, by burghers in Cape Town and burgher farmers in the southwestern regions of the settlement. By the end of VOC rule in 1795, there were reportedly 16 839 slaves in the Cape.[10]

Markus Vink quotes Dutch minister François Valentijn (1666–1727), who stated that slavery was 'the world's oldest trade'.[11] When the Dutch entered the world of the Indian Ocean in the seventeenth century, they encountered a longstanding tradition of slavery in Arab, Indian and Asian countries. Kerry Ward recounts how the leading Indian scholar Mirza Abu Taleb Khan visited Cape Town in 1799. In his travelogue he comments on many aspects of life at the Cape, 'but in contrast to contemporary European travel accounts of the Cape, he was not the least bit surprised by the

---

7 Ross 1989:43 (Structure and culture in pre-industrial Cape Town).
8 Huigen, S. 2009. *Knowledge and Colonialism: Eighteenth-century Travellers in South Africa*. Leiden: Brill, 22–26.
9 Countless articles and books about slaves and slavery at the Cape have been written and published. It is not my intention to repeat that here.
10 Armstrong & Worden 1989:122–136.
11 Vink, M. 2003. The world's oldest trade: Dutch slavery and slave trade in the Indian Ocean in the seventeenth century. *Journal of World History* 14(2): 131–177, 132.

institution of slavery.[12] And his intended readership back home would have been quite familiar with it. The acceptance of slavery was reflective of the time and place. By modern standards, however, it is a detestable institution.

The Dutch could have made the choice not to continue the custom because slavery did not exist in the Netherlands. In principle, the Dutch Republic recognised '*vrije grond*' (free land): all people held in slavery were automatically regarded as free on entering the territory of the Netherlands. But it was often up to the individual to claim this right and if he or she did not know about it or did not have the means to demand freedom, and if owners were not inclined to make their slaves wiser, those brought from overseas could remain enslaved out of sight of the authorities. Towards the end of the eighteenth century, this situation became more official when the States-General decided several cases in favour of slave-owners. The laws against slavery in the Netherlands were not applied to slaves imported from the colonial settlements.[13]

The Dutch authorities picked the side of commerce, as they often did. Recent research has shown that a much larger group of Dutch entrepreneurs and merchants were involved in underwriting and insuring slave ships than has been assumed. This type of insurance business contributed to the continuation of the slave trade. Slavery insurance was part of the ordinary business activities of a large group of affluent Dutch business people.[14] It is likely that these men used their influence and connections, particularly with the big trading companies, to protect their financial interests.

The VOC was trying to build a trading empire, and the directors realised the advantages of having access to cheap labour and the financial gain that could be made from the trade in slaves. Perhaps to ease their conscience, the Dutch used a combination of theological, juristic and pragmatic arguments to support and justify the practice of slavery and the slave trade. The biblical argument was that Africans and Asians were the children of Ham who were cursed by God to be servants of the Western people. Great Dutch legal minds like Hugo Grotius defended the slavery of people captured in a just war, the sentence of slavery as an alternative to death, and voluntary sale into slavery to escape famine. Slavery was also justified in humanitarian terms by stating that the slave's body and soul could be saved from the infidels who owned

---

12 Ward, K. 2012. Southeast Asian migrants. In N Worden (ed.). *Cape Town between East and West. Social Identities in a Dutch Colonial Town*. Cape Town: Jacana, 84–100, 84.

13 Hoonhout, B. 2018. Vrije grond onbereikbaar voor slaven. In M 't Hart et al (eds). *Wereldgeschiedenis van Nederland*. Amsterdam: Ambo Anthos, 323–328.

14 Lurvink, K. 2019. Underwriting slavery: Insurance and slavery in the Dutch Republic (1718–1778). *Slavery & Abolition* 40(2).

and traded him or her. The institution of slavery was never principally condemned by Dutch opinion-makers in the seventeenth and eighteenth centuries. Some of them objected only to the excesses of slave treatment and punishment.[15]

Undoubtedly, inherent in the attitude of Westerners towards Africans and Asians was a sense of superiority. The Dutch settlers in the Cape were most certainly aware of and pointed out the differences between various population groups. However, it cannot simply be concluded that official discrimination in law or institutionalised racism were natural consequences of such awareness. Attempts to do so have resulted in doubtful interpretations, both of official rules and laws as well as of personal and social interactions. The actual situation was more nuanced than many historians would like us to believe. My study of the group of free blacks, based on their experience and position, offers alternative interpretations of some long-established narratives regarding race during VOC rule.

The free blacks or *vrijswartes* can arguably be called the extras of Cape historiography. Almost every other group in Cape society has been researched extensively. In some of these studies free blacks are mentioned, but often in no more than a supporting role.[16] But unlike slaves, who were bound to the lowest level of Cape society, free blacks and their descendants occupied all social levels.

Historians have found it difficult to define free blacks. Even the Company administration was not very precise in describing them in their official documents. Though the name 'free black' originated at the Cape, it was at first not used consistently to refer to a particular group and members

---

15 Vink 2003:149–153. See also Douma, J. 1999. Slavernij in het Nederlandse koloniale tijdperk: Waarom een zwarte bladzijde? *Transparant* 10(3): 4–12.

16 For information on free blacks see: Böeseken, AJ. 1977. *Slaves and Free Blacks at the Cape, 1658–1700.* Cape Town: Tafelberg; Elphick, R & Shell, R. 1989. Intergroup relations: Khoikhoi, settlers, slaves and free blacks, 1652–1795. In H Giliomee & R Elphick (eds). *The Shaping of South African Society, 1652–1840.* Cape Town: Maskew Miller Longman, 184–239; Ross 1993; Ross, R. 1999. *Status and Respectability in the Cape Colony, 1750–1870: A Tragedy of Manners.* Cambridge: Cambridge University Press, 32–34; Keegan, TJ. 1996. *Colonial South Africa and the Origins of the Racial Order.* Cape Town: University of Virginia Press; Heese, HF. 2005. *Groep sonder grense: Die rol en status van die gemengde bevolking aan die Kaap, 1652–1795.* Cape Town: Protea Boekhuis; Worden, N. (ed.). 2012. *Cape Town between East and West. Social Identities in a Dutch Colonial Town.* Cape Town: Jacana, 64–65; Schoeman, K. 2007. *Early Slavery at the Cape of Good Hope 1652–1717.* Pretoria: Protea Book House; Groenewald, G. 2010. Slaves and Free blacks in VOC Cape Town, 1652–1795. *History Compass* 8/9: 964–983.

of the group were sometimes classified differently. It was only by 1720 that free blacks were named as a separate group in the tax lists.[17]

There is a narrower definition of free blacks: 'persons who had been born in slavery and later freed, whether by their owners, by themselves, or by a third party'.[18] But free blacks were not only freed slaves. The Company administrators considered the Cape an excellent place of banishment, because of its isolated and remote position in the VOC's Indian Ocean world.[19] And so they sent a small group of people, political exiles and convicts, from Batavia and other parts of the Dutch Asian territories to the Cape. These people were mostly Asians, but there were a few European Company employees among them. Convicts became free once their sentences had expired, and if Asian they came to be regarded as free blacks together with freed slaves. Some historians therefore state that free blacks were not only ex-slaves, but that the group included a small number of ex-convicts and even the 'occasional free immigrant'.[20]

In the Asian VOC settlements, there were also freed slaves, but they were called *mardijkers*.[21]

At the Cape, the free blacks remained a relatively small group throughout the eighteenth century in comparison with slaves, burghers or Company employees. A 1731 census calculated that they made up a mere 6 per cent of the total population of the Cape District. By 1773 there was a total of only 390 free blacks.[22] One reason for the small size of this group is that not many slaves obtained freedom. Robert Shell estimates that between 1652 and 1833 there were 4 200 manumissions.[23] He points out that the crude manumission rate (number of manumissions per thousand slaves per year) 'began in the seventeenth century at about five slaves per thousand per year and steadily declined until it was just above one-tenth of 1 percent of the total population in the years before the general emancipation of all slaves in 1834'.[24] Most freed slaves were females and were often concubines and wives of the many (European) bachelors at the Cape.

Most free blacks lived in Cape Town and they were not a significant group in economic terms. They made their living as craftsmen, retailers,

---

17 Ross 1993:72.
18 Newton-King 2012:153–175, 243 n8.
19 Ward 2009:116–125.
20 Elphick & Shell 1989:184; Ross 1999:33; Worden 2012:64.
21 Böeseken 1977:77.
22 Worden 2012:50; Heese 2005:29.
23 Shell 1994:371–394.
24 Shell 1994:383.

hawkers and fishermen. After obtaining their freedom from slavery, they had to start out with next to nothing and that made it difficult for them to succeed in a highly competitive and constrictive economic environment. Some may have fared better than others, but overall, they were only marginally successful.[25]

The legal status of free blacks

Free blacks and burghers had different legal status, each group with its own rights and privileges as well as duties. This may seem an obvious distinction, but it must be noted that in some respects free blacks were rather like burghers: they were not in Company service and were not slaves; they could own property (including slaves); and they engaged largely in the same sort of business ventures and crafts. In June 1752 the government even declared that free blacks also had to pay taxes, because, 'they enjoyed all the privileges of burghers'.[26] The administration was rather disingenuous in this regard because the main differences between the two groups were in fact quite substantial. Free blacks could not be elected to public office, because this prerogative was awarded only to freeborn burghers and Company employees. Consequently, free blacks did not have a direct influence on political decision-making in the Cape. Free blacks also did not have representation on the Council of Justice, unlike the burghers. These significant political and judicial differences illustrate that there was a distinction between the legal status of the groups. However, this should not necessarily be translated into evidence of a sense of racial superiority among the burghers.

The different legal status of burghers and free blacks had a parallel in Dutch cities. Many cities recognised a second legal category of residents: those who were established but had no burgher rights, the so-called *inwoners* or *ingezetenen* (inhabitants). These inhabitants were not legally protected in the same way as burghers were, they could not be elected to public office, and they did not have access to guilds and therefore could not operate as independent craftsmen or shopkeepers. They could, however, own property and their property rights were respected. The major advantage of *burgerschap* was membership of the guilds and, related to that, the possibility of building up a relatively independent economic existence. This was probably the main reason for *inwoners* wanting to become burghers. In Amsterdam after about 1680, to protect the burghers' economic power, most guilds issued strict

---

25 Elphick & Shell 1989:221–224.
26 Council of Policy. *Resolution C 130*, Cape Town: WCARS, 1752.06.06, 185.

rules against accepting *ingezetenen* in their ranks. As a result, the number of these inhabitants decreased dramatically, while the number of burghers increased. The *ingezetenen* were now forced to buy *burgerschap* if they wanted to survive economically.[27]

The free blacks of Cape Town were remarkably like the *ingezetenen*. Although there was no guild activity in the settlement, and therefore burghers and free blacks in principle had equal access to economic opportunities, the burgher group was more organised and connected, which gave them the upper hand. And there was a manifest political and judicial distinction between the two groups as there was between burghers and *ingezetenen* in Dutch cities.

How the lens of race obscures the facts

It is my opinion that by removing race from the discussion about free blacks and burghers, we gain a better understanding of Cape society. Free blacks originated mostly from Africa or Asia or, if their parents mixed with Dutch and other Europeans, were of African or Asian descent. This has given the group a racial aspect which seems to have been predominant in the minds of most historians who have written about free blacks. They have focused on the 'black' part of 'free black' as opposed to the 'free' part, the latter referring to their legal status within society. Some have claimed that the level of racial discrimination in the Cape settlement increased considerably towards the end of the eighteenth century.

In their chapter in *The Shaping of South African Society*, Robert Shell and Richard Elphick are, to my mind, oblivious of the proper context of rules and laws. They write: 'By the second half of the eighteenth century the laws had ceased to be colour-blind.'[28] They give two examples. The first refers to the sumptuary laws issued in 1755. The government had noticed, in 1765, that free black women were attempting to show themselves equal to, or sometimes even above, burgher women by dressing in the same manner. To put a stop to this the administration ordered that free black women could no longer appear in public 'in coloured silk clothing, hoopskirts, fine laces, adorned bonnets, curled hair or ear-rings'.[29] This was a clear instance of racial discrimination according to Elphick and Shell.

---

27 Kuijpers & Prak 2002:125–127; Prak 1997:407 (Burgher into citizens); Streng 1997: 91–92.
28 Elphick & Shell 1989:215.
29 Ibid.

These rules further defined the already very specific sumptuary laws that had been enacted a decade earlier by the VOC in Batavia and its other settlements, which detailed exactly the type of carriages, number of horses, type of decoration, and the number and dress of servants that could be used by each rank in the Company hierarchy and by members of the different status groups in the general population. The regulations also specified the type of clothing, the material of this clothing, and the amount of money that could be spent on it, for each rank and status. Members of the highest level of society were thus allowed to have gold or silver embroidery on their clothes and wear lace; those immediately below them in rank could not go further than velvet; the rest could wear only wool or silk garments. Robert Ross points out that these laws were created to preserve 'distinction and subordination' within society.[30] The Company directors were attempting to ensure that the VOC remained supreme and to reinforce the societal hierarchy. The sumptuary laws dictated that every status group would demonstrate their status in outward display, visible to all members of society. They were not an attempt to construct a difference between races.

The second example used by Elphick and Shell to show that Cape legislation had become increasingly racial was the law of 1771 against the buying or bartering of clothing provided by the Company to slaves or convicts. They claim that the punishment for transgression by 'Europeans' was a fine, whereas free blacks were to be flogged and sentenced to 10 years of hard labour. However, the wording of the original *plakkaat* has been changed in their Afrikaans translation, 'Europeans' becomes *blankes* (whites),[31] which suggests that the difference in punishment was racially motivated.

When reading the *plakkaat* in Dutch, as issued in 1771, one discovers that there is no racial qualification or reference in it whatsoever.[32] The law sets out the penalties for buyers and sellers of slave clothing. The buyers could be anybody in Cape Town and they were to be punished with a fine for the first two offences and if caught a third time they would be banished. The sellers, however, would receive the harsh punishment of flogging and 10 years of hard labour. It was a matter of chance that the sellers were likely

---

30 Ross, R. 2007. Sumptuary laws in Europe, the Netherlands and the Dutch colonies. In N Worden (ed). *Contingent Lives. Social Identity and Material Culture in the VOC World.* Cape Town: UCT Press, 382–390.

31 Elphick, R & Shell, R. 1989. Onderlinge verhoudings: Khoikhoi, nedersetters, slawe en vryswartes, 1652–1795. In H Giliomee & R Elphick (eds). *'n Samelewing in Wording, 1652–1840.* Cape Town, 188–246, 221.

32 Council of Policy. *Placaat Books C 2285,* Cape Town: WCARS, 1771.06.19.

mostly slaves or free blacks (in this case convicts) simply because they were the ones who received the clothes from the Company. Thus, the difference in punishment is between sellers and buyers, not between whites and free blacks.

Eighteenth-century Cape official documents were mostly written in direct language. They can be taken at face value without having to look for hidden meaning and agendas. The VOC was confident that it was firmly in charge of the Cape throughout the eighteenth century and there was no need for Company officials to disguise their intentions. If they had wanted to create a racial difference in punishment, they would have stated this clearly. It is my opinion that the 1771 law did not distinguish between races, and that it is a misrepresentation of facts to state otherwise.

In 1779, the petition submitted by the protesting burghers, who are the main subject of this book, made demands that targeted other groups. They proposed that no foreigners originating from European countries should be allowed to engage in burgher trade or become burghers without first having been in Company service. This point was followed by one that stated that Chinese or Javanese immigrants, or convicted criminals (*bandieten*), should not be permitted to live among the burgher population, trade or have shops, because — among other reasons — they were 'buyers of stolen goods and would tempt slaves to become thieves'.[33] It could be argued that this demand was dangerously close to stigmatisation and expressed the desire to create a social distance between the burghers and other groups. If the VOC administration had acceded to these requests, it could easily have led to terrorisation, in the form of racist and discriminatory behaviour.[34] However, the Company and the government did not agree to these demands. Seen in the entire context of the burgher protests the 1779 proposal should be interpreted as a reaction of the burghers to a perceived threat to their advantages and status as burghers from the many other types of residents: foreigners from European countries, Africans and Asians. I argue that their demands were based on a sense of entitlement born from a historical social reality and not from a sense of racial superiority.

What the Cape burghers did in the 1770s and 1780s was not that different from what happened in many Dutch cities and had been happening for at least two centuries: they asserted the differences between insiders and outsiders when times were difficult. The Dutch have widely

---

33 Council of Policy. *Cape Disputes C 2689*, Cape Town: WCARS, 1779.10.09, 69.
34 See for this theory: Van Arkel, D. 2009. *The Drawing of the Mark of Cain. A Socio-Historical Analysis of the Growth of Anti-Jewish Stereotypes*. Amsterdam University Press.

been described as tolerant of outsiders and people who were different from them. This tolerance was pragmatic attitude; it opened doors when the skills or economic advantages of the outsiders were needed but changed to animosity when political and economic positions and privileges were under threat. Their so-called tolerance was perhaps more an attitude of indifference when advantages were not threatened. But when they were, status and privilege linked to *burgerschap* suddenly became paramount and outsiders were prevented from moving into burgher territory. For example, in the 1770s in 's Hertogenbosch, bakers from surrounding villages bought burgher rights and rented rooms in the city, which gave them the right to buy grain earlier than outsiders. But they would then return to their homes, which meant that they did not share in and contribute to the duties of resident burghers. The burghers therefore urged the city administration to put a stop to this practice.[35]

Another case which is often quoted to substantiate the point about increasing racial discrimination at the Cape was the petition submitted in 1788 by a group of Stellenbosch burghers who refused to serve under a corporal in the burgher militia because he was 'of a black colour'.[36] This corporal, Jan Hartog junior, sued his principal detractor, Daniel Bosman, for serious verbal insult and defamation in March 1789.[37] Apparently, Bosman had quoted the Bible (Deuteronomy 23:3) to justify why Hartog should not be made corporal. The verse he quoted refers to the Moabites and Ammonites, who had not assisted the Israelites when they fled from Egypt and was used to imply that Hartog was a heathen and a traitor. In court, Hartog stated that he was a Christian and had never done anything to harm the community. Bosman had allegedly also claimed that Hartog was *bruijnachtig van Couleur* (brownish in colour). Hartog countered that his colour did not disqualify him from being a corporal, and that if that criterion were to be used, a complete overhaul of the burgher militia, as well as governmental structures at the Cape, would have to take place. Many brown people served in various high positions and nobody had ever made an issue about this. Hartog added that colour had nothing to do with being a good and upstanding member of the burgher community. What was important to consider was whether one was honest and peace-loving

---

35 Prak, M. 1999. *Republikeinse Veelheid, Democratisch Enkelvoud. Social Verandering in het Revolutietijdvak, 's-Hertogenbosch 1770–1820.* Nijmegen: SUN, 35–44.
36 Keegan 1996:24.
37 Council of Justice. *Civil Cases: Original Rolls and Minutes CJ 883*, Cape Town: WCARS, 1789, 228–229; Council of Justice. *Civil Cases: General Series CJ 1163*, Cape Town: WCARS, 1789, 246–305.

and Hartog claimed that he was just that. The matter was eventually settled amicably and the men shook hands in friendship. Bosman officially declared Hartog to be an honourable person.

A few observations can be made about this court case. Even though race or colour seemed to have played a role, it was not the main one. The court papers give the distinct impression that it was a case of sour grapes and that Bosman had some personal problem with Hartog, which was exacerbated when Hartog was promoted to corporal over him. Perhaps Bosman had ambitions to be promoted and was upset that he did not get the post.

It is further noteworthy that the racial aspect was an exception. Between 1772 and 1791 there were at least 91 defamation and insult cases before the Council of Justice in Cape Town.[38] But in only two of these was a reference made to colour or racial descent, and in both cases, it seemed that the underlying cause of the dispute was about something else.

Another notable point is that Hartog, despite being 'non-white', was a burgher and was qualified as such in the records of the Council of Justice, and there were many like him. He was not wrong when he stated that descendants of unions between whites and (former) slaves as well as between whites and free blacks filled all kinds of public roles in Cape society, some more prominent than others. It is well established that mixed marriages were a regular occurrence in the eighteenth century and were not discouraged by the authorities. This is borne out by a study about the origin of Afrikaners, published in 1971 by JA Heese.[39] Controversially (for the time) he estimated that 7 per cent of Afrikaner families had a non-white foremother. This was mainly because, during the VOC period at the Cape males outnumbered females within the European population, and so they sought sexual partners and spouses in other population groups. Consequently, there were a fair number of unions, legitimate and illegitimate, between European men and slave women or women from slave descent.[40]

It follows that the offspring of these unions became an accepted part of life at the Cape. For instance, in 1788 and 1789, when the Hartog case played out, two of the five active burgher councillors were descendants of Angela van Bengalen, a former slave of Jan van Riebeeck. One was a leading

---

38 I have made an inventory of these cases. Baartman, T. 2012. *The most precious possession: Honour, reputation and the Cape Council of Justice*. Unpublished paper, Cape Town.
39 Heese, JA 1971. *Die Herkoms van die Afrikaner 1657–1867*. Cape Town: AA Balkema.
40 See on this subject: Ross 1993 ('White' population of South Africa); Malherbe, VC. 2006. Illegitimacy and family formation in colonial Cape Town, to c. 1850. *Journal of Social History* 19(4): 1153–1176; Heese 2005; Elphick & Shell 1989:194–204.

burgher protester of the late 1770s, Christiaan George Maasdorp, who was the great-grandson of Angela van Bengalen. Before she married Maasdorp's great-grandfather, Arnoldus Willemsz Basson, she had a daughter called Anna de Koningh, who would later marry Olof Bergh. Their daughter Christina married Jacobus de Wet and one of their sons, Hendrik Justinus de Wet, was the other burgher councillor referred to above. Anna Böeseken writes about Angela van Bengalen: 'What is remarkable about this woman from Bengal is the perfectly natural way in which she fitted into a white community without disregarding the friends she had made when she was still a slave.'[41]

The Free Corps

In 1787 the Burgher Military Council submitted to the Council of Policy that there were men among the population who were born illegitimately, but not in bondage, and that these men should not serve in the burgher militia, presumably because they would bring down the standing of burghers. But they would also not fit in the category of men who were freed slaves, and who served as firemen, because they were born free.[42] These men apparently could not be classified as burghers or as free blacks and it was therefore difficult to fit them into the existing militia structures. The Burgher Military Council suggested instituting a *Vrij Corps* (Free Corps) to accommodate these men. The Council of Policy subsequently approved this plan.[43] The establishment of the Free Corps has been explained by some researchers as a further sign that racial divisions became stronger towards the end of the eighteenth century. Timothy Keegan, for example, writes that the 'implication was that one had to be of putatively European ancestry to be fully accepted within the ranks of the dominant, respectable free burgher population.'[44] And Richard Elphick and Hermann Giliomee conclude that 'increasing tension between Europeans and persons of mixed blood was evident in disputes concerning the militia.'[45]

---

41 Böeseken 1977:81; De Villiers, CC & Pama, C. 1981. *Geslagsregisters van die Ou Kaapse Families.* 2 vols. Cape Town and Rotterdam: AA Balkema, 1124–1127. For more on Angela van Bengalen see Schoeman, K. 2001. *Armosyn van die Kaap: Die Wêreld van 'n Slavin 1652–1733.* Cape Town: Human & Rousseau. See also the first chapter of Heese 2005.
42 A militia of free black firemen was created in the 1720s.
43 Council of Policy. *Resolutions C 174,* Cape Town: WCARS, 1787.01.26.
44 Keegan 1996:23–24.
45 Elphick, R & Giliomee, H. 1989. The origins and entrenchment of European dominance at the Cape, 1652–c. 1840. In H Giliomee & R Elphick (eds). *The Shaping of South African Society, 1652–1840.* Cape Town: Maskew Miller Longman, 521–566, 547.

But these interpretations become questionable when considered from an eighteenth-century perspective. The documentation regarding the Free Corps did not make any reference to race. What rather seemed to be the case was that, by the 1780s, the Cape government was trying to deal with an increasingly complex society in which they had to accommodate the rights and position of several different groups. Issues of status had become especially topical during the 1780s when the burgher group made a huge effort to protect and fight for their rights. It was certainly not desirable to give the influential burgher population any reason for further dissatisfaction and possible unrest. The establishment of the Free Corps could thus be seen, as were the sumptuary laws, as an attempt by the government to make sure that each group in Cape society knew its place and that people could not be left free to usurp the rights of others. This was considered important in a culture where status, and especially its outward signs, played a significant role.

The possibility of an alternative interpretation of the establishment of the Free Corps would put the matter of Jan Smook, which is often quoted to argue that racism had taken hold in (late) eighteenth-century Cape Town, in a different light. Jan Smook was married to Johanna van de Kaap, a former slave. In 1790 Smook complained to the Council of Policy that his son had not been allowed to serve in the burgher militia, but had been ordered to join the Free Corps instead.[46] Most researchers who write about Smook blame racism for the decision and claim that the young man had not been allowed to join the burgher militia because he was of mixed descent. However, Jan Smook stated in his complaint that he believed this was a matter of 'a personal gripe of Muller against [him]'.[47] Smook referred to Petrus Jesse Möller, the militia captain who had given the order not to enrol his son. Smook thought it was a personal issue because Möller did not prevent other sons of former slave women to become members of the burgher militia. As an example, Smook mentioned that Möller had enrolled Pieter Voges junior, the son of the burgher Pieter Voges, who was married to Nelletje van de Kaap, a freed slave. This aspect is often not mentioned by scholars. For instance, Robert Shell in *Children of Bondage*, includes a transcription of Smook's request but omits the section

---

46 Council of Policy. *Resolutions C 190*, Cape Town: WCARS, 311–320; Keegan 1996:24; Shell 1994:372–374.
47 Council of Policy. Resolutions C 190, Cape Town: WCARS, 1790.11.19; Heese, JA & Lombard, RTJ. 1986–2007. *Suid-Afrikaanse Geslagregisters / South African Genealogies*. Pretoria and Stellenbosch: GSSA, 316.

about the personal antagonism between Smook and Möller.[48] When reading the request of Jan Smook in its original version one gets the impression that he had been most concerned about preserving his standing in the burgher community, of which he was a respected member. Smook had been appointed corporal in 1787 and held the important position of one of the butchers contracted to supply meat to the VOC. His high social status in the Cape community was thus without question.[49] All he wanted to do was to protect his reputation and this naturally extended to his family. He was highly upset that, even though he was lawfully married, and his children were all legitimate and had received a proper Christian upbringing, 'his children were not distinguished from those who were born illegitimately'.[50]

It was unfortunate for Smook that his request resulted in the Burgher Militia Council becoming more specific about the men who were to join the Free Corps. They replied to the Council of Policy that it was their intention that this corps would accommodate those men 'born in wedlock, but whose father and mother had been slaves'.[51] What mattered here was the significance of a person's descent: a son of a slave was not equal in standing to a son of freeborn burghers. Social and legal status were referred to, and whether race was implied is arguable.

Fluid boundaries

Hans Heese writes in *Groep sonder grense* (translated from Afrikaans): 'It later became the practice to place free-blacks and freeborn last on the [*opgaaf*] roll. More than one explanation could be offered for this, for example that they were considered inferior because of their skin colour or because they had few possessions and were therefore economically the lowest group.'[52] In fact, neither of these is correct. The Dutch administrators of the Cape divided the various groups in society according to their legal status. They compiled separate tax rolls for Company employees and for free residents. The last roll contained burghers and free blacks. First came the burghers and then the free blacks, which was simply because the latter had a different, albeit lower, legal standing in society than burghers, which had nothing to do with race, but everything to do with descent.

---

48 Shell 1994:372-374.
49 Ross 1993:73–74.
50 Council of Policy. *Resolutions C 190*, Cape Town: WCARS, 319.
51 Council of Policy. *Resolutions C 197*, Cape Town: WCARS, 1791.10.11, 242–250, 246.
52 Heese 2005:70.

Perhaps the most important illustration that there was no racial ideology in Cape society in the eighteenth century and that people were not primarily defined in racial terms is the fact that there was a fair amount of social mobility between the various status groups there. We know about the many Company servants who decided to leave the service and settle as burghers. What is less well-known is that children of free blacks were assimilated into the burgher group. There are several well-documented examples of the fluid boundaries between the status groups.

In the archives of the burgher council is a tax list of burghers dated 1783.[53] On this list are Abram Ventura (junior) and his brother Adriaan. They were the sons of Abraham van Ventura, the grandson of the slaves Ventura (from Ceylon) and Helena van de Kaap. Abraham van Ventura was named a free black in 1746 in a request to manumit a slave, yet his sons were burghers.[54] Brothers Adriaan and Abram Ventura took the burgher oath in 1770.[55]

On the 1783 tax list is also Abraham Adehaan, who was the grandson of Abdul Basir Sultania, the Rajah of Tambora, who was banished to the Cape in 1698. The Rajah stayed at Vergelegen, the estate of Governor Willem Adriaan van der Stel, and married the daughter of the well-known Shaykh Yusuf, Sitti Sara Marouff. After several failed requests the Rajah was finally allowed to return to the Indies in 1710, but because of his continued opposition to the Company, he was again exiled to the Cape in 1714.[56] The eldest son of the Rajah and Sitti Sara Marouff, Ibrahim Adehan was born in 1699. He converted to Christianity and was baptised in 1721. Under his new name, Abraham de Haan, he married Helena Valentijn, a daughter of the free blacks Hercules Valentijn of the West Coast of India and Cecelia van Bengalen. Their son, Abraham Adehaan, was born in 1731. In 1767 he married a Dutch woman, Christina Alesia Eversdijk of Amsterdam.[57] We do not know what Adehaan looked like, but in the light of his background, it is highly likely that he had distinctive Asian or Indian features. Adehaan swore

---

53 Burgher Council. *Quotisatie Rolle over den jaaren 1783, BRD 24,* Cape Town: WCARS, 1783.09.16.
54 Heese, JA & Lombard, RTJ. 1986–2007. *Suid-Afrikaanse Geslagregisters / South African Genealogies.* Pretoria and Stellenbosch: GSSA, 169–170; Leibbrandt, HCV. 1906. *Precis of the Archives of the Cape of Good Hope. Requesten (Memorials) 1715–1806.* Vol II. Cape Town and London, 632.
55 Council of Policy. *Oath Book C 2663,* Cape Town: WCARS, 1770.10.18, 96.
56 Ward 2009:210–212; Morris, M 2004. *Every Step of the Way: The Journey to Freedom in South Africa.* Cape Town: HSRC Press, 66–67.
57 Morris, *Every step of the way,* 67; Heese 2005:41; De Villiers & Pama 1981:276.

the burgher oath on 21 October 1750.[58] The significance of the occasion should not be downplayed: a descendant of Asian eminence swearing allegiance to the Dutch Republic and the VOC together with European men, promising to protect each other even if it would cost them their lives. After that Abraham Adehaan was consistently referred to as a burgher in all official VOC records. He was a well-respected and active member of the burgher community and an entrepreneur who acted as financial surety for and with other burghers.[59] In the period 1775–1799, he was one of the top 10 central individuals in the networks of private credit transactions that existed in the Cape, and he owned more than 25 slaves, which was indicative of his prosperity.[60]

A third case is that of Moses Davids, who was born in 1742 as the son of free black Martha van de Kaap. On 18 October 1758, he took the burgher oath in Cape Town.[61] In 1762 he married Anna Elizabeth Knoetzen, the illegitimate child of Elizabeth Knoetzen and Joachim Prinsloo. Moses Davids was a fully fledged member of the burgher community, who in 1779 was one of 404 burgher protesters against the VOC administration and in 1783 was identified as a burgher on the *Quotisatie Rolle* (tax list based on financial means). Also noteworthy is that in 1794 he was nominated to become a teacher in the District of Stellenbosch and was described as a 'Cape burgher and a member of the Dutch Reformed Church'.[62]

There is at least one known example of a man born as a slave who achieved burgher status in his lifetime. He was Frans Smiesing, the son of Jan Smiesing and Anna van Dapoer, both of whom were slaves in the Slave Lodge in Cape Town.[63] It is not known exactly when Anna van Dapoer became free. It could have been in 1731 when she married Jan Smiesing. In any case, in 1739 she was described as a free black when she requested the Council of Policy to manumit her two sons, Jan and Frans, who were slaves

---

58 Council of Policy. *Oath Book C 2663*, Cape Town: WCARS, 1750.10.21, 69.

59 See for instance civil matters heard in the Court of Justice in 1794 and 1795: Council of Justice, *Documents in Civil Cases, General Series, 1708–1827 CJ 1221*, Cape Town: WCARS, 1794.12.18, 253–261, and 1795.01.15, 239.

60 Swanepoel, C. 2017. The Private Credit Market of the Cape Colony, 1673–1834: Wealth, Property Rights, and Social Networks. PhD thesis, Stellenbosch University, 67–94.

61 Council of Policy. *Oath Book C 2663*, Cape Town: WCARS, 1758.10.18, 78.

62 Heese & Lombard 1986–2007 *Suid-Afrikaanse Geslagsregisters*. Vol 2: 33; Vol 4: 348; Leibbrandt *Precis*. Vol I: 12; Council of Policy. *Resolutions C 222*, Cape Town: WCARS, 1794.03.14, 358.

63 Shell, R. & Dick, A. 2012. Jan Smiesing, Slave Lodge schoolmaster and healer, 1697–1734. In N Worden (ed.). *Cape Town between East and West. Social Identities in a Dutch Colonial Town*. Cape Town: Jacana, 128–152.

in the Slave Lodge.[64] Frans was born in 1729, while his mother was still a slave and therefore he was one as well. By the time he was freed, he must have been about 10 years old. He entered the service of the Company in 1745 as a smith's apprentice. When his contract ended in 1751, he requested the Council of Policy to favour him with the burgher rights of Cape Town.[65] On 18 October 1751, he swore the burgher oath.[66] Frans Smiesing followed the same process as many Europeans did to become a burgher, but in contrast, he made the full transition from slave to free black to Company employee to burgher. He was a perfect example of the possibilities of social mobility that existed in eighteenth-century Cape Town.

The above cases illustrate established practice under VOC rule. Free blacks were named thus because they had obtained freedom from slavery, yet because of their status as former slaves, they could not become burghers. However, the 'stain of slavery'[67] did not apply to their children, who, if they were born free, were automatically regarded as burghers. This was the decisive factor: not that they were black, Asian, mixed or from slave descent, but that they were born free. And being free they had the right to be classified as burghers, which they later confirmed by taking the burgher oath.

Apart from the other reasons mentioned earlier in the chapter, it now appears that the fact that children of free blacks were assimilated into the burgher group was likely the biggest factor in the continued small size of the free black group. Basically, there was no natural growth.

The main determinant of the status of free blacks in eighteenth-century Cape society was that they were free, not that they were black. The children of free blacks (and thus descendants of slaves) became burghers. It is important to realise that this would not have been possible if access to the burgher group was based purely on race. This has implications for the composition of the burgher group. Because most burghers were of European descent, historians have tended to see the burgher group as strictly European or white. Often the terms 'burgher', 'European' and 'white' are used as if they were interchangeable. This is a fundamental mistake and results in unnecessary confusion because it creates the impression that Cape society before 1800 was divided along strict racial lines. Instead, the burgher

---

64 Council of Policy. *Petitions and Nominations C 1101*, Cape Town: WCARS, 1739, 8–9; Council of Policy. *Resolutions C 110*, Cape Town: WCARS, 1739.04.28, 42.
65 Council of Policy. *Petitions and Nominations C 1118*, Cape Town: WCARS, 1751, 81–82.
66 Council of Policy. *Oath Book C 2663*, Cape Town: WCARS, 1751.10.18, 69.
67 Ross 1993:74.

group was racially mixed. There never was a stipulation that burghers had to be of European descent and that the group was closed to blacks. Therefore, the burghers should be defined as a group of people who were not employed by the VOC or were slaves and whose status in society was tied to certain rights and duties that other groups did not have.

The Cape indeed consisted of a 'multitude of statuses'. The slaves, being on the lowest rung, were in no conceivable manner able to influence burgher politics. The middle layer, consisting of free blacks and poorer white servants and overseers, was too small and insignificant to have much of an impact. This book does not set out to exclude these groups, but when it comes to the politics of the Cape, it must be clear that the power struggles that are the topic of this book played out in the 'haute bourgeoisie': between elite Company officials and burghers of wealth, position and rank.

CHAPTER 5

Traditions of protest

It did not take long for the first clash between Cape burghers and the VOC administration to occur. On the afternoon of 23 December 1658, two burgher councillors, Steven Jansen of Wageningen and Hendricq Boom of Den Overtoom, submitted a petition signed by themselves and 12 other burghers to Commander Van Riebeeck and the Council of Policy. Van Riebeeck's *Daghregister* (logbook) has a running commentary on the Council meeting during which the VOC administrators replied to the burgher petition.[1] The petition was submitted 'with the necessary reverence'. Van Riebeeck, however, noted with some irritation that it was 'actually a seditious request and document. The supplicants claim to be respectful in the beginning, but then they continue to present an ultimatum'.

The petition aimed to change VOC economic policies, which, according to the burghers, were restrictive and oppressive. The petitioners wanted the Company authorities to honour a promise they had made: to give burghers the right to freely barter for cattle with the indigenous population. In response, the Council read out the burghers' letters of freedom to demonstrate that although they were free they were subject to all orders issued by the Company and its representatives. They were mistaken in their belief that they could trade freely with the Khoi. Visiting VOC commissioner Rijkloff van Goens had allowed them some free trade under certain conditions, but it was soon found that the burghers had abused this right. So in May 1658 a law had been passed prohibiting all private trade in cattle.

The burghers further claimed that they had not been informed of the exact price they would be paid for the corn and barley they produced. They demanded that a price be set on the spot, and that this price be guaranteed in writing by the Council of Policy, because 'they did not believe any word which was said, as they were appeased by all kinds of fine words, but no deeds'. Furthermore, the burghers threatened to strike and stop cultivating their lands, because they 'were not the Company's slaves'.

The belligerent tone of the burghers' petition angered Van Riebeeck. He wondered what motivated 'the free settlers to submit to their compassionate

---

1 Bosman, DB & Thom, HB (eds). 1955. *Daghregister Gehouden by den Oppercoopman Jan Anthonisz Van Riebeeck, Deel II, 1665–1658*. Kaapstad: Balkema, 435–447.

commander such a bold demand, which left a taste of subversion rather than the required obedience'. The burghers were not regarded as slaves, but they were obliged, as stated in their letters of freedom, to be loyal and obedient to the Company authorities. To Van Riebeeck it seemed that the free burghers wanted 'to be masters above their lawful government, and even over the honourable Company and its directors'. He told the petitioners to leave lawmaking to the government and to behave as obedient subjects should. Van Riebeeck then made a clever move by saying he was giving in to the demand to disclose the price that the VOC directors intended to pay for the burgher produce. He said he had not done so yet, because he had not wanted to create a situation in which the burghers would try to sell their corn illegally, and he had planned to negotiate a better price without interference. As it turned out, the price was indeed lower than the burghers expected.

The outcome of the meeting was that the burghers were forced to admit that the commander was on their side, and that they had been wrong in submitting the petition. With egg on their faces, they asked for forgiveness, to which Van Riebeeck replied that he could forgive this assault on his authority, but he cautioned that their real problem was with the Heeren XVII, who would disapprove of this attempt to force their hand. He pointed out that the burghers were not indispensable. There were enough other men who would jump at the opportunity to take their place. The burghers were then each given a glass of wine, and once 'the pleasing peace and order was restored', they left the council chamber in good spirits.

Van Riebeeck's superiors could only have approved of how the commander dealt with the burgher protesters. Van Riebeeck had demonstrated he was a skilled politician. He had listened to what the burghers had to say and had pretended to be interested but replied without giving in to their demands. He had made it seem as if he was on their side but made sure that he did not give assurances he would later have to renege on and which could embarrass his superiors. He admonished the burghers like petulant children and embarrassed them about coming to him with such unreasonable demands.

Van Riebeeck's performance was so convincing that among the Cape burghers his reputation as a 'wise Commander' was still standing 125 years later, when the burghers again protested against Company rule. François Bernard, author of *Nederlandsch Afrika*, wrote in 1783 that during the first years of settlement 'only Riebeek was able to maintain good order, peace, harmony, and unity'. He mediated in conflicts among the settlers, and in those between settlers and Company servants, and 'he always acted like a loving father rather than a harsh judge'.[2] Bernard continued to heap praise on Van Riebeeck and concluded that 'the short period, during which Justice and Equity ruled at the Cape, while Riebeek was in charge, can be called the golden age of the Settlement'.[3]

The significance of this event is not in Van Riebeeck's accomplishments as Company commander of the Cape. It is rather that it was the first recorded event of a Cape burgher protest and that the process the burghers used to express their dissatisfaction with Company policies mirrored a longstanding tradition of protest widely used in the Dutch Republic.

Rulers in Western Europe traditionally (at least since the late Middle Ages) used a conventional rhetoric to underline their authority. They disguised this in benign terminology, in which they portrayed themselves as the (often divinely anointed) leader, who took care of their subjects but were severe when their authority was challenged. It was vital that they alone remained in political, fiscal and religious control without any room for power-sharing or interference.[4]

But times were changing. Cities in the Netherlands were flourishing and commanded an ever-increasing economic power. Urban elites were less inclined to put up with an autocratic ruler who limited their ambitions, and they started to demand a greater say in government. Cities formed coalitions against the centralisation of power in the hands of one sovereign. This resulted in a series of rebellions lasting from the early fourteenth to the late fifteenth century, which were labelled the Great Tradition of Revolts by Wim Blockmans.[5] This urban opposition was not republican in nature. The cities did not want to remove their monarchs, but they were adamant that they should be given the opportunity to share power so that they could protect their urban freedom and autonomy. Overall, their aim was to establish a political model in which the central powers of the traditional ruler were bounded by a framework of co-operation.

An important outcome of the Great Tradition was the Little Tradition of urban revolt, described by Marc Boone and Maarten Prak.[6] They argue that the struggle for urban independence was fought in the name of the urban

---

2   *Nederlandsch Afrika*, 18–19.
3   *Nederlandsch Afrika*, 22–23.
4   Blockmans, WP. 1988. Alternatives to monarchical centralisation: The great tradition of revolt in Flanders and Brabant. In HG Koenigsberger (ed.). *Republiken und Republikanismus im Europa der Frühen Neuzeit*. Munich: Oldenbourg Wissenschaftsverlag, 145–154, 146–148.
5   Ibid 148–152.
6   Boone, M & Prak, M. 1995. Rulers, patricians and burghers: The great and little traditions of urban revolt in the Low Countries. In K Davids & J Lucassen (eds).

community in general, and that this created a political awareness among large groups of city dwellers who in turn began to demand representation from local authorities.

Urban residents had the ideal structures in place through which to organise their protests. There were many kinds of corporations, such as craft guilds, civil militias, churches, universities and even organised groups of residents of a street or neighbourhood. The city itself could be regarded as the overarching corporation. The existence of corporations in Dutch society was based on the principle of privileged exception. This meant that members of these organisations claimed to have rights and privileges that others could and should not have, and that they had a measure of autonomy within the larger community. Their membership further showed that they were making a positive contribution to the community at large by fulfilling duties like paying taxes and being involved in the security of the town. There was no room for individuality in this environment. Personal identity in urban society was defined by membership of a group. It follows that residents would strive to become members of a corporation (hence the desire to obtain official *burgerschap* for instance), because this offered them the opportunity to maintain the fundamental elements of their way of life: economic independence, political assertiveness, virtue and honour.[7]

The Great Tradition had legitimised revolt as a political weapon, it had appointed corporate organisations as modes of mobilisation, and it had established the strength of the urban community versus the government. The Little Tradition differed from the Great Tradition in scale. It occurred within the confined boundaries of cities and towns as opposed to the context of a wider regional conflict. Yet the two cannot be regarded independently of each other.[8]

The people on the opposing side were the members of the ruling elite which had evolved from a group of major entrepreneurs who engaged in international freight shipping and trading, fishing and local industries. They were the ones with whom the landlords and nobility communicated and from their midst the members of town councils were chosen. Up to the sixteenth and early seventeenth century, these men still divided their time between public office and their private business. From the second half of the seventeenth century the regents were forced to concentrate more on their

---

A Miracle Mirrored: The Dutch Republic in European Perspective. Cambridge: Cambridge University Press, 99–134.
7   For more on the Dutch corporate society of the early modern period see: Streng 1997:33–45; M. Prak 1999:22–27, 132–136
8   Prak 1999:140.

enterprises because of an economic downturn. At the same time continued growth of the cities caused the workload of the councillors to become heavier and more time consuming. Increasingly, the regents divided administrative tasks among family members. Some of them became professional administrators and politicians, while others remained involved in business and trade. The regents gradually became a distinct professional governing elite, which owned the land in the city centre, traded across vast distances and ran the city industry. They began to separate themselves from the rest of the city community by entrenching themselves in grand townhouses. They also bought property outside the cities on which they built conspicuous country houses. The regents formed only about 3 to 4 per cent of the city population, but their mark on Dutch society was greater than one might expect. Because most regent families were deeply involved in business and enterprise, local policies were heavily geared towards economic interests.[9]

Even though a small group of regents monopolised power, this power was not absolute. Dutch political structures were not set up as a dictatorship and local urban politics were not exclusively the domain of members of the ruling elite. Burghers belonging to the lower and middle social strata of the city actively and persistently challenged the authority and rule of the regents throughout the seventeenth and eighteenth centuries in what was described as the Little Tradition of revolt. The involvement of ordinary burghers in local politics generally manifested itself in two ways.

Riot as a form of protest

First, burghers expressed their discontent with the policies of the local rulers through riots. The early modern Dutch Republic has been described as peaceful and prosperous, where disputes were resolved through compromise. Riots are rarely mentioned in the books of Dutch historians. But Rudolf Dekker challenges this perception in his study of riots in cities in the most populous and urbanised province of the United Netherlands, Holland, in the period 1600–1800.[10] He defines a riot as 'a local action of a group of at least twenty people, who express a protest against the government over a period of at least half a day, but not longer than two weeks, whereby the public order is disrupted and violence occurs'.[11] He shows that rioting

---

9 Prak 2000:349; Leupen 2002:27–29; De Jong 1987:16; Roorda, DJ. 1978. *Partij en Factie. De Oproeren van 1672 in de Steden van Holland en Zeeland, een Krachtmeting tussen Partijen en Facties.* Groningen: Wolters-Noordhof, 38–41.
10 Dekker, R. 1982. *Holland in Beroering. Oproeren in de 17e and 18e Eeuw.* Baarn: Ambo.
11 Ibid 12–13.

was a regular occurrence in the cities of Holland. He divides the types of riot into food riots, tax rebellions, religious conflicts and political upheaval. These riots each had different motives and the participants varied from type to type. While religious and political disturbances tended to bring together residents from all walks of life, food riots were usually started and carried out by members of the lower ranks of urban society.[12] To pacify the rioters the city administrators sometimes gave in to some of their demands, but quite often these decisions were reversed once peace and order had returned. It is therefore questionable if the riots had a lasting impact on local policies.

Two of Dekker's conclusions are rather remarkable. The first is that the riots were exclusively urban. There were no disturbances by farmers in the countryside. Second, he concludes that the riots were not overly violent in nature. They did not involve attacks on people. The number of deaths in two centuries was less than six. Violence was contained and was directed at the goods of the intended targets via looting and destruction. Together with the fact that most city riots lasted only a few days, this may have contributed to the perception that the Dutch Republic was peaceful during the seventeenth and eighteenth centuries.[13]

One reason for the lack of physical violence during Dutch riots was that participants followed rules of engagement which hardly changed during the two centuries of Dekker's study. Riots were highly organised and structured, because the leadership was based in corporations. The burghers who were organised via the corporate structures were mostly economically independent residents, people of the middle layers of society. The riots mobilised the common people but were often controlled and well organised by more affluent members of the urban communities. They wanted to bring their point across, but they did not want to place themselves outside the existing structures, because that would threaten the social order and harmony they needed to give their lives meaning and to prosper economically. This explains why most Dutch turmoil was 'limited in scope and relatively non-violent'.[14]

---

12 Dekker 1982:22–50. See on food riots also: De Bont, F. 2014. *Op het Vorige is Genoeg Gewoekerd. Een Vergelijkende Studie naar Voedseloproeren in Holland, 1690–1770.* Nijmegen: Radboud Universiteit. De Bont concludes that the motive for food riots was not primarily a lack of food or hunger, but rather a demand for a just and fair price for food items at times when prices tended to increase.

13 Dekker 1982:142–144.

14 Prak, M. 2008. Challenges for the Republic: Coordination and loyalty in the Dutch Republic. In A Holenstein, T Maissen & M Prak (eds). *The Republican Alternative. The Netherlands and Switzerland Compared.* Amsterdam: Amsterdam University Press, 51–74, 59.

The petition — a tool of protest

Apart from rioting, there was another, more peaceful, way of influencing local politics available to the burghers. This second means, perhaps an even more significant aspect of the Little Tradition of protest, was petitioning. Here our story again becomes relevant to the Cape settlement. There are records of many petitions in Cape VOC history, starting with the one submitted to Jan van Riebeeck in 1658.

'Petitions were seen as a specific political right that the Republic's citizens were entitled to'[15] and they were a frequent instrument of protest used by individuals and organisations throughout the seventeenth and eighteenth centuries. The petition was an excellent means through which government at all levels and their subjects could resolve problems, and burghers could influence politics. Henk van Nierop argues that 'the regent class was able to keep the common burghers out of politics precisely because they were relatively open to informal pressures. Common burghers were able to influence administration and even to participate in legislation by presenting their grievances and suggesting solutions to those in power.'[16]

A petition could be submitted to ask for permission for something, like executing a trade or opening a shop, or to request assistance in a conflict with neighbours (for example, when a neighbour had encroached on another's property by extending his house), or with relatives where it concerned a disputed inheritance. These kinds of petitions were procedural and dealt with the execution of policies and customs already in place. The requests for *burgerschap* of the Cape settlement were procedural petitions. The regents received a considerable number of this type of request and they spent a lot of time dealing with them. In Amsterdam three of nine judges were on duty for a week at a time to consider and dispose of these requests. Even though the right of petition was not recorded officially, it was a customary privilege, and the administrators had the duty to carefully reflect on requests and agree to them if they were reasonable. Only then could they rightfully claim that they represented the burgher population.[17]

A different kind of petition was one with which a group of residents took the initiative to try to change an existing policy or to propose a new one. Many of the requests made via these petitions were economic in nature: they

---

15 Prak 2008:61.
16 Van Nierop, HFK. 2000. Private interests, public policies: Petitions in the Dutch Repubic. In AK Wheelock & A Seeff (eds). *The Public and Private in Dutch Culture of the Golden Age.* London: Associated University Presses, 33–39, 35.
17 Ibid 35–36.

asked for the adjustment of wage levels or prices of products, or a relaxation or tightening of trade regulations. Certain trade guilds pointed out, for example, that outsiders were encroaching on their territory, and asked for the issue of an order to stop this from happening. The 1658 burgher petition to Van Riebeeck fell into this category in that it was presented by a group of burghers who had organised themselves to ask to be allowed to trade freely and for a price directive for their produce.

It was not uncommon that a petition would be drawn up after a lengthy process of negotiation. Local city councils and representatives of the petitioners would meet to discuss the matter and the nature and contents of the complaints. Then the petition would be drafted according to strict rules and submitted to the relevant authorities. The regents embarked on an extensive investigation into the complaints and various parties were consulted. Only after all these steps had been taken were any decisions made. These petitions often resulted in the passing of a new law or bylaw, which sometimes copied the solutions that were proposed in the petition exactly. It was through this means, then, that ordinary burghers had the most direct voice in the creation of legislation.[18]

The burghers of the Cape settlement were undoubtedly familiar with the instrument of petition, and regularly made use of it to try to shape local economic policies in their favour. Throughout the period of VOC rule of the Cape, groups of burghers, in the true Little Tradition of protest, organised to petition the government for changes in policies. Sometimes they were successful, other times they were not. But the study of petitions has largely been neglected in South African historiography. They are mentioned in a few cases to provide argument and background in the discussion of specific subjects or people, but a substantial study of petitions has not been undertaken. Joris van den Tol writes that 'petitions can be studied in three ways: [1] for their opportunities to provide access to rulers; [2] for their rhetorical content; [3] for their influence on decision-making'.[19] The last approach studies petitions for their effectiveness or functionality. It is a useful approach in the context of the Cape settlement before 1800, to establish if the burghers were really the perpetual underdogs they are often portrayed as, or if they managed to wield some influence on Company policy. The following examples suggest that the latter was the case.

18 Van Nierop 2000:36–37; Prak 2008: 61–62.
19 Van den Tol J. 2016. *Petitions and the duality of structure: Lobbying in the seventeenth-century Dutch Atlantic* in *The Many-Headed Monster*. https://manyheadedmonster. wordpress.com/2016/11/21/petitions-and-the-duality-of-structure-lobbying-in-the-seventeenth-century-dutch-atlantic/ (Accessed 30 July 2019).

In the 1670s a burgher petition led to an important reform of the alcohol trading business. By 1673 the Council of Policy realised that it could make money from selling the right to retail alcohol to certain burghers. Until then a tap concession had been granted free of charge to those burghers who requested it and who were deemed suitable by the administration. This changed when the Council decided that the licensees (*pachters*) had to purchase the right to sell liquor. But the Company authorities still limited entry into this market by deciding which burghers could buy the tapping right and had the necessary funds to afford it. As a result, the licences were simply renewed year after year and a closed system of privileged alcohol *pachters* was created. Several burghers were unhappy about this state of affairs. They petitioned the government to remove the restrictions to the alcohol trade by selling the rights to sell liquor at a public auction to the highest bidder. The Council of Policy agreed to these requests in 1679, probably not only because of burgher pressure, but also because the members of local government realised that this could be a money-spinner. The burghers who submitted the petitions to the authorities were almost certainly not the poorest, because they had to have money to take part in the auctions.[20]

The licensed butchers of the Cape, again a group of well-to-do burghers, submitted a petition to the Council of Policy in 1747. They stated that the maximum price they could charge for meat was too low, given that the price they had to pay for cattle and sheep was very high. They claimed that they operated their businesses at a loss, and this would ruin them if the situation continued. They humbly asked that the government allow them to sell meat at a higher price. The Council agreed to increase the meat price from 1.5 to 2 *stuijvers* per pound.[21]

Another example was an action by the licensed teachers of the Cape. If a person wanted to educate the youth of the Cape settlement in subjects such as reading, writing and calculus, he or she had to ask the government for permission to start a school. An examination by the authorities and the church council of the Dutch Reformed Church followed and a licence would be issued if the applicant was found to be suitable. But there were people who evaded government control. Some did so as private tutors to the children of wealthy families. The licensed teachers regarded them as a

20 Groenewald, G. 2012. More comfort, better prosperity, and greater advantage: Free burghers, alcohol retail and the VOC authorities at the Cape of Good Hope, 1652–1680. *Historia* 57(1): 1–21.
21 Council of Policy. *Resolutions C 125*, Cape Town: WCARS, 1747.02.07, 48–67.

threat to their income and during the eighteenth century submitted several petitions to the government to curb this practice.[22] On 29 May 1779 seven of the official teachers complained to the ministers of the Dutch Reformed Church that the growing number of unlicensed teachers in Cape Town drew pupils away from their legal schools and that this eventually would lead to the 'collective ruin of the licensed schools'.[23] They asked that action be taken against the illegal schools and private tutors. The church council handed the request to the Council of Policy, which decided that the committee of *Scholarchen* (supervisors of the schools), consisting of Independent Fiscal Willem Cornelis Boers, two ministers of the Dutch Reformed Church and the elder Jan Serrurier, would thoroughly investigate the complaint of the licensed teachers as well as the condition of the schools in the town. A few months later the *Scholarchen* submitted their report to the Council of Policy.[24] They declared that the complaints of the licensed teachers were completely unfounded. According to them, teachers who were prepared to work hard would always have a large influx of pupils, sometimes even more than they could handle if they intended to teach the children properly. Some of the private tutors taught subjects that were not available in the schools, like French and certain sciences, and were therefore not competitors, but offered supplementary education. The *Scholarchen* found that no measures needed to be taken and that the situation could continue as it was.

In 1716, 12 prominent farmers of the Cape District petitioned the Company for an exemption of tax on wine harvested for their own use.[25] And during the 1740s, grain farmers complained that the wheat price was too low and taxes too high. They petitioned for a revision of this situation, and that they might be allowed to trade more freely.[26]

Although Cape burghers clearly did not hesitate to use petitions to get the VOC authorities to reconsider their political and economic stance it must be recognised that this form of protest was used predominantly by burghers of the middle and upper classes. The petitioners in the above examples were entrepreneurs of prominent standing in the community. Their actions were civilised and non-violent. Other, more violent and disturbing ways of protest, like rebellion, mutiny, strikes and direct physical attacks,

---

22 Du Toit 1937:137–142.
23 Council of Policy. *Resolutions C 157*, Cape Town: WCARS, 1779.07.06, 309–313.
24 Council of Policy. *Resolutions C 157*, Cape Town: WCARS, 1779.09.02, 355–365.
25 Groenewald, G. 2009. An early modern entrepreneur: Hendrik Oostwald Eksteen and the creation of wealth in Dutch colonial Cape Town, 1702–1741. *Kronos* 35(1): 7–31, 25.
26 Van Duin, PC & Ross, R. 1987. The economy of the Cape Colony in the eighteenth century. *Intercontinenta*. Leiden: Centre for the History of European Expansion, 30.

were mainly used by the popular classes — low-ranking VOC employees (soldiers and sailors), slaves and indigenous labourers.[27]

There was a period in the beginning of the eighteenth century, however, when burgher protests and petitions resulted in severe political unrest. The outcome of this unrest was significant and had potential similarities with the conflict of the 1770s and 1780s.

A stronger attack

In 1699, Willem Adriaan van der Stel succeeded his father, Simon, as governor of the Cape settlement.[28] The directors of the VOC made it clear to him that food production in the Cape was considered insufficient to supply the passing ships and the Cape itself. He managed to turn this situation around. The problem was that, while doing this, he put his own and his families' interests ahead of those of the Cape and the burgher population. He made sure that his family and network of supporters were awarded large tracts of land for farming, even though Company officials were officially forbidden to do so. For himself, his father and his brother Frans, he claimed the largest properties. Willem Adriaan's estate was called Vergelegen, and apparently was a grand affair. The ground measured 525 hectares. His father owned Constantia, which was set on 763 hectares. By 1705 about a third of the total farming land of the Cape settlement was in the hands of only 20 Company officials, who all happened to be closely related to the Van der Stels.

However, while agricultural production increased, the markets did not. The Company failed to look for new outlets for the crops of the Cape. The market was also subject to various restrictions. The burghers had to sell their produce to the Company at prices determined by the VOC and the Company controlled the shipping routes. Van der Stel's actions resulted in a situation in which officials and burghers competed, and that had never been the Company's intention. Van der Stel and his clientele had the upper hand in this battle, simply because of their access to valuable resources and official

---

27 See: Ulrich, N. 2015. Cape of storms: Surveying and rethinking popular resistance in the eighteenth-century Cape colony. *New Contree* 73: 16–39.
28 Information regarding Willem Adriaan van der Stel and burgher protests can be found here: Schutte 1989:303–309; Giliomee 2003:23–26; Ward 2009:164–168; Penn, N. 1999. *Rogues, Rebels and Runaways: Eighteenth-Century Cape Characters.* Cape Town: David Philip, 22–30; Böeseken, AJ. 1964. *Simon van der Stel en sy Kinders.* Cape Town: Nasou. For a detailed account of the issues and people involved see Schoeman, K. 2013. *Here & Boere. Die Kolonie aan die Kaap onder die Van der Stels, 1679–1712.* Pretoria: Protea Boekhuis, 343–459; Schoeman 2013:93–121 (*Twee Kaapse Lewens*).

channels, which gave them the opportunity to manipulate the market to their own advantage.

In 1705, the governor moved to take over control of two of the most important sectors of the Cape economy. One of these concerned the so-called meat *pacht*, the licence to sell meat to the VOC. The Company sold this right at a public auction to raise revenue. In the past, the sole *pachter* or leaseholder had been Henning Hüsing. Though initially he was an ally of Van der Stel there must have been some disagreement between the two men. Maybe it was about the fact that Hüsing was obliged to buy a large number of Van der Stel's cattle to sell to the Company with the result that he could sell fewer of his own. He may have wanted to make himself more independent. That did not fit with the governor's plans and in December 1705 the meat licence was taken away from Hüsing and divided in four parts, each of which was given to a different licensed butcher, all of whom happened to be the governor's men.

Van der Stel made a similar strategic move with regards to the liquor trade. The right to sell Cape wine was sold in four parts at an annual auction. But Van der Stel changed the rules so that one person could buy all four parts of the licence. He subsequently arranged for a certain Johannes Phijffer to buy the consolidated licence. This benefited Van der Stel, because by then he owned a quarter of all the vines in the Cape settlement and he could now sell his own wine through his crony Phijffer without competition.

Within a few years, Willem Adriaan van der Stel had set up himself, his family and a few close friends with a monopoly on the trade in meat, wine and wheat. He apparently did not think there was anything wrong in doing so. His regent background had conditioned him to act in this manner. He was the highest authority at the Cape, and as a highly placed regent, he felt he was entitled to exploit all the advantages at his disposal. It was widespread practice among the Dutch ruling elite that family and supporters were awarded favours, which could be called in when needed.

However, the policies and actions of Governor Van der Stel and his allies were a threat to the economic position, as well as the reason for being, of the burgher population. If a small group of VOC officials could produce everything to satisfy the Company's needs, there was no need to have burghers at the Cape. This naturally did not sit well with the settlers. Under the leadership of Henning Hüsing, a group of prominent farmers drew up a petition against the governor, which was sent to the VOC authorities in Batavia. Among the petitioners were Jacob van der Heijden, Pieter van der Bijl, Ferdinand Appel and Hüsing's nephew by marriage, Adam Tas. When no official reaction from Batavia was forthcoming, a second petition was set up under the direction of Adam Tas and smuggled from the Cape to the Netherlands at the beginning of 1706.

Tas was born into the Dutch middle class and was well educated. He knew how to compose an effective petition. It was addressed to the Heeren XVII and signed by a group of 63 burghers, almost half of whom were French Huguenots. It was divided into 38 clauses, which were mostly economic in nature. It was a collection of general and personal grievances against Governor Van der Stel and several other members of his administration. It exposed the illegal land holdings of the officials and their extensive farming operations. Tas and his fellow dissidents were careful to frame their complaints in a general concern for the Company's interest by accusing the VOC officials of being incompetent and of stealing from the Company. They further called on the directors to protect the Cape burghers against the abuses of the administration and hinted that they could disrupt the local order if their complaints were not taken seriously.

Van der Stel had no intention of taking the threat to his authority, status and business interests lying down. He clamped down on those who opposed him and had several ringleaders of the protest movement arrested and imprisoned. He made sure that some were banished to Mauritius, while Hüsing and three others were sent to the Netherlands to account for their behaviour. He also organised a counter petition, for which he collected 240 signatures, most of which were from people who were favoured by the governor in one way or another or were dependent on him as a business patron. In the end, it was all to no avail. The VOC directors were not keen on entertaining a public scandal that could harm the reputation of the Company. They also recognised that the Cape was a vital strategic station for the VOC and did not want this position threatened by having a potentially disloyal population. In October 1706, the directors decided to relieve Van der Stel of his duties as governor and recalled him to the Republic. Furthermore, ownership of all his land and that owned by other officials was restored to the Company.

More importantly, the Company directors issued orders aimed to prevent a repeat of the situation in which the Cape settlement had found itself under Van der Stel. They specifically stated that no Company employee, from the highest to the lowest rank, was permitted to be involved in any form of trade or enterprise in corn, cattle, wine or any other produce. And furthermore, no Company employee could own or rent any land. It was a major victory for the Cape settlers. It was also a good example of how Cape burghers could bring about a policy shift through protest and petition, even though they did not have the same strong legal position as their counterparts in the Republic, and they were supposed to be subject to the VOC rulers.

A further remarkable aspect of the conflict is that it played itself out among the wealthy elite of the settlement. Burghers engaged in many other occupations apart from farming. There were bakers, brewers, millers, barbers, teachers and artisans of various kinds. Some fared better than others, but burghers who turned to wheat and wine farming, and those who became alcohol *pachters*, and were situated in the immediate proximity of Cape Town, did exceptionally well and soon evolved into a wealthy burgher elite. The burgher community became increasingly socially stratified. Governor of Ceylon and VOC commissioner at the Cape on his return to the Netherlands, Cornelis Joan Simons, stated in 1708, just after the Van der Stel affair, 'that the lesser burghers ... are oppressed and kept in too great dependency by the wealthiest ones'.[29] We saw in the previous chapter that historian Gerrit Schutte divided the Cape residents into 'a labouring class, a modest middle class and a well-established haute bourgeoisie'.[30] Leonard Guelke writes that 'wealth was unevenly distributed among the colonists of the southwestern Cape. There were wealthy planters with several farms, hard-working cultivators burdened by debt and many poor landless single men'.[31] Research by economic historian Johan Fourie and others, who use a wide variety of archival sources and information, has backed up the income inequality among Cape burghers during the Dutch period with hard facts.[32]

The burghers who opposed Governor Van der Stel without a doubt belonged to the new burgher elite. Henning Hüsing was a German from Hamburg, who had started out as a lowly shepherd at the Cape, but through clever entrepreneurship, a fortunate marriage, government favour and the meat *pacht*, he had become one of the wealthiest men of the Cape. He owned several farms, among them Welmoed and Meerlust, as well as property in the town itself. As a man of distinction, he became a burgher councillor and served in several other official positions. Adam Tas initially worked as secretary for Hüsing, but soon married the widow Elisabeth van Brakel, a

---

29 Schoeman 2013:120 (*Twee Kaapse Lewens*).
30 Schutte 1989:300.
31 Guelke 1989:101.
32 See for instance: Fourie, J & Von Fintel, D. 2011. A history with evidence: Income inequality in the Dutch Cape Colony. *Economic History of Developing Regions* 26: 16–48; Fourie, J. 2013. The remarkable wealth of the Dutch Cape Colony: Measurements from eighteenth-century probate inventories. *Economic History Review* 66(2): 419–448; De Zwart, P. 2013. Real wages at the Cape of Good Hope: A long-term perspective, 1652–1912. *Tijdschrift for Sociale en Economische Geschiedenis / The Low Countries Journal of Social and Economic History* 10(2): 28–58.

niece of Hüsing. As her husband, he controlled his wife's substantial purse and became the owner of the farm Libertas. From his own diaries and from accounts of others, he appears to be someone who liked the comforts of life and surrounded himself with all kinds of luxuries. He behaved like a landed gentleman, who enjoyed the fruits of his farms, while the actual work was carried out by his European overseers (*knegte*) and of course his many slaves. Jacob van der Heijden was also a Dutch immigrant who managed to do well at the Cape. He owned six farms and was 'a very rich farmer, money-lender and livestock dealer'.[33] A sure sign of his prominent standing in the community was that he served several times as *heemraad* (the equivalent of burgher councillor in the country districts) in the Stellenbosch district. Much the same can be said about the other men who joined Hüsing and Tas in the protest movement. They all were wealthy farmers with extensive economic interests and high social standing.[34]

These rich burgher men held the highest and most important official positions in the administration, burgher militia and church. They called lesser burghers simply by their name, but in turn expected to be addressed as *baas* (master) or *monsieur*. The *knegte* of these farmers would not dare to wear the same expensive clothing as their masters, and their lower social status made it almost impossible for them to be regarded as suitable candidates to wed a farmer's daughter. The well-heeled had their own benches and seats in front of the church, and after death they were buried in the church, whereas the burghers of lower rank ended up in the graveyard. Adam Tas thought it beneath him to attend the funeral of the farm supervisor of Henning Hüsing, even though he was a fellow burgher and European, and Tas must have known him socially.[35]

In their petition to the VOC authorities to oust Willem Adriaan van der Stel, Hüsing, Tas and their fellow protesters had painted a picture of an arrogant and unjust governor who oppressed the burghers and treated them worse than slaves, even though they were freeborn. They had complained that the Cape settlers had become poorer and poorer, while VOC officials thrived. They had made it seem as if they represented the burgher population in general, but their motives were far less righteous and principled. These wealthy farmers were not seeking to protect the welfare of burghers lower on the social ladder. They were interested, rather, in personal gain. Adam Tas testified that high-placed Company officials had taken the best and

---

33 Schutte 1989:304.
34 Schoeman 2013:167–192 (*Here & Boere*).
35 Ibid 207–210; Biewenga 1999:269; Schutte 1989:303.

largest estates for themselves to own, to cultivate and ultimately to profit from.[36] This is essentially what worried the burgher farmers: that Van der Stel and his network of friends and families encroached on their, until then exclusive, territory, and in doing so formed a direct threat to their livelihood and economic position. The petition to the VOC directors had been a means for several wealthy individuals to organise themselves around a common, but limited, interest and to lobby the authorities to make a change in their favour. They had been seeking to deal a decisive blow to another section of the ruling elite.

Hermann Giliomee describes the Van der Stel conflict as 'a feud between two sets of elites who had fallen out in a fight over the spoils'.[37] Robert Ross writes, after stating that political conflict during the 1770s and 1780s was caused by Company employees grabbing too large a share of the economic activity in the Cape settlement: 'In this sense it was a replay of the WA van der Stel affair earlier in the century'.[38] In the following chapters I will analyse the later conflict in detail and I will demonstrate that this was indeed the case and that the Cape burghers continued to use the Dutch traditions of protest.

---

36 Schoeman 2013:410 (*Here & Boere*).
37 Giliomee 2003:24.
38 Ross 1989:42 (Structure and culture in pre-industrial Cape Town).

CHAPTER 6

The burgher troubles spread like wildfire

An angry woman unintentionally set in motion a period of serious political unrest at the Cape. Maria Jacoba Theron went to the authorities during the first days of January 1779 to complain about her husband, burgher Carel Hendrik Buijtendag. She could not take his abusive behaviour any longer. 'Driven by domestic quarrels and rage' she spoke to the assistant prosecutor, George Elias Timmer, to ask for permission to be separated from her husband.[1] Buijtendag was known as a man who was quick to lose his temper, and often reacted violently to his family, slaves and neighbours. After several complaints from fellow farmers, he had been banned from the Stellenbosch District in 1776. The VOC authorities had wanted to expel him from the Cape settlement altogether, but after an appeal by Buijtendag he was given permission to live in Cape Town on condition that he behaved himself.[2] Following Theron's complaint, Timmer wanted to arrest Buijtendag immediately. This response startled Theron. She realised that her action could lead to her being without a husband and breadwinner. Taken aback by the potential consequences of her complaint, she asked if Buijtendag could rather be summoned to appear in civil court. A warning might set him straight. In the following days no summons appeared, and Maria Jacoba Theron assumed, or hoped, that the authorities had forgotten the matter. Whatever the case, she patched up things with her husband.

Unfortunately, the wheels of justice had begun to move and the Buijtendag matter caught the attention of the prosecutor, Independent Fiscal Willem Cornelis Boers. He saw this as the perfect opportunity to deal with troublemaker Buijtendag once and for all. Boers brought the matter before the Council of Policy on 20 January, and requested that Buijtendag, because of his 'continuous improper behaviour', be drafted back into Company service and banished from the Cape. The Council gave him permission to arrest Buijtendag and send him to Batavia as a soldier in VOC service.[3] Boers wasted no time. He sent his *geweldiger* (enforcer) Hendrik Matthijsen[4] to the

---

1 Council of Policy. *Burgher Complaints C 2665*, Cape Town: WCARS, 1779.04.09, 93. A full statement by Theron and her daughter, Anna Catharina Buijtendag, is on pages 93–98.
2 Penn 1999:131–146.
3 Council of Policy. *Resolutions C 157*, Cape Town: WCARS, 1779.01.20, 75–76.
4 He was the subordinate of the fiscal in charge of the town's law enforcement.

Buijtendag household to collect him. Buijtendag's daughter, Anna Catharina, told Matthijsen that her father was not at home, but that she would pass on the message. Matthijsen then went to look for Buijtendag. The two men ran into each other in town and Buijtendag promised that he would go to the fiscal, but he would first go home to change and have something to eat. While Buijtendag was enjoying his lunch, Matthijsen again came to his house and this time he meant business. He had brought his *caffers*, Company slaves who acted as policemen and assisted the executioner.[5] Anna Catharina opened the door, but he pushed her out of the way. Buijtendag came to see what all the noise was about. He lost his temper, swore at Matthijsen and refused to go with him. Matthijsen ordered his men to grab Buijtendag. They wrestled him to the floor and tied him up. A bewildered Buijtendag was then dragged through the streets of Cape Town to the harbour, while 'his hands were tied and the *caffers* pushed, shoved and punched him'.[6] His wailing daughters ran alongside the procession. Buijtendag was placed on board the ship *Honcoop*, which was about to leave for Batavia.[7]

News of the arrest spread fast in the small Cape community. Burgher councillors Cornelis van der Poel, Christiaan George Maasdorp and Gerrit Hendrik Meijer immediately went to the governor, Baron Joachim van Plettenberg, to object to the mistreatment of Buijtendag.[8] They argued that 'a burgher by birth' should never be handled in such a violent manner. As burgher, he should have been arrested by burgher law enforcers and not by Company employees. Buijtendag's privileged position as burgher and his honour were severely compromised. The burgher councillors further claimed that, because Buijtendag was a burgher, they should have been consulted about the decision by the Council of Policy. Instead, they were ignored. The governor countered that one of the conditions of Cape *burgerschap* was that a burgher could be forced back into Company service if he misbehaved. The Company had therefore acted within its rights. Once the Council of Policy had taken its decision, Buijtendag had lost his burgher status. As a servant of the Company he was subject to Company rules and

---

5   An interesting article on the history of the term '*caffre*' has been published recently: Arndt, JS. 2018. What's in a word? Historicising the term 'caffre' in European discourses about Southern Africa between 1500 and 1800. In *Journal of Southern African Studies* 44(1): 59–75. In my opinion, the author too easily reaches the conclusion that the word had a racial connotation from the start. I also find it a glaring omission that he does not mention anything about the *caffers* as they are referred to here.
6   Council of Policy. *Cape Disputes C 2689*, Cape Town: WCARS, 1770.04.12, 111.
7   Buijtendag arrived in Batavia, where he appealed against his banishment. He was permitted to return to the Cape but died on his way there.
8   Council of Policy. *Cape Disputes C 2689*, Cape Town: WCARS, 1779.01.21, 113.

the Company could do with him what it wanted. The burgher councillors warned the governor that the events would lead to great unrest among the burgher population. Burghers would be worried that 'what had happened to Buijtendag today, could happen to somebody else tomorrow'.[9] None of their arguments persuaded the governor. On 25 January 1779, the governor's journal recorded that 'in the evening the South Easter came up, and the ship *Honcoop* used the opportunity to leave for Batavia'.[10]

The burgher councillors were right in their warning to the governor, because Buijtendag's arrest immediately led to a flurry of activity among the burghers.[11] In many parts of the Cape settlement burghers were mobilised. According to Fiscal Boers 'they openly use about 2 or 3 young and inexperienced upstarts, who ride around the whole country, to let gullible commoners sign papers of which they will perhaps never know the contents'.[12] They were seeking burgher support for a request to be submitted to the Council of Policy. On 30 March 1779 the burgher councillors and the *heemraden* of the Stellenbosch and Drakenstein District, with the backing of about 400 burghers, handed in a petition. They asked for permission to send a delegation of burghers to the Dutch Republic to inform the Company directors about 'the condition of the burghers of this colony and the violence caused to the burgher Carel Hendrik Buijtendag, which had violated the rights of the burghers'.[13] In response, the Council of Policy expressed their severe displeasure. An irritated Boers observed that the administration saw the petition as 'an extremely disrespectful deed, through which one demonstrated that one did not expect much of the good intentions of the local government'.[14] The Council of Policy made clear that they would not allow the burghers to bypass the chain of command and go directly to the Heeren XVII with their complaints. They were the government of the Cape, appointed to look after the interests of the entire population, and any grievance should be addressed to them first. Only if it transpired that they could not deal with the issue, would they refer the matter to their superiors.[15]

By now the tension between VOC officials and burgher councillors was palpable. When the burgher councillors came to the Castle to submit their petition to the Council of Policy they were kept waiting. They were

---

9   Council of Policy. *Cape Disputes C 2689*, Cape Town: WCARS, 113.
10 Council of Policy. *Journals C 2057*, Cape Town: WCARS, 1779.01.25, 12.
11 Council of Policy. *Cape Disputes C 2689*, Cape Town: WCARS, 1779.05.22, 13.
12 Schutte 1982:102.
13 Council of Policy. *Cape Disputes C 2689*, Cape Town: WCARS, 1779.05.22, 14.
14 Schutte 1982:102.
15 Council of Policy. *Cape Disputes C 2689*, Cape Town: WCARS, 1779.05.22, 16;
    Resolutions C 157, Cape Town: WCARS, 1779.03.30, 149–154.

not invited to enter the council chamber but were made to stand outside like common underlings. A lowly messenger was sent to collect the request from them and then they were dismissed. A few days later the burgher councillors were summoned, not requested, to appear before Governor Van Plettenberg to explain what all the meetings and unrest were about and what the intentions of the burghers were.[16] This was unprecedented, because the relationship between the burgher councillors and members of the Company administration was based on mutual respect. Letters from the government to the Burgher Council usually started with the cordial *Goede Vrienden* (Dear Friends). Burgher councillors were notables, so to be treated like commoners was a serious affront to the importance of these high office-bearers. The disgrace was clearly intended to show who was in charge.

If the members of the Council of Policy thought that the denial of the March petition would put an end to the burgher protests, they soon found out that they were sorely mistaken. The burgher movement was progressing at full steam. A second petition was drawn up, dated 7 May 1779 and signed by 404 burghers, who wanted to send a delegation of four people to the Netherlands 'to submit to the judgment of the Lords Directors the current disputes and the concerns of the burghers as well as the fair accusations against the honourable government and certain other people'.[17] The four people chosen to represent the burghers were former burgher councillor and entrepreneur Jacobus van Reenen, former burgher militia lieutenant Barend Jacob Artoijs, and the burghers Tieleman Roos and Nicolaas Godfried Heijns. At the time nobody could leave the Cape and travel to the Republic without permission of the government, because the journey had to be made on one of the VOC ships of the return fleet from Asia. Therefore, the four delegates had to inform the Council of Policy of their travel plans and ask for passage on one of the ships. Each of the delegates submitted their own separate request.

Barend Jacob Artoijs had in December 1778 asked to be relieved of his burgher duties and tendered his resignation as lieutenant of the burgher cavalry because he wanted to travel to the Netherlands. Although he gave no specific reason for his trip, it was generally assumed that it was for study purposes.[18] Artoijs also asked that if he should return to Cape Town in future, he would be reinstated as burgher lieutenant. The Council of Policy granted his request and gave him permission to travel on one of the

---

16 Council of Policy. *Cape Disputes C 2689*, Cape Town: WCARS, 1779.04.05, 164–165.
17 Council of Policy. *Cape Disputes C 2689*, Cape Town: WCARS, 1779.05.07, 75–76.
18 Schutte 1982:97.

Company's return ships for the normal fee.[19] In May 1780 Governor Van Plettenberg complained to his friend Hendrik Swellengrebel junior that he felt personally betrayed by Artoijs, because Artoijs had, without being prompted, assured the governor that he would not involve himself with matters concerning the Cape burghers or their protests.[20] Artoijs left the Cape on 3 March 1779 on board the *Amsterdam*, which arrived in Holland on 3 July 1779.[21]

Getting permission to travel proved to be more problematic for Tieleman Roos. He had asked the Council of Policy for consent to travel on 19 January 1779. He stated that he had recently started to plant tobacco and he wanted to take a few specimens to the Republic to get the opinion of some experts, while at the same time trying to gain knowledge on how to prepare the tobacco.[22] The Council of Policy, however, replied that they were aware that Tieleman Roos was a troublemaker in the Dutch Reformed parish of Drakenstein and one of the people 'who continuously fans the fire of discord in that parish'.[23] Since 1771, Roos had been embroiled in a fight with the Drakenstein Dutch Reformed church council, church leaders and Company, because he disagreed with the appointment of Jacobus Arnoldus Theron as a church elder. What had started as a dispute between neighbouring farmers over the use of water streams ended up as a church conflict, which almost resulted in the breakup of the local parish. The various parties involved in the quarrel sued each other in civil matters before the Council of Justice during the 1770s. The Council of Policy believed the tobacco story was just a cover-up and that Roos was really planning to take his issues with the Drakenstein church council to the leaders of the Dutch Reformed Church and perhaps even the VOC directors. Therefore, his request was initially refused. On 6 April 1779 Roos again tried to get permission to go to the Netherlands. This time he solemnly swore that he would not go to the church authorities with any issues concerning the Drakenstein parish, nor would he make trouble 'about other matters concerning the Colony'.[24] After he made this promise the Council had no further grounds to refuse his request.

---

19 Council of Policy. *Petitions and Nominations C 1172,* Cape Town: WCARS, 42–43; *Resolutions C 156,* Cape Town: WCARS, 1778.12.01, 396.
20 Schutte 1982:121.
21 Schutte 1982:89.
22 Council of Policy. *Petitions and Nominations C 1173,* Cape Town: WCARS, 17–18; *Resolutions C 157,* Cape Town: WCARS, 1779.01.19, 64–68.
23 Council of Policy. *Resolutions C 157,* Cape Town: WCARS, 1779.01.19, 66–67. See for more on this story Beyers 1967:118–126.
24 Council of Policy. *Petitions and Nominations C 1173,* Cape Town: WCARS, 140–142; *Resolutions C 157,* Cape Town: WCARS, 1779.04.06, 140–142.

Clearly Artoijs and Roos had already planned to go to the Netherlands before their selection as burgher delegates. This convenient coincidence may be the reason they were chosen in the first place, but it did not augur well for their fight for the burgher cause.

On 13 April 1779, Jacobus van Reenen and Nicolaas Godfried Heijns had asked for consent to travel overseas in separate requests that did not offer specific explanations for their trips. Both were given permission.[25]

The delegates had not wanted to raise any untoward suspicion about the main reason for their travel. As was apparent from the case of Tieleman Roos, permission to travel was not a given, and if they were known to be rabble-rousers or had stated they intended to submit complaints about the Cape government, the administration would have found reasons to refuse their requests. Even though the members of the government must have suspected ulterior motives, based on the information provided, the Council of Policy had no choice but to allow the delegates to leave the Cape. Perhaps the Council also did not want to fuel the burgher unrest further. Van Reenen, Roos and Heijns travelled together on the *Morgenster*, which sailed from the Cape on 26 May 1779 and docked in Amsterdam on 10 September 1779.[26] With the same ship arrived a letter from the governor to the Heeren XVII about the agitation among the burgher population and his misgivings regarding their plans.[27] This was not nearly enough for Independent Fiscal Boers, who expressed dismay and objected to the 'far-reaching leniency and indulgence' demonstrated by the government towards the burgher protesters.[28]

On arrival in Amsterdam the delegates first made sure that they were officially recognised as representatives of the Cape burghers by handing over the proof of their deputation — the petition of 7 May 1779 — to Jacob Temminck, a mayor of Amsterdam and treasurer of the VOC. He submitted this to the VOC Chamber of Amsterdam on 27 September 1779 to have it recorded.[29] The four men then set out to properly compile a petition, which had likely already been prepared on the long sea voyage from the Cape. On 12 October they submitted it with supporting material to a notary public, Kier van der Piet, and the next day they swore an oath to the truth of

---

25 Council of Policy. *Petitions and Nominations C 1173,* Cape Town: WCARS, 150–154; *Resolutions C 157,* Cape Town: WCARS, 1779.04.13, 196.
26 http://www.historici.nl/Onderzoek/Projecten/DAS/detailVoyage/98860 (Accessed 23 April 2017).
27 Council of Policy. *Cape Disputes C 2689,* Cape Town: WCARS, 1779.05.22, 13–14.
28 Schutte 1982:102.
29 Beyers 1967:30.

these documents before the town council of the City of Amsterdam. After all these formalities, the four delegates appeared in person on 16 October 1779 at the meeting of the Heeren XVII and presented them with 'a bulky Memorandum and appendices'.[30]

The petition was submitted according to the long-established rules of protest tradition.[31] The supplicants identified themselves as 'representatives of the entire burgher population' of the Cape of Good Hope. They humbly appeared before the 'noblest and eminent lords' and respectfully wanted to submit the nature of their grievances and the causes, and to propose certain remedies. Accordingly, the *Memorie* consisted of three parts: a description of the 'deteriorating state of the burghers and free colonists of the Cape of Good Hope', the reasons for this situation, which were the 'unjustified oppression and illegal trade by certain Company servants', and lastly 'the best and most necessary means to improve the situation'.

The document started with a description of the adverse economic situation of the burghers at the Cape.[32] The fertility of the soil at the Cape had enabled the farmers to produce enough grain, wine and other produce to supply the Cape settlement, the ships of the Company and to fulfil the demand from Batavia. The prices for produce paid by the Company had been good and costs relatively low. Farming had proved to be a profitable business and more burghers had gone into agriculture, so that it spread quickly from the immediate surrounds of Cape Town into the outer districts. But then the Company had begun to lower the prices it paid for agricultural produce. At first the farmers had not been concerned about this, because they were promised that all their produce would be bought. But these conditions changed. The demand from Batavia had diminished, the costs of material had steadily increased, the Company demanded a high tax and the number of farmers kept growing. Besides this, trade was unreliable because it depended on the amount of VOC and foreign vessels that visited the Cape. This ship traffic was far from regular.

The burghers of Cape Town proper made their living from trade. They sold agricultural and fresh produce to passing ships and bought European and Indian goods from the sailors, which in turn they sold to the residents in town and the farmers in the outer districts. Company employees were supposed to leave to the burghers 'this way of making a living as a privilege'. Here the petition cleverly referred to the instructions of 1706 issued by the

---

30 Council of Policy. *Cape Disputes C 2696*, Cape Town: WCARS, 1779.10.22, 101–102.
31 The full text of the *Memorie* can be found in: Council of Policy. *Cape Disputes C 2689*, Cape Town: WCARS, 1779.10.09, 29–72.
32 Council of Policy. *Cape Disputes C 2689*, Cape Town: WCARS, 1779.10.09, 30–35.

Heeren XVII themselves. Trade of grain, cattle or wine was supposed to be the exclusive terrain of burghers. The *Memorie* pointed out that, despite these orders, there were some powerful VOC officials who dominated the most profitable trade with passing ships by using their influence and access to Company warehouses, boats and slaves. The burghers were forced to buy the most essential goods from these officials at high and often unaffordable prices. The officials were taking the bread out of the mouths of burghers.

The *Memorie* continued to describe 'the signs of the state of suffering of the free colonists'. In the main town many houses were standing empty, because two or three families were forced to move in with each other. In the country, many farmers stopped growing produce and started to try their hand at cattle-farming. They moved further away and lived under harsh and dangerous conditions, while they eked out a meagre living from the supply of cattle for slaughter and the sale of butter and soap. From their little earnings they had to pay a high rental for their farms to the Company, while prices for their basic materials soared. The situation had grave consequences. The farmers hardly had money to feed and clothe their families. Many families shared one dwelling and pooled their earnings and costs. The children did not get a good education, because the parents could not afford proper teachers. Perhaps one of the worst results, according to the burghers, was that the young men had to remain unmarried 'or dwell with the Hottentots and this mixing will lead to an offspring which should be feared more than the Bosjesmans Hottentots are now'.[33]

The burgher rhetoric was that their situation was miserable and dire, and that this was caused by the oppression and behaviour of Company servants, the topic of the second part of the petition. This section consisted of 16 articles in which the burghers complained about several VOC officials who had abused their position to harm the burgher population.[34] The writers pre-empted accusations that these personal attacks were sour grapes or personal gripes by stating that they merely wanted to expose these Company servants, 'forced by the utmost distress and out of love for their fatherland and fellow burghers'. They reinforced their words by undertaking to present the plain truth and refrain from abusive remarks.

The first VOC official about whom the burghers complained was Independent Fiscal Willem Cornelis Boers. 'In the execution of his duties, he is so arbitrarily oppressive and irresponsible towards the burghers and settlers, that anyone with the least sense of liberty, cannot think about this

---

33 Council of Policy. *Cape Disputes C 2689*, Cape Town: WCARS, 1779.10.09, 34.
34 Council of Policy. *Cape Disputes C 2689*, Cape Town: WCARS, 1779.10.09, 35–63.

without getting emotional.'[35] The burghers stated that because of this the settlers were not free, as they were supposed to be, but were virtually equal to slaves — a status which was considered far below that of burgher. The Fiscal's behaviour flew in the face of the privileges and security of the burghers. The *Memorie* provided several examples of this, the most important and recent being the arrest and banning of Carel Hendrik Buijtendag. Besides this, Boers had fined the burghers excessively for minor offences and had gone as far as confiscating their goods, even though they were sometimes innocent of any offence. It was said that he habitually blackmailed the burghers into paying him a bribe by threatening that he would punish and publicly shame them. It was furthermore alleged that Boers wanted to ensure that he financially benefited from his position and punished only those from whom he could get money. To underpin this, the burghers claimed that he was much more lenient towards slaves, because they did not have money.[36]

The *Memorie* continued to name and shame several other Company officials, and to expose them as openly breaking the VOC rules. Most were accused of arbitrary behaviour towards the burghers and trying to make as much money as possible by forcing them to accept low prices or to pay kickbacks for using their services or the right to sell their products to the Company. There were several high-ranking VOC officials who owned farms and market gardens, where they grew vegetables and fruit which they sold to burghers and visitors to the Cape. Some of these men owned cattle and wine farms and they sold meat and wine 'even per bottle in public wine-houses or so-called taverns'.[37] The burghers felt that the Company officials caused great harm to their livelihoods and interfered with their privileges.[38]

The last part of the *Memorie* consisted of recommendations to improve the situation for the burghers.[39] These proposals and requests concentrated on two main topics: first, the economic, and second, the judicial and administrative position of the burghers.

The burghers primarily wanted the VOC to renew and enforce the 1706 orders to keep the VOC employees out of their way. The burghers wanted to cut out the middleman — ie, an official buyer from the VOC — which would

---

35 Council of Policy. *Cape Disputes C 2689*, Cape Town: WCARS, 1779.10.09, 35.
36 Council of Policy. *Cape Disputes C 2689*, Cape Town: WCARS, 1779.10.09, 35–41; Beyers 1967:37.
37 Council of Policy. *Cape Disputes C 2689*, Cape Town: WCARS, 1779.10.09, 50.
38 See Chapter 8 for more detailed information on the complaints made against other officials.
39 Council of Policy. *Cape Disputes C 2689*, Cape Town: WCARS, 1779.10.09, 63–72; Beyers 1967:49–61.

enable them to deliver their own products and farm produce directly to the Company. They did not want any involvement from Company officials in the trade because this resulted in higher costs, as they had to pay fees and, on top of that, they had to grease the palms of officials to allow them to deliver their produce. The control over the delivery and distribution of products should be transferred to the burghers. The Company could still determine the prices it paid for the products, but because the costs of having to pay many employees and feed and clothe slaves would be reduced, it was expected that these prices would be reasonable and satisfactory to both parties.

The burghers furthermore requested that they be allowed to freely sail to Dutch and foreign vessels in Cape Town harbour and sell their fresh produce directly to the crew. But they would do so only if there was a surplus after the Company had been sufficiently provided. They also suggested that the burghers be allowed to have their own ships with which they could import products from Europe, which they could sell on auction to the highest bidder, while they could also use these ships to export their produce to Europe and the Asian settlements. This last request would be on the condition again that first the demand of the Company at the Cape had been satisfied.

Regarding the position and rights of burghers the petition referred directly to the case of Carel Hendrik Buijtendag. It asked that no burgher be arrested by Company officials, but only by other burghers and that they be imprisoned under burgher authority and not in the Castle. It should be prohibited that any burgher, both those born as burgher and those having gained burgher freedom after serving out their contract with the Company, could be forced into Company service or be banished to Batavia 'because that was contrary to the Burgher rights'.

Another suggestion was that the Council of Justice should consist of an equal number of burghers and Company employees, while the longest-serving burgher councillor would be vice-president of this body. They wanted more influence over and greater burgher participation in the judicial processes concerning burghers.

They proposed that there should be seven burgher councillors (instead of three) and that only two of these would resign every year, to allow for greater consistency and stability. The burgher councillors would then freely elect two replacements, whose final appointment would still be subject to approval by the governor. More importantly, the seven burgher councillors would be allowed to take part in the meetings of the Council of Policy — exclusively a VOC domain — when this body discussed burgher affairs or matters regarding the general welfare of the Cape settlement. The participation of the burgher councillors in the administration should be strengthened by giving them the authority to submit an annual report to the Heeren XVII about the state of the burghers.

After the presentation of the *Memorie* to the board of directors of the VOC the chairman replied that the complaints would be investigated. The Heeren XVII believed that the complaints of the Cape burghers were a matter 'of severe importance, which should be treated with the utmost care'. The documents were handed to the Amsterdam and Zeeland chambers, which would head the inquest. A letter was sent to the Cape administration in which the governor and various officials were asked to reply to the accusations levelled against them and comment on the proposals made by the burghers. As a special instruction to the governor, he was informed 'that the Directors trusted that he would do everything to restore peace and order and mutual trust'.[40]

This was easier said than done, because the protesting burghers had no intention of toning down their actions. At the very same time that the deliberations in Amsterdam were taking place, there was a standoff between the burgher militia and the VOC government at the Cape. It was the closest to a riot the Cape came during the burgher protests.

The annual burgher militia review was held in October 1779 and lasted for a week. All the burghers of the Cape District gathered in Cape Town to demonstrate that they were ready and able to defend the settlement.[41] The militias held exercises and marched through the town to show off their military prowess. There was a festive atmosphere and every burgher took part in this. It was a boost for the local economy, because the burghers had to be housed and fed, and they looked for ways to enjoy themselves. The festivities ended with a parade on the square in front of the burgher Watch House.[42]

This time, instead of dispersing after the parade, the burghers remained on the square. Certain burghers and officers were seen going through the ranks and speaking to the men. A hostile and agitated mood descended over the gathering. Eventually a delegation of the highest officers made their way from the square to the Castle. The officers demanded, in the name of all the burghers, that the incumbent burgher councillors (Cornelis van der Poel, Christiaan George Maasdorp and Gerrit Hendrik Meijer) should

---

40 Council of Policy. *Cape Disputes C 2696*, Cape Town: WCARS, 1779.10.22, 102.
41 Burgher Military Council, *Diverse Papers BKR 8*, Cape Town: WCARS, 18–19.
42 Now known as Greenmarket Square.

remain on the council after December and that there would not be the usual replacement of two of them. The burghers wanted these men to remain burgher councillors until a reply from the Heeren XVII to the *Memorie* had been received.

The events of that day were highly significant. The militia members had not laid down their arms as they should have done. This meant that about 1 200 to 1 600 fully armed militia members could potentially march on the Castle, the seat of the Company administration. According to François Bernard, they were 'well exercised in the handling of weapons and exceptionally skilled in shooting, an armed Cape farmer seldom misses his mark'. In contrast, the 500-men strong Cape VOC garrison consisted of 'a hodgepodge of European wretched folk and vagabonds' and would not stand a chance against the burghers.[43] The writer probably exaggerated, but nevertheless the potential for a violent clash was there. A highly volatile stage in the burgher protests had been reached. The message was clear: should the government not give in to the demand, the militia would not hesitate to intervene with force. An anonymous commentator summarised the situation: '[H]ere a gang of armed burghers is openly showing off under the eye and in the heart of their government and seems to defy that same government. My worthy and beloved fellow burghers! What else can one call this, but Rebellion?'[44]

This view was echoed by Company officials, who were upset about the threatening and intimidating actions of the burghers. Cellar Master Jacobus Johannes le Sueur exclaimed: '[I]s that the way to submit a request?'[45] He should have known better. In Dutch cities burghers were mobilised via the militias and the guilds in times of political crisis, and they would not hesitate to use a show of force if they felt it was needed in order to support a petition.[46] The Cape burghers were merely following Dutch protest tradition.

Independent Fiscal Boers was strongly opposed to the burgher demand. He believed that the three burgher councillors should have stopped the burgher unrest a long time before. That they had not done so, showed they were not fit to hold their office.[47] Boers was among the members of government who urged the governor to counter the burgher actions harshly. They advised that the militia officers should be placed under arrest. This

---

43 *Nederlandsch Afrika*, 55.
44 Verbatim Copies, *VC 161, Nieuw-Jaars Gift aan de Caabse burgerije*, Cape Town: WCARS, 16.
45 Schutte 1982:96.
46 Prak 1999:145–146; Van Nierop 2000:37.
47 Schutte 1982:103.

would show that the VOC government was in charge and would crush any further opposition.

But the governor kept a cool head. He recognised that a crackdown could have the opposite effect and 'that it would be better to spare innocent blood, than to try and risk the spilling of innocent blood with these rascals'.[48] He minimised the gravity of the event and stated that 'this was such a small matter and a curt refusal would only lead to unpleasant incidents'.[49] The governor managed to convince the other members of the Council of Policy to accede to the burgher demands and let the burgher councillors remain in their posts. He personally conveyed the decision to the burgher militia officers, who then returned to the square where the members of the militia were waiting anxiously.

The resolution of the administration was officially announced in the meeting room of the Burgher Military Council in the Watch House and greeted with cheers and applause. Boers remarked that it was unheard of that there were also lower officers present at this meeting and, to add insult to injury, that they did not just observe quietly, but commented loudly that the governor had been forced to agree to the burgher demands 'otherwise blood would have flowed'.[50] However, the governor had made a wise decision. This became even more evident when two days later the new burghers and young men swore their oath of allegiance to the VOC, governor and administration. This was originally planned on the day of the militia protest but did not take place for obvious reasons. Two days later emotions had calmed down sufficiently for the militia and governor to face each other in a dignified manner.

Whether the militia members would have followed through with their threat of violence remains uncertain, but the fact that the mighty VOC government was intimidated by the burghers to this extent made this a serious incident. It is also hard to believe that this action by the burghers was on the spur of the moment. It had all the signs of a well-planned and organised event, which indicates that influential people were most likely behind it.

Bolstered by their success, the burgher councillors continued to oppose and test the patience of the VOC government at every opportunity. The wealthy farmer Hendrik Cloete informed his friend Hendrik Swellengrebel in January 1780 that 'the burgher troubles spread like wildfire. If they do

---

48 Verbatim Copies, *VC 161, Nieuw-Jaars Gift aan de Caabse burgerije*, Cape Town: WCARS, 17.
49 Council of Policy. *Burgher Complaints C 2674*, Cape Town: WCARS, 52.
50 Schutte 1982:104.

not get what they want, I fear grave consequences'.[51] During 1780, several more petitions and documents were spread and signed by burghers, who expressed their support for the protest movement and pledged money to be sent to the delegates in the Republic.[52]

The VOC administrators tried to stem the tide of the dissenting movement by persuading some burghers to withdraw their support. In April 1782 the burgher ambassadors in the Republic composed a *Nadere Memorie* (Further Memorandum) which they sent to the VOC directors.[53] They explained that they had received word from the Cape that several burghers were going around with 'statements and other documents, which revoked the complaints brought against certain Company servants, as well as exonerated or excused them, with the aim to solicit the burghers to sign these and even persuade them to do such with promises and threats'.[54]

The delegates claimed that Jan Coenraad Gie had visited the former burgher councillor Andries Brink, who was old and frail, to coax him to sign a declaration in support of the VOC administration. Gie attempted to do so twice without success and Brink had instructed his married children to stand strong. However, Gie came back a third time and this time he brought Petrus Ludovicus le Sueur, a member of the Council of Justice, and Jan Fredrik Willem Böttiger, a former burgher councillor. They took Brink into a room, prevented his wife and children from entering, and convinced Brink to sign the required statement.[55]

The burgher Willem Lutsche spoke to several burghers. He told them that if any of them had signed the protest documents and now had regrets, they could just write a small note or request to the governor to ask for forgiveness. The governor would then make sure that they were crossed off the list of signatories and that everything would be forgotten. But Lutsche also intimated that things would end badly for them if they continued their support of the protest movement.[56]

The burgher delegates in the Netherlands based their second petition on letters and statements they had received from the Cape.[57] This is how they knew that Jan Coenraad Gie, Johannes van Sittert, Jan Hendrik Ekhard

---

51 Schutte 1982:95.
52 See for example: Council of Policy. *Cape Disputes C 2690*, Cape Town: WCARS, 189–190 (11.02.1780), 209–210 (09.09.1780), 190–191 (14.09.1780), 210–211 (03.10.1780), 191–192 (14.11.1780).
53 Council of Policy. *Cape Disputes C 2690*, Cape Town: WCARS, 1782.04, 94–101.
54 Council of Policy. *Cape Disputes C 2690*, Cape Town: WCARS, 98.
55 Council of Policy. *Cape Disputes C 2690*, Cape Town: WCARS, 99.
56 Council of Policy. *Cape Disputes C 2690*, Cape Town: WCARS, 99–100.
57 Council of Policy. *Cape Disputes C 2670*, Cape Town: WCARS, 1780.12.20, 2–68.

and Andries Gous had been recruited by the Company administration to convince other burghers to withdraw their complaints against the government and officials. Apparently, these burghers had good reason to choose the side of the government. Johannes van Sittert was given half a block of property in Cape Town on which he built eight houses and two warehouses and still had space left for a pleasure garden. Andries Gous was a common man, who was very much indebted to Independent Fiscal Boers and Provisions Master Staring, who had recommended him for a post as officer of the burgher cavalry, a prestigious position in the burgher community. Jan Coenraad Gie made his money in the *Fransche commercie* (French trade) and if the burghers were to be allowed to trade freely on Madagascar and the coast of Africa it would harm him personally. Ekhard was one of Gie's partners.

But there was also the familial link between these men and Company officials. The burgher delegates in the Republic and the burgher councillors were keen to point out these relationships. The son of Jan Coenraad Gie was married to a daughter of junior merchant Jan Fredrik Kirsten, while through his own marriage Gie was related to Olof Martini Bergh, a member of the Council of Policy. It so happened that complaints had been made against both these officials.[58] The only daughter of Jan Fredrik Willem Böttiger was married to the junior merchant and landdrost of Stellenbosch Olof Goblieb De Wet and this linked him to the brothers Le Sueur, who both were married to sisters of De Wet.[59]

The late eighteenth-century VOC administrators were following the same approach as had Willem Adriaan van der Stel. They were attempting to sow division and organise a counter movement by using the means at their disposal: handing out favours and positions, as well as access to their relationship networks. Regent tactics had not changed much.

The protest movement and counter actions had a severe impact on Cape society. Willem Cornelis Boers elaborated on this by stating that confusion and disorder reigned and

> *hate and anger, always so common in these circumstances, are playing a remarkable role in our current drama. One needs to be here to truly experience the real nature of what is going on. The nearest relatives begrudge each other the light in their eyes and only self-preservation is just about preventing an unspeakable*

---

58 Council of Policy. *Cape Disputes C 2690*, Cape Town: WCARS, 98.
59 Council of Policy. *Cape Disputes C 2690*, Cape Town: WCARS, 1780.12.20, 2–68.

persecution, which would surely be followed by murder and mayhem.[60]

Even in 1788 the traumatic effect of the political turmoil of previous years was still apparent. In February of that year, the Council of Policy was informed by Johannes Isaak Rhenius, the president of the Council of Justice, that former burgher councillor Cornelis van der Poel had asked permission to sue VOC merchant Christoffel Brand for some offensive remarks he had made about Van der Poel in 1779. Van der Poel was regarded as one of the ringleaders of the disturbances, and the council members immediately recognised that allowing him leeway in this matter could spell trouble. They feared

> *the immediate revival of the ruinous divisions, which had dominated this Settlement, and which had caused separation and animosity between residents, yes, even between those who before were united by the loving bonds of kinship, so much so that one had feared the most harmful consequences for this Settlement.*

The rekindling of the unrest had to be prevented, so the government instructed the Council of Justice to stop in their tracks any legal procedures relating to the conflict of the previous years.[61]

It was only on 3 December 1783 that a report on the burgher complaints was submitted to the Heeren XVII and subsequently adopted as a resolution.[62] These decisions reached the Cape a few months later, where they were discussed in the Council of Policy on 25 May 1784.[63]

The VOC directors concluded that the allegations against the Cape officials were partly insignificant, partly unproven and partly unfounded. The accused Company officials were mostly acquitted of the charges brought against them. The status quo at the Cape remained largely unchanged. One major transformation was that the Council of Justice would consist of six Company employees and six burgher councillors and that the *secunde,* the deputy governor, would be the chairman. VOC officials were therefore still in the majority. Members of the council, including the burgher councillors, would be appointed on a permanent basis and no longer be changed annually. But a free election of the burgher representatives was out of the question. The directors also resolved that the burghers had the right to

---

60 Schutte 1982:104 *(31.01.1780).*
61 Council of Policy. *Resolutions C 177,* Cape Town: WCARS, 1788.02.19, 249–287.
62 Council of Policy. *Cape Disputes C 2696,* Cape Town: WCARS, 115–128.
63 Council of Policy. *Resolutions C 166,* Cape Town: WCARS, 365–404.

appeal court sentences to the Council of Justice in Batavia, according to the status quo, thus not in the Republic as the burghers had wanted.

Regarding the trade and economic proposals of the burghers, the directors decided to confirm the 1706 orders, which placed restrictions on the involvement of individual VOC officials in economic life. However, the burghers were not given more control nor would conditions of trade be relaxed. Further decisions were postponed until after the end of the Fourth Anglo-Dutch war, which had started in December 1780.

CHAPTER 7

The 404 burghers

The petition of May 1779 was signed by 404 residents of the Cape settlement.[1] This group was the core of the protest movement. Because we know their names, we can find information about them in the Company archives. This gives us some insight into what kind of people supported the protests, and tells us whether they had a similar background to the burghers of Dutch cities who organised to petition their rulers.[2] The information further helps to establish if the overseas burghers echoed the actions of their counterparts in the Republic and operated within the Little Tradition of urban revolt and politics.

Several of the protesters wrote down their public position or their militia rank after their name. Most of these were highly placed burghers: (former) burgher councillors, *heemraden*, captains and lieutenants. The rest (357) wrote that they were '*burger*'. It seems a humble epithet, but this was an especially meaningful and deliberate action. These men wanted it known that they were members of an exclusive, privileged group. The designation of burgher set them apart from slaves, who were not free, could not own property and did not have any rights. Slaves were the lowest status group. These protesters were full burghers: they were men of a certain age, had property rights, were born at the Cape as free burghers or had been granted burgher freedom there, and they served in the burgher militia. Only these men had the right of petition, and, therefore, their protest action was completely legitimate and acceptable. Writing 'burgher' behind their names was making a statement.

This statement was strengthened by making the petition in the name 'of the entire burgher population' of the Cape of Good Hope. The same phrase was used in the introduction to the *Memorie* presented to the Heeren XVII in October. This was not just the hollow rhetoric of a group of dissidents, who wanted to impress or intimidate their opponents. The petition was drawn up following an understood protocol, in which each sentence had an explicit meaning, which was also known to the opposing party.

---

1 Council of Policy. *Burgher Complaints C 2665*, Cape Town: WCARS, 2–9.
2 See for the more technical details on researching the Cape burghers and protesters: Baartman, T. 2011. Fighting for the Spoils. Cape Burgerschap and Faction Disputes in Cape Town in the 1770s. PhD thesis, University of Cape Town, 88–102.

Maarten Prak has written extensively about Dutch *burgerschap*. He describes the constant interplay between the regents and the burghers.[3] He sets out the choices available to government and citizens in this political interaction based on the theory of 'exit, voice and loyalty' developed by Albert Hirschman.[4] The premise is that members of an organisation have two options when they are dissatisfied with the organisation and what it has to offer: they can withdraw from the relationship (exit) or they can complain, raise their concerns and try to improve the relationship (voice). In political circumstances, the first option would be to leave: emigrate to another country or become a refugee. The second option would be to stay and negotiate or protest. To resolve tensions and prevent citizens from going for the exit or voicing their dissatisfaction in protest, it is important for governments to promote loyalty to the state.

When Hirschman's theory is applied to the political world of the Dutch Republic, it is evident that city administrations generated loyalty by making it attractive for people to become active members of the urban community. They gave *burgerschap* exclusive advantages, in the form of political and economic privileges and welfare schemes. The ruling elite further strove to instil loyalty by showing that they were equally committed to the community as a whole. They did this through a tax system. In most European countries, the poorest citizens were the ones who paid most towards the tax base. But in the Netherlands of the eighteenth century, 'the Dutch elite not only paid taxes like everybody else, but even experimented with progressive taxation.'[5] The urban rulers, despite having become a largely exclusive group by this time, were still burghers and as such wanted to be seen to be looking after the common good with their initiatives and investments.

Even burghers on the lower rungs of the societal ladder, mostly craftsmen and shopkeepers, regarded themselves as the backbone of the urban community. They argued that their skilfulness, industry and thrift were just as, if not more, beneficial to the public interest[6] and they also paid taxes as part of their *burgerschap* duties. In the event that some of them wanted to voice concern, they organised to petition the rulers for economic or political changes. Usually, the first thing they emphasised was that they acted in the interests of the entire community, and not against them.

---

3   Prak 2008: 56–64.
4   Hirschman, AO. 1970. *Exit, Voice, and Loyalty: Responses to Decline in Firms, Organizations, and States.* Cambridge MA: Harvard University Press.
5   Prak 2008:64.
6   Kloek & Tilmans 2002:2–3.

So, when the Cape protesters declared that they were burghers and that they represented the Cape burgher population, they did so to demonstrate that they were loyal community members and not just troublemakers. They knew that most petitions in the Dutch Republic followed similar formulas and that the meaning of their declaration would be well understood by the administration. It was thus an important statement to make.

Of course, the VOC officials at the Cape were just as familiar with the protocol of petitions and therefore knew exactly what was implied by the burgher statements. Their response was to try to discredit the protesters and portray them as nothing more than a small band of agitators. Governor Joachim van Plettenberg stated that 'the Burgher Councillors in this matter can and must not be regarded as anything else than exceptions, or at the very best leaders of the signatories, whom altogether are only a small portion of the Free Burghers and Colonists'. He further claimed that 'the largest and most distinctive part of the burgher population, do not approve of the actions of their fellow Residents and certainly do not recognise the quality, which Burgher Councillors and Heemraden have given themselves'.[7]

Independent Fiscal Willem Cornelis Boers, true to his vocation as lawyer, wrote a long exposé on the authority of the burgher councillors which, he concluded, did not extend to anything other than minor burgher matters and was subject to strict oversight from the Council of Policy. They were most certainly not 'entrusted with anything like general care or supervision and therefore they cannot in the least be considered Representatives of the Burgher nation'.[8] He stated that wanting to present a request of just a few hundred of the many thousands of burghers as being representative of all of them was ridiculous and presumptuous.[9]

Other officials also commented on the small number of signatories. Because of good record-keeping by the VOC, it is not too difficult to establish whether they were right. The total male burgher population of the Cape settlement in 1779 numbered 2 873.[10] The 404 protesters were 14 per cent of this total. However, only residents of the Cape District (247) and the District of Stellenbosch and Drakenstein (157) signed the petition.[11]

---

7 Council of Policy. *Cape Disputes C 2692*, Cape Town: WCARS, 1781.03.20, 6.
8 Council of Policy. *Cape Disputes C 2692*, Cape Town: WCARS, 1781.02.02, 99.
9 Council of Policy. *Cape Disputes C 2692*, Cape Town: WCARS, 1781.02.02, 100.
10 Information on the total male burgher population figures from: Van Duin & Ross 1987:115, 117, 120, 122, 124.
11 Council of Policy. *Resolutions C 157*, Cape Town: WCARS, 149; *Petitions and Nominations C 1173*, 1779.03.30, 88; Council of Policy. *Burgher Complaints C 2665*, Cape Town: WCARS, 1779.05.07, 2. This is confirmed by Governor Van Plettenberg in his official response — Council of Policy. *Cape Disputes C 2692*, Cape Town: WCARS, 1781.03.20, 8.

Nobody in the Swellendam District did so and when this district is left out, the percentage of signatories as part of the male burgher population in the Cape and Stellenbosch districts increases to 17.75 per cent. The picture changes again slightly if we consider that 60 per cent of the protesters lived in the central and most important Cape District, where they formed 25 per cent of the burgher population.[12] At face value, the protesters were indeed a minority among the burghers and it seems that the governor and other VOC officials were correct.

François Bernard blamed the relatively small number of signatories on the controlling effect of multiple connections and relations between burghers and VOC employees at the Cape. Many burghers did not want to create bad feelings within their families by taking a stand against the government. He wrote that most of the wealthy families in the Cape were in one way or another closely linked to members of the administration.[13] Even more significant, in his opinion, was that 'at the Cape there are many less-prominent burghers who are favoured by the administration' and were therefore dependent on the good graces of members of the government.[14] It was in fact surprising that still so many had shown the courage, resolution, selflessness and virtue to sign a petition against these 'earthly demi-gods, who would destroy them with their lightning, if the High Authority would not wrench it from their hands'.[15] In other words, Company patronage and intimidation were the reasons that so few had signed the protest documents, and the protest movement had, in fact, more supporters than the numbers showed, according to Bernard.

Despite their efforts to dismiss the protest movement as trivial, the Company administrators were irritated by this thorn in their side and expressed this by making derogatory comments. Based on information provided to him by his rich farmer friend Hendrik Cloete, Hendrik Swellengrebel wrote: '[T]he disgruntled at the Cape are not the most prominent settlers, but people of lower standing.'[16] Fiscal Willem Cornelis Boers called the 404 signatories 'rabble'.[17] And Governor Van Plettenberg wrote to Hendrik Swellengrebel 'that the people who started this whole game for the larger part have such a bad reputation, that one does not

---

12 See for the more technical details on the number of Cape burghers and protesters: Baartman 2011:88–102.
13 *Nederlandsch Afrika*, 114.
14 *Nederlandsch Afrika*, 114.
15 *Nederlandsch Afrika*, 114.
16 Schutte 1982:17.
17 Ibid 102.

want to have much to do with them, as I concluded from the Register of Signatories.[18] Provisions Master Damiaan Hugo Staring was most vitriolic in his judgement of the protesters: '[A]t least three quarters are the lowest kind of Europeans, most of whom had to leave that continent because of their criminal behaviour, mixed with Hottentotten and slaves.'[19]

Company officials also alleged that the signatories had been misinformed and hoodwinked by the protest leaders, and once they had found out the true nature of the movement, they had wanted to withdraw their support, thereby making the numbers of protesters even smaller. Governor Van Plettenberg maintained that most signatories thought they had signed a petition only to prevent 'that what happened to Buijtendag would happen that evening or another day to them or theirs.'[20] VOC official Jacobus Johannes le Sueur wrote to Hendrik Swellengrebel that 'among those who signed the petition, are several, who in hindsight felt very misled.'[21] And Fiscal Boers declared in his reply to the burgher accusations that most signatories of the protest petition 'did not know the content of the paper they signed, and that some only days after having signed regretted it, and insisted that their names would be removed, and informed him in person of this desire, so that this ill-considered deed would not be held against them later.'[22] Boers stated that the signatures had been obtained by means of deception, force or even had been bought. In his book *Nederlandsch Afrika*, Bernard disagreed with this view, saying that Boers' claims had no foundation and that he had offered no affidavits from those who were supposed to have been lured, stating otherwise or withdrawing their support officially. Despite the many measures available to the fiscal, 'a little Prince, who can demand and obtain everything he wants', he was not able to get any proof to back up his claims.[23]

The VOC officials were most probably stretching the truth. After all, there had been meetings among burghers where what the protest movement stood for had been discussed. The signatories must have been informed or at least had an inkling of the nature of the objections against the administration. The burghers who signed the protest petition were not uneducated: only four of the 404 burghers were illiterate and signed

---

18 Schutte 1982:121.
19 Staring, A. 1948. *Damiaan Hugo Staring. Een Zeeman uit de Achttiende Eeuw. 1736–1783*. Zutphen: Thiem, 190.
20 Council of Policy. *Cape Disputes C 2692*, Cape Town: WCARS, 1781.03.20, 9.
21 Schutte 1982:85.
22 Council of Policy. *Cape Disputes C 2693*, Cape Town: WCARS, 1781.02.02, 100.
23 *Nederlandsch Afrika*, 113.

the May 1779 petition with a cross. These were certainly not all gullible low-lifes.

The Company officials attacked the status and integrity of the burgher dissenters because they realised that using arguments based on the number of protesters would not be enough. So they called the prominence of the protesters into question, hoping to convince their superiors, and perhaps themselves, that the protesters were not of any significance. But there was indeed cause for concern, because a considerable section of the burgher elite had joined the protests. First among them were the three burgher councillors, four incumbent and eight former *heemraden*, and several other members and former members of administrative colleges. Furthermore, 12 of the 18 highest officers of the burgher militia, among them five of the six captains, had signed the petition. These men were certainly not the kind of people who could just be dismissed as people of lower standing. We know the occupations of 107 of the 404 signatories.[24] There were bakers, butchers, bricklayers, carpenters, smiths, tanners, shoemakers, watchmakers, wigmakers, tailors, innkeepers, shopkeepers and farmers. These were people who had set up successful businesses and made their living independently, despite the constraints of VOC regulations. They were entrepreneurs who belonged to the middle and upper strata of Cape society.

This argument is supported by financial and property data available in the VOC archives. Among the most revealing documents are the *opgaafrollen*, which captured detailed information from the burghers for tax collection purposes. Burghers were asked to declare how many members there were in the household, and how many slaves, cattle, horses, sheep and pigs they owned. The lists further recorded data on agricultural and business activities. It is assumed that many burghers would have underreported their harvest figures, because they had to pay 10 per cent of their gross production to the VOC. But numbers of slaves, stock and vines are more reliable, because these assets were highly valued and are therefore an indication of wealth.[25]

The *opgaafrol* of 1773 contains the records of 289 of the 404 burgher protesters of 1779, and thus constitutes a fair sample (71.5 per cent). The number of slave-owning burghers among them was 175. Cape historians have identified a group of 'relatively prosperous, market-oriented farm owner-operators' as the so-called Cape gentry.[26] The farmers belonging

---

24 See database of Cape burghers: Baartman 2011.
25 See a detailed analysis of the *opgaafrollen*: Fourie, J & Von Fintel, D. 2010. The dynamics of inequality in a newly settled, pre-industrial society. *Cliometrica* 4(3): 229–267.
26 Ross, R. 1983. The rise of the Cape gentry. *Journal of Southern African Studies* 9(2): 193–217, 193.

to this group owned more than 16 slaves.[27] According to the 1773 tax return, 26 of the 289 protesters on the list fell into this category and could be considered as gentry. Another measure of wealth was the number of vines owned: having 10 000 or more vines was a sign of a well-established and wealthy farmer. Fifty-seven of the 289 dissidents had well over 10 000 vines, with the highest number being 116 000.

Of the 289 protesters, at least 167 owned one horse or more (37 of them owned more than 20 horses). A horse was considered almost as valuable as the highest valued property of a burgher, an adult male slave. Another *Taxatie Lijst* (taxation roll), compiled in 1773, contained the names of 400 burgher residents of the Cape District who were required to contribute financially to the building of a new road between Cape Town and the outer suburb of Rondebosch.[28] Among these burghers were 124 of the protesters, representing half the total number of protesters in the Cape District. The burghers on this list were owners of horses and carriages; they were licensed as private butchers, bakers and wood transporters.[29] They were entrepreneurs who were wealthy enough to own modes of transport, but also displayed this prosperity through their horses and carriages (so much so that the VOC government became concerned that they were trying to surpass Company officials in splendour, and in 1755 felt it necessary to issue sumptuary laws to prescribe how carriages could be decorated and limit the number of horses burghers could have drawing their carriages).[30]

A further archival source of information about the wealth of the protesters is the 1783 *Quotisatie Rolle* (tax list based on financial means).[31] The *quotisatie* tax was raised by the burgher councillors to provide for a fund from which several expenses were paid, such as the killing of dangerous animals, maintenance of roads and bridges, and the wages of the men serving in the night watch.[32] A new *Quotisatie Rolle* was made up every year around September[33] and consisted of two parts: one for burghers

---

27 Giliomee 2003:29.
28 Burgher Council. *Taxatie-Lijst der Burger Collegianten en andere onder dit Caabse district gehoorende burgers (September 1773) BRD 24*, Cape Town: WCARS, 1773.09.10.
29 Burgher Council, *Minutes BRD 1*, Cape Town: WCARS, 1773.05.29, 28.
30 Ross 1999:9–10.
31 Burgher Council. *Quotisatie Rolle over den jaaren 1783, BRD 24*, Cape Town: WCARS, 1783.09.16.
32 Council of Policy. *Resolutions C 132*, Cape Town: WCARS, 1754.08.27, 311; Burgher Council. *Inventory no. 1/82*, Cape Town: WCARS, 1970, JC Visagie. 'Inventory of the Archives of the Secretary, Burgher Council, 1695–1803', 8.
33 The *Quotisatie Rol* of 1783 was compiled by the *Burgerraaden* Johannes Smuts, Hendrik le Sueur and Adriaan van Sittert together with the Council of Policy members Adriaan van Schoor and Jacobus Johannes le Sueur and approved by the Council of Policy on

and burgher widows and one for VOC employees and VOC widows.[34] The 1783 roll is a list of 1 011 burghers, among whom were 27 females and five males who did not reside in the Cape District, but owned property there. When they are excluded, one ends up with a list of 979 males. According to the *opgaafrol* of 1783 there were 958 male burghers in the Cape District.[35] The difference between the two figures can be explained by the fact that the *opgaafrol* was compiled in April and the *Quotisatie Rolle* in September 1783. It is possible that in the period between 21 more persons could have registered to become burghers. Whatever the case, the difference is minimal, and the 1783 *Quotisatie Rolle* should be considered as a complete burgher roll or at least a complete roll of all burghers who were required to pay tax. The tax amounts were based on financial means, income and property. Thus the *Quotisatie Rolle* provides good insights into the wealth of the burghers.

Of the 979 male burghers on the 1783 roll, there were 701 residing in the Cape District in 1779. Among these 701 residents there were 499 non-protesters and 202 identified protesters, forming 81.8 per cent of the 247 Cape District protesters. The two groups are compared in Figure 7.1. The tax brackets of the burghers are divided into three tiers. The first tier represents the young and lower income burghers, who did not own property (and were taxed 0–4 guilders). The next one comprises the property-owning burghers and is divided into two sections, thereby creating a middle-income bracket (6–15 guilders) and a higher income bracket (18–30 guilders).

Immediately, several differences between the protesters and non-protesters stand out. First, the percentage of protesters in the lowest income group is significantly lower than that of the non-protesting burghers. If one considers the criterion for being taxed 2 guilders — that one was an unmarried young man[36] — only 6.9 per cent of these young men were among the protesters, which contrasts sharply with the 25.3 per cent among the non-protesting burgher population. Presumably, unmarried young men were at the beginning of their career. That only a few of them were protesters suggests that most of the protesters were already well-established burghers. Second, in the middle-income group the situation is almost the other way around: the percentage of protesters is almost double that of non-protesters.

---

16 September 1783. Council of Policy. *Resolutions C 165*, Cape Town: WCARS, 1783.09.16, 154–176.
34 According to the Resolutions of the Council of Policy, the VOC employees, burgher councillors and their widows were included in the *Quotisatie Rolle* only after 1754. Council of Policy. *Resolutions C 132*, Cape Town: WCARS, 1754.08.27, 316–317.
35 Beyers 1967:347.
36 Council of Policy. *Resolutions C 132*, Cape Town: WCARS, 1754.08.27, 313–314.

And third, the combined percentage of protesters in the middle- and high-income groups is nearly 30 per cent higher than that of the non-protesters. Most of the protesters were indeed older and wealthier burghers.

The image that emerges of the Cape burgher protesters of 1779 is that they were mostly economically independent, and that many of them were prosperous settlers. They were people in the middle and top layers of society, the same social ranking of residents who formed the core of protest movements in Dutch cities. The disparaging comments made by VOC officials about the dissenters are largely contradicted by the facts. Cape society was small, and it is hard to imagine that the officials did not know exactly who they were dealing with. It can therefore only be concluded that the comments were a deliberate and concerted attempt to create a narrative that was hostile to the protest movement. It is also likely that the Cape administrators wanted to deceive their superiors in the Republic, who were not familiar with the Cape burgher group, by describing the protesters in a way that showed that they would not be a threat, and all was under control. This effort failed miserably once the burgher delegation managed to directly lobby the Company directors.

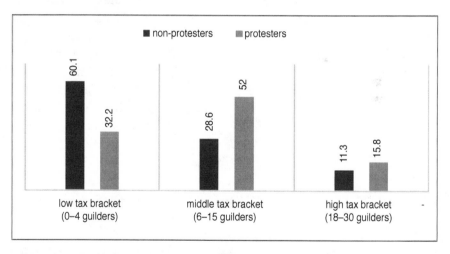

Figure 7.1: Comparison of tax brackets between protesters and non-protesters, according to the 1783 Quotisatie Rolle
Source: Author

Standing up to a government is not an easy thing to do. The burghers who took part in the protest had much to lose, but it did not stop them. What exactly motivated them to take this risky step and voice their dissatisfaction with the administration?

CHAPTER 8

Motives for protest

The Buijtendag arrest was a relatively insignificant event, and not particularly unusual. Why then did it trigger a major political upheaval? In the literature about the late eighteenth-century protests several explanations are often repeated, sometimes in combination with each other. In this chapter I aim to pick apart and evaluate some of the motives that have been suggested.

The 1778 'Revolution'

For the directors of the Company it was a foregone conclusion. They wrote in 1780 that the disturbances in the Cape settlement 'began, and became worse, and probably were caused by the distributed ... documents'.[1] Also, the most important official of the VOC, First Advocate Frederik Willem Boers, wrote in a letter to a friend that the Cape turmoil of the late 1770s began the moment these 'inflammatory' documents appeared.[2] In a pamphlet written at the Cape at the end of 1780, the anonymous author stated that the 'strife, hatred, envy, selfishness and arrogance' that were rife among the burghers found their roots in the papers 'full of slander and all kinds of incorrect and dangerous claims' that had been distributed.[3] The documents referred to were contained in mysterious parcels which some Cape burghers had found on their doorstep on a May morning in 1778. The drops had been done secretly and under cover of darkness and there was no clue as to who was responsible. The notion that the burgher protests began in 1778, instead of 1779, and that there was a continuity from the one to the other, has been perpetuated in South African historiography to this day. But was this really the case?

One document in the package was a pamphlet entitled '*The power and the liberties of a civil society defended by the principal legal minds, submitted to the judgment of the Cape burghers*'.[4] It argued that it was the primary

---

1 Council of Policy. *Cape Disputes C 2696*, Cape Town: WCARS, 138.
2 Beyers 1967:183. The letter was dated 4 March 1780.
3 Verbatim Copies. *VC 161, Nieuw-Jaars Gift aan de Caabse burgerije*, Cape Town: WCARS, 3.
4 '*De magt en de vrijheden eener Burgerlijke Maatschappij verdedigt door de gevoelens der voornaamste Regtsgeleerden, opgedraagen aan 't oordeel der Caabsche Burgerij*'. The full

duty of each member of society to improve their own welfare and that of their fellow residents to the best of their ability and knowledge. The task of looking after and improving the general welfare of the population, and to safeguard individual liberties was delegated by the people to the government. But this did not mean that the people could sit back and neglect their responsibilities. They always had to hold the government to account. If the government failed in its duties and 'when a nation sees its burgher society deteriorate and decay and be submitted to the most extreme danger, all signs of a bad delivery, and everybody is suffering, resulting in complete collapse',[5] then the people had the right and duty to stand up for themselves and protest. This should not happen in a violent manner, but according to prevailing laws.

The other document was a letter addressed to the 'fellow burghers of the settlement of the Cape of Good Hope'.[6] It maintained that the state of decline at the Cape had indeed reached danger level and it was now time for the burghers to intervene. The letter accused employees of the ruling VOC of running businesses and shops and owning farms, which were in direct competition with those of the burghers. This practice brazenly flouted the orders of the Company directors. This was to the detriment of the burgher trade, because these Company servants used their positions and privileges to squeeze out the burghers and to position themselves as 'Master of Commerce'.[7] The burgher entrepreneurs suffered greatly and many of them lost their sources of income and had no other choice than to look for financial support from church and charity. The letter named and shamed several VOC officials. The document appealed to the burghers to stand up and defend their rights, and those 'who will be the most zealous in this matter will earn our respect and esteem and will be named protector of the Burgher Liberties'.[8]

The Cape burghers were asked to sign a petition which urged the governor and the administration to address the undesirable conditions for the burghers. In case that should not have the required effect, the burghers would look for recourse from higher authorities and present their position directly to the Dutch States-General and the *stadholder*, 'who, next to

---

text of this pamphlet can be found in: Council of Policy. *Cape Disputes C 2689*, Cape Town: WCARS, 18–27 and has been reproduced in Beyers 1967:299–309.

5   Council of Policy. *Cape Disputes C 2689*, Cape Town: WCARS, 26.
6   Council of Policy. *Cape Disputes C 2689*, Cape Town: WCARS, 16–18; Beyers 1967:310–312.
7   Council of Policy. *Cape Disputes C 2689*, Cape Town: WCARS, 16.
8   Council of Policy. *Cape Disputes C 2689*, Cape Town: WCARS, 18.

God, are the only ones we recognise as our sovereigns.'[9] Significantly the documents ended with the motto of the United Netherlands: 'Eendragt maakt magt' (In unity is strength). This indicated that the writers considered the Cape to be part of the Dutch Republic, but also that they wanted to show that this was not a revolt against the Dutch administration.

Naturally, Company officials were dismayed once they became aware of the documents. One of them remarked that the documents were 'so full of malice and rebellious language that one could only label it as the filthiest slander'.[10] The Cape government reported the incident to their superiors in the Netherlands.[11] They noted that the documents stated that burghers and residents of a free state had the right to replace their government if it did not execute its duties properly. The VOC officials regarded this as a direct threat. In their reply to the Council of Policy the Heeren XVII labelled the writings 'most unfortunate and dangerous', while at the same time indicating that the Cape government had failed by not preventing their distribution.[12]

There is no indication of an investigation by the Council of Policy to find out who was behind the secret night-time drop of the rebellious documents. And nowhere else in the Company documents of the time is a guilty party named. But the report to the VOC directors contains a clue. It noted that shortly after the papers were spread there were 'several unusual movements and gatherings' among the residents of the Cape and other districts. The government had managed to lay its hands on two invitations to these gatherings which were signed by the burgher Barend Hendrik Taute. From these it appears that Taute convened a meeting of almost 200 people 'in which matters concerning the burghers will be discussed'. He further specifically asked that the meeting would be kept a secret. The meeting was held on 24 June 1778 in the garden of Domburg, the home of Jacob Schreuder.[13] According to a 1785 map of Cape Town, Schreuder's garden was situated directly to the south-east of the Company Gardens and next to the Tuijnhuijs, the residence of the governor. The choice of venue for the burgher meeting was perhaps made to add insult to injury.

The connection of Barend Hendrik Taute to the 1778 documents and meetings resurfaced at the beginning of 1795 when Johannes Henricus Redelinghuijs wrote an open letter to the burghers of the Cape of Good

---

9 Council of Policy. Cape Disputes C 2689, Cape Town: WCARS, 27.
10 Schutte 1982:83.
11 Council of Policy. Cape Disputes C 2689, Cape Town: WCARS, 1779.05.22, 13–14.
12 Council of Policy. Cape Disputes C 2689, Cape Town: WCARS, 1779.10.23, 138.
13 Council of Policy. Cape Disputes C 2689, Cape Town: WCARS, 1778.06.23, 28; Schutte 1982:49.

Hope from Amsterdam.[14] Redelinghuijs addressed it to the 'Burghers of my unhappy Fatherland'. That fatherland was the Cape. In several of his publications he claimed to be a 'native burgher of the Cape settlement'.[15] Redelinghuijs was proud to be a 'Kapenaar', and regarded this as his first affiliation, even though he was born as the son of an immigrant, Johan Herman Redelinkhaus, who originated from the German territory of Brandenburg.[16]

Via his maternal grandmother, Redelinghuijs was a descendant of Abraham de Villiers, a French Huguenot refugee to the Cape, and he made special mention of this ancestry in his letter: 'Proud of my kinship to the French people, as descending of these great souls, who, after the Edict of Nantes was broken in the year 1683, rather decided to leave their Fatherland, then bend their free necks under the despotic feet of Louis XIV.' Redelinghuijs pointed out that the French had defeated 'the pack of villains' known as the Directors of the VOC, who had shackled the Cape burghers for 150 years. French revolutionary forces had entered the Netherlands in 1795 and contributed to the demise of the Dutch Republic. Redelinghuijs now called on the Cape burghers to follow their example and to 'break the chains by which you have been bound ever since the beginning of the Colony'.

Most relevant to our story, however, is that Redelinghuijs disclosed in his letter to his countrymen that he and his fellow burgher Barend Hendrik Taute had been 'the instrument of the first Revolution in my Fatherland', even though by admitting this he 'exposed himself to all the dangers which threatened him'. He had been betrayed by former comrades. Attempts had been made to corrupt him, but he had stood strong and had resisted. He now publicly and solemnly renewed the oath 'which he once consecrated to the cause of mankind: TO LIVE IN FREEDOM, OR DIE'.

There were several similarities between Redelinghuijs and Taute. They were both born in 1756 at the Cape to German immigrants. On reaching the age of 18 they officially became part of the burgher population and joined

---

14 I have used a version of the letter which was handwritten by Redelinghuijs himself: Non-public records, *FS Malan 1795–1941 A 583*, 38, Cape Town: WCARS, 1795.02.05. The letter can also be found in: Redelinghuijs, JH. 1796. *Verzameling van Authentieke en Andere Stukken, Betreffende de Zaak tusschen Johannes Henricus Redelinghuijs aan de Eene, en Pieter Paulus en Reinier Leendert Bouwens aan de Andere Zijde; Voorzien van Ophelderende Aanmerkingen*. Amsterdam: PE Briet, 2–6. A version of the letter was published in, among others, the *Nationaale Courant* (Amsterdam, 26 January 1795).
15 Redelinghuijs, JH. 1795. *Memorie Overgegeeven aan de Provisioneele Representanten des Volks van Holland*. Amsterdam: PE Briet, iv; Redelinghuijs 1796:69.
16 Master of the Supreme Court. *Wills General Series MOOC 37/1/39*, Cape Town: WCARS, 1764.05.27, 42.

the burgher militia, where they ended up in the second company of the infantry.[17] On 3 June 1777 the Council of Policy dealt with a request from Redelinghuijs to 'teach the youth of this place reading, writing, calculus as well as the basics of the Christian reformed religion, in which he was confirmed'.[18] He was given permission to start a school and by August 1779 he was educating 102 pupils. His was the third largest of the eight registered schools at the time.[19] Taute's father and grandfather were also teachers. With these similar backgrounds, and within the rather small Cape community, it is not surprising that the two connected and became friends. The friendship was strong enough for Redelinghuijs to remember Taute fondly 20 years later in his letter to his Cape countrymen, while he hardly had anything positive to say about other former associates. In 1792 Redelinghuijs published his book *De Eerloosheid Ontmaskerd* (The betrayal unmasked), in which he fiercely criticised the 'traitors, burgher scum and scoundrels' who once were his comrades in arms.[20]

Both Taute and Redelinghuijs must have had an above-average education. In his writings of the 1790s Redelinghuijs reveals himself as an intelligent man, and one gets a glimpse of his sharp and street-smart mind from a court case that was held in 1782.[21] He had just teamed up with Johannes Augustus Bresler to become the contractor for the building of the French hospital in Cape Town.[22] Redelinghuijs bought some goods on behalf of his newly formed company from the burgher Daniel Fredrik Lehman, but apparently was slow in settling the bill. Lehman reminded Redelinghuijs several times of the outstanding account, but he kept avoiding the issue. Eventually Susanna Fleck, Lehman's wife, who was clearly closely involved in her husband's business and perhaps fed up with her husband's slack handling of the matter, decided that stronger measures were called for. She wrote to Redelinghuijs that he would have to pay and if he did not do so immediately, they had no other choice but to take legal action against him. After this ultimatum Redelinghuijs finally made payment, but he also wrote a note to go with the money. In the note, addressed to Lehman, he observed 'that the threat by your friendly wife, to send the court messenger

---

17 Council of Policy. *Oath Book C 2663*, Cape Town: WCARS, 1773.10.18, 103 (Taute); Council of Policy. *Oath Book C 2663*, Cape Town: WCARS, 1774.10.18, 105 (Redelinghuijs).
18 Council of Policy. *Resolutions C 155*, Cape Town: WCARS, 1777.06.03, 246–248.
19 Council of Policy. *Resolutions C 157*, Cape Town: WCARS, 1779.09.02, 363–365.
20 Redelinghuijs, JH 1792. *De Eerloosheid Ontmaskerd*. Amsterdam: JA Crajenschot.
21 Council of Justice. *Civil Cases: Original Rolls and Minutes CJ 876*, Cape Town: WCARS, 225; Council of Justice. *Civil Cases: General Series CJ 1125*, Cape Town: WCARS, 55–71.
22 Council of Policy. *Resolutions C 168*, Cape Town: WCARS, 1785.03.15, 263–268.

for me, was so extraordinarily well-mannered, that one can only conclude, that it shows her noble character, because a mere commoner would never be able to display such a courtesy'.[23] The note was dripping with sarcasm, but Redelinghuijs was smart enough to phrase it in such a way that he could deny having said anything negative about Fleck. Lehman was not fooled. He was a respected member of the community. He was an entrepreneur, who had just been appointed to the prestigious office of *brandmeester* (fire master) and was responsible for the fire safety of many Cape Town residents.[24] He stated that 'this letter was composed deliberately to taunt and disrespect [Lehman] and his Wife'.[25] The insult could not be ignored, and he decided to sue Redelinghuijs and demand reparation for his bruised reputation. It did not take much to convince the mediators appointed by the court to agree with him, and they strongly urged Redelinghuijs to apologise and to state that Lehman and his wife were honourable burghers about whom he had nothing negative to say. Redelinghuijs agreed to do so. Besides the observation that Redelinghuijs may not have been the most reliable person to do business with, this case also illustrates that he was a bright young man who had a way with words.

And that is exactly what Redelinghuijs and Taute were in 1778: young men. They were about 22 years old, not even mature (the age of maturity was 25) and had no social standing or influence in the burgher community. Redelinghuijs obviously had a flair for drama, but to say that he and Taute were instrumental in the first revolution at the Cape would be overstating their role. They may have caused some unrest with their actions, but it is doubtful whether the Cape burghers, or the government for that matter, took them very seriously. The aftermath of the secret distribution of their pamphlet shows that.

After discovering what was in the packet left on their doorstep, the recipients did not distribute the contents further. There were no signs that the burghers were gripped by the letters and lining up to become 'protectors of burgher liberties'. Instead, they rushed to hand in the documents to the authorities. The government noticed that shortly after the papers were spread there were 'several unusual movements' among the residents of the Cape and other districts. These were the meetings convened by Barend Hendrik Taute. These events indeed drew some publicity. In the small and rather dull Cape settlement any social gathering would have excited residents. But nothing

---

23 Council of Justice. *Civil Cases: General Series CJ 1125*, Cape Town: WCARS, 65.
24 Council of Policy. *Resolutions C 159*, Cape Town: WCARS, 1781.04.10, 262.
25 Council of Justice. *Civil Cases: General Series CJ 1125*, Cape Town: WCARS, 59.

came out of the meetings. A high-placed Company official commented that 'the opinions among them [the burghers] were at the time divided and these meetings were severely disrupted'.[26] Soon there were no gatherings anymore and 'everything returned to the previous calm'.[27] The distribution of the papers in May 1778 and the subsequent meetings did not make a serious impression on the Cape government either. No mention of them was made in the daily journals of the governor or in the minutes of the meetings of the Council of Policy. In fact, Governor Van Plettenberg announced to the Council of Policy on 26 May 1778 that he was planning an inspection tour of the outer districts of the Cape settlement and that he would be leaving at the beginning of September.[28] The governor stayed away for three months and only returned at the end of November 1778.[29] Clearly, Van Plettenberg was not in the least bit worried that the pamphlets would have disturbing consequences for the peace and quiet in the Cape settlement. It seems that the governor recalled the papers only when he wrote to his superiors about the burgher unrest of 1779, and only then did he and his VOC colleagues make a connection between the events of 1778 and 1779. But this was more to place the dissidents in a bad light, which they did by using words like 'rebellious' and 'inflammatory' in referring to the 1778 documents.

Whatever intentions Taute and Redelinghuijs may have had, they did not create much of a stir. The Cape settlement settled back into its normal routine and the young men did not persevere with their 'revolutionary' path. Barend Hendrik Taute signed the protest petition of the Cape burghers of May 1779, but left Cape Town for the Dutch Republic almost immediately after doing so, on 26 May on the ship *Morgenster*, the same ship that the burgher delegation were travelling on. He gave as a reason that he wanted to study.[30] He was not seen or heard of again with respect to the Cape burgher protests. He became a lieutenant at sea in Dutch service and visited the Cape only when his ship passed there. In November 1783 his mother, Elisabeth de Bruijn, wrote to her uncle that Barend was about to leave for Ceylon because all the warships had been ordered to go there.[31] He died in the Cape

---

26 Schutte 1982:83.

27 Council of Policy. *Cape Disputes, C 2689*, Cape Town: WCARS, 13.

28 Council of Policy. *Resolutions C 156*, Cape Town: WCARS, 1778.05.26, 299.

29 Council of Policy. *Resolutions C 156*, Cape Town: WCARS, 1778.12.01, 379; See the following for a report of the governor's trip: Schutte 1982:51–54, 61–62; Panhuysen, L. 2011. *Een Nederlander in de Wildernis. De Ontdekkingreizen van Robert Jacob Gordon (1743-1795) in Zuid-Afrika*. Amsterdam: Nieuw Amsterdam/Rijksmuseum, 73–81.

30 Council of Policy. *Petitions and Nominations C 1173*, Cape Town: WCARS 171–172.

31 Master of the Supreme Court. *Liquidation and Distribution Account MOOC 14–66 (part 1, vol.14, 10)*, Cape Town: WCARS 1783.11.

in 1791. Johannes Henricus Redelinghuijs was also a signatory of the May 1779 protest petition, but that appears to be the extent of his involvement, because no mention of him was made in any of the records and documents of the protest movement. His claim that he was instrumental in the start of the Cape protest movement was exaggerated. The 1779 protests were not a continuation of the 1778 unrest. Redelinghuijs gave himself a role which is not supported by facts.

The Enlightenment

The eighteenth century was an era of new thinking. It was the age of science, reason and humanism, in which philosophers touted the view that humankind was not subject to circumstance and divine law but shaped its own environment and progress through knowledge. In this new world, all people had equal opportunities and privileged groups would be no longer. Governments were of the people and by the people. Thinkers who influenced these ideas were Voltaire, Hutcheson, Rousseau, Smith, Raynal, Grotius, Pufendorf and Locke.

The ideas of the Enlightenment were widespread in Europe, and undoubtedly also found their way to overseas settlements like the Cape. In Chapter 2 we saw that there were several book collectors at the Cape. Often the individual writers and titles in their collections remain unknown, but from the ones that were recorded in more detail it appears that works by Enlightenment philosophers were present.[32] A public library was created in 1761, after the German Joachim Nikolaus von Dessin died and bequeathed his collection of almost 4 000 books to the Dutch Reformed Church council.[33] The Von Dessin library held an impressive set of works on subjects ranging from politics to history, philosophy, theology and geography, which some people described as having distinct enlightened elements. It contained the complete works of Voltaire and books by legal philosophers Hugo Grotius and Samuel Pufendorf.[34]

These men were among the thinkers who influenced the ideas of the American independence fighters and politicians. Although there is no evidence that the thoughts and the events of the American Revolution, which came to a head in the early 1770s, were discussed at the Cape, it is

---

32 Schoeman, K. 2016. *Swanesang. Die Einde van die Kompanjiestyd aan die Kaap, 1771–1795.* Pretoria: Protea Boekhuis, 104–107.

33 Van der Walt, T. 2004. The German contribution to South African librarianship. *Innovation* 28: 41–51.

34 Von Manger, JHW & Kaufmann, FJR. 1821. *Catalogue of the Dessinian Collection in the Public Library of Cape Town.* Cape Town.

likely that residents of the settlement were aware of what was happening on the other side of the ocean. After all, the Cape was regularly visited by Dutch, French and English fleets, which brought many visitors and news from all over the world. And there was correspondence between Cape residents and people in the Republic.

But there were no printing presses or newspapers at the Cape, so it is almost impossible to establish if the latest ideas were entertained. And there is just not enough proof that Enlightenment theories had an influence on the thinking or actions of the Cape dissidents. The only hint of evidence is in the pamphlet that was distributed in May 1778. It was copied nearly word for word from a work which first appeared in the Dutch Republic in 1754, entitled *'Het Gedrag der Stadhoudersgezinden verdedigt door Mr. A. V. K. Rechtsgeleerden'* or *'The behaviour of the supporters of the Stadholder, defended by Mr. A. V. K., lawyer'*.[35] This pamphlet had been written by the Dutch lawyer, printer and publisher Elie Luzac, who had meant it to be a defence of the Doelisten movement, which opposed the power of the regent oligarchy and contributed to the end of the second *stadholder-less* period in the Republic in 1747. Luzac often defended the right of the people to stand against their government when tyranny and miscarriages of justice threatened to replace good governance. He believed that the powers of the government had to be prescribed and counterbalanced, because only then was the freedom of the people guaranteed. Luzac's support for the role of the *stadholder* made him more conservative than other political thinkers of his time, who wanted to remove the *stadholder* and patriciate altogether and form a government of the people. But despite his more conventional stand, Luzac's influence on Enlightenment ideas in the Dutch Republic cannot be denied.[36]

So, even though books by philosophers of the Enlightenment continued to be published, and political culture in the Dutch Republic was dominated by a constant stream of pamphlets and lampoons, this was the best that Cape protesters could come up with: one pamphlet from 1754. And even this one publication did not manage to impress.

---

35 Beyers 1967:214–215, 299.
36 Schutte, GJ. 1974. *De Nederlandse Patriotten en de Koloniën. Een Onderzoek naar hun Denkbeelden en Optreden, 1770–1800.* Groningen: HD Tjeenk Willink, 8; Velema, WRE. 1993. *Enlightenment and Conservatism in the Dutch Republic. The Political Thought of Elie Luzac (1721–1796).* Assen/Maastricht: Van Gorcum; Van Vliet, R. 2003. 1756–1757: Elie Luzac geeft de republikeinse Cato's letters uit. In: *Mededelingen van de Stichting Jacob Campo Weyerman 26-3*, 181–196; Velema, WE. 2007. *Republicans: Essays on Eighteenth-Century Dutch Political Thought.* Leiden: Brill 93–114; Blaak, J. 2009. *Literacy in Everyday Life. Reading and Writing in Early Modern Dutch Diaries.* Leiden, 237.

The burgher petition of 1779 to the Heeren XVII did not contain quotes from or references to any Enlightenment thinkers. In fact, the content was not new at all. The accusations may have been directed at the VOC officials of the time and the complaints were obviously set in the contemporary framework, but the message was the same one that had been put forth by the Cape burghers since their first petition of 1658. It was repeated in the complaints against Governor Van der Stel, and in several petitions after that.

On 18 July 1719, a petition was submitted to the administration by the burgher councillors in which they stated that agriculture was no longer sufficient to provide income for the burghers, and that they would be plunged into poverty if other areas of commerce were not opened up to them.[37] They asked for 'a kind of licensed sea trade' with Mozambique and Madagascar and other islands. The goods for this trade could be sold to the burghers by the Company, and the burghers would also pay import and export duties. Therefore, the Company would profit from this, while it was another potential source of income for burghers.

On 23 March 1745, burgher councillors, *heemraden* and burgher militia officers petitioned the Heeren XVII via the Council of Policy.[38] The heading of their petition stated that 'the residents of this land unanimously had decided that the poverty and miserable condition in which they found themselves', because of high taxes and low produce prices, needed to be exposed to the directors, so that they could implement measures to improve the situation.

Every time the burghers wanted to challenge the Company restrictions, they repeated the same complaint: that they were suffering and could not make a decent living under the oppressive regime; that they wanted the local economy to become more inclusive and wanted more freedom to trade and grow. The petition of 1779 was much the same. It was an expression of the enduring tradition of popular politics in Dutch Africa and not the dawn of a liberation struggle against colonial oppression inspired by Enlightenment theories.

The 'deteriorating state of the burghers'

The protest *Memorie* of 1779 painted a picture of dismal circumstances for the burghers of the Cape settlement, caught between unfavourable economic circumstances and VOC policies. The writers claimed that they had presented a fair and realistic assessment of the situation. Historians

---

37 Council of Policy. *Resolutions C 49*, Cape Town: WCARS, 1719.07.18, 93–107.
38 Council of Policy. *Resolutions C 123*, Cape Town: WCARS, 1745.03.23, 94–138.

have not challenged the anecdotal accounts of burghers and some travellers, which described the Cape settlement as a place with a static economy where poverty reigned supreme (with mention of a few exceptions for measured contrast). The narrative of the downtrodden burghers was perpetuated.

What has not been sufficiently acknowledged is that the 1779 petition was a biased document full of political rhetoric. This should put a question mark behind the validity of the complaints. Pieter van Duin and Robert Ross were the first scholars who, in the 1980s, took an objective look at the Cape economy during the eighteenth century.[39] They write:

> it has been too commonly assumed that the farmers' own complaints on their poverty and on the absence of markets reflected economic reality. As a matter of course, historians should consider such expressions of grievances to be special pleading, and they should therefore subject them, where possible, to independent testing. This we have done, and we consider that in general they cannot be corroborated.[40]

Van Duin and Ross used the rich material available in VOC archives in the Netherlands and Cape Town. They took the data of tax rolls, annual reports on production and harvests, export and import figures, and had a thorough look at the statistics. The outcome of their research was that:

> it becomes clear that the market for Cape agricultural produce was much larger, more dynamic and quicker growing than has previously been thought, so that a very considerable rate of agricultural growth was possible. This implies that capital accumulation occurred in the eighteenth century Cape to an extent that has generally not been appreciated.[41]

Economic historian Johan Fourie clarifies that Ross's work was a reinterpretation of the economic history of the period.[42] Unfortunately this largely remained ignored by historians until about two decades later, when a new generation of economic historians took an interest.

The Company had made it compulsory for all its ships to stop at the Cape. This order was so effective that over the entire period of Dutch rule

---

39 Van Duin & Ross 1987:88.
40 Ibid 88.
41 Ibid 3.
42 Fourie, J. 2014. Subverting the standard view of the Cape economy: Robert Ross's cliometric contribution and the work it inspired. *Stellenbosch Economic Working Papers* 16.

93 per cent of all VOC ships anchored there. Also, many ships of other nationalities arrived at the Cape regularly. Ship traffic fluctuated, depending on wars between European nations, harsh weather, concern about local unrest stemming from the indigenous populations and periods of disease like the smallpox epidemic of 1713. But generally, there was a constant increase of ship traffic from 1652 onwards, which declined only in the second half of the eighteenth century, when the VOC increasingly succumbed to its own mismanagement and corruption and started to experience more competition from its British and French counterparts.[43]

The ships arrived at the Cape for three important reasons, and each of these created a demand and a market. First, in line with the main function of the station, supplies of food, water and fuel had to be replenished. Second, the VOC ships bought products like wheat, wine and brandy for export to the Asian settlements. At the same time, they brought products that were needed in the Cape. Third, the crews had to be fed, accommodated and entertained. Cape Town came to be known as the 'Tavern of the Seas', where almost every house was an inn or offered lodging.

The function of the Cape as a refreshment station had a profound effect on its development as a settlement. Johan Fourie and Willem Boshoff have investigated this in detail,[44] and have concluded that ship traffic acted as a stimulus for growth of the Cape economy. There was a strong relation between the amount of ship traffic and the growth of agricultural activity close to Cape Town with regards to wheat and wine, which by then was produced not only for export but also for local use. This indicates a vibrant tertiary sector which fed thousands of sailors and soldiers.

Fourie's analysis of probate inventories and other statistics illustrates that the living standards of the average Cape settler were comparable to, and often better than, those of people in the most developed European countries.[45] His research further shows that the Cape experienced an economic boom, which started in the early 1770s and lasted until 1795. Even the poorest farmers in the outlying districts profited from this and improved their standard of living.

These studies confirm what contemporary observers had stated, in contradiction of the burgher claims. One anonymous opponent of the

---

43 Boshoff, WH & Fourie, J. 2008. Explaining ship traffic fluctuations in the early Cape settlement: 1652–1793. *Stellenbosch Economic Working Papers 01/08*.
44 Boshoff, WH & Fourie, J. 2008. The significance of the Cape trade route to economic activity in the Cape colony: A medium-term business cycle analysis. *Stellenbosch Economic Working Papers 23/08*.
45 Fourie 2013:419–448.

burgher protesters wrote that 'our land is a land where the Jehovah pours out the one bountiful blessing after the other'.[46] VOC cellar master Jacobus Johannes le Sueur wrote in 1780 to his cousin Hendrik Swellengrebel how the prosperity in the colony had visibly increased over the last years. According to him, burghers could make a good living in any trade and enterprise, and if they did not, they had only themselves to blame. He pointed to the signs of extreme opulence among the farmers living closest to Cape Town and commented that 'the lifestyle among those people has transformed, not only in the altering of their houses, [but also in] excessive furniture and clothing'.[47]

The burgher petition of 1779 was by nature a complaint, so it would not have been credible if the burghers had painted a rosy picture of their situation. Detailed research in recent years has convincingly demonstrated that the account of a poor, suffering burgher population was misleading. New techniques of analysis, assisted by software as well as a wider set of available economic data, have provided a clearer understanding of the Cape economy. It was dynamic, and the settlement was a thriving, affluent society. As a motive for burgher unrest, especially as this was supported mostly by the burghers of middle and top layers, the argument of a 'deteriorating state' does not bear scrutiny.[48]

Banishment and burgher honour

A banishment like that of Carel Hendrik Buijtendag was not unique. The Council of Policy every so often decided that a burgher, because of undesirable behaviour, needed to be removed from the community, drafted into Company service and sent elsewhere. In his response to the burgher complaints, Independent Fiscal Willem Cornelis Boers provided a list of 33 names of burghers who had been banished between 1738 and 1779.[49] According to this list, the requests for this action had been made by the burgher military council, Council of Justice, guardians, orphan masters and burgher councillors. The initiative was therefore taken not only by Company officials, but also by fellow burghers. So why did the protesting burghers make such a fuss about the arrest and banishment of Buijtendag?

---

46 Verbatim Copies, *VC 161, Nieuw-Jaars Gift aan de Caabse burgerije*, Cape Town: WCARS, 2.
47 Schutte 1982:128–129.
48 More about increasing wealth among Cape farmers in Chapter 9.
49 Boers 1779: *Verantwoording*, Bylaag (Appendix) no. 18: 'Notitie van zodanige Perzoonen welke volgens Resolutie des Politique Vergaderinge, in dienst der E. Comp. Zyn getrokken, en van hier gedimoveert.'

When the three burgher councillors went to the governor to object to Buijtendag's arrest, they made the point that he was a burgher by birth. In other words, he had been born at the Cape as the son of a burgher, he was not a former Company employee who had become a burgher. The burgher councillors understood that letters of burgher freedom cautioned the new settlers that they could be forced back into VOC service if they misbehaved, and that their burgher status was a form of indefinite leave from the Company. But that position, of 'freed burgher', was not transferred to their children, which meant that Buijtendag was in name and deed free in the full meaning of the word. So, according to the burghers, the government had acted unlawfully and against burgher rights by taking Buijtendag into custody.

Independent Fiscal Boers countered this argument by stating that there was no distinction between burghers released from Company service and those born as burghers at the Cape. And he was backed up in this by the VOC directors, who had approved that all 'undesirable elements' at the Cape, whatever their background, could be removed if the administration thought this was in the interest of the settlement.[50] Boers made it clear that 'this whole settlement solely exists on account of the Company and for the sake of the Company; that the whole administration and government of this land is entrusted solely to Company servants' and, if the Company decided to discipline a burgher if there was a need for it, they would not hesitate to do so.[51]

In Boers' list of 33 banished burghers, there were 11 men who had been born at the Cape and had never been in Company service. Some of them had been exiled on request of burgher councillors and *heemraden*. It was therefore rather disingenuous of the burgher representatives to complain about Buijtendag's arrest and to base their objections on rights they had happily ignored on previous occasions. The reason for few complaints coming from the burgher councillors about the previous banishment of burghers could have been that in those cases the burghers concerned were lower on the social ladder than Buijtendag was. They were poor and seemingly operated on the fringes of burgher society. The abrasive and unpleasant Buijtendag may not have been a much-loved person, but he was by no means a poor man and he fully took part in burgher life.[52] The burgher councillors were trying to protect one of their own social standing,

---

50 Boers 1779:45–47.
51 Ibid 50.
52 Schoeman 2016:78–82.

but were less caring when it concerned burghers whom they considered to be beneath them.

Perhaps it was the treatment that was meted out to a burgher of Buijtendag's status that had enraged the burghers and caused them to act against the government. First, there was the public nature of the scene. Buijtendag was tied up and taken through the streets for everyone to see. In the eighteenth century, sentences were deliberately carried out in public. These events were not spontaneous affairs but were carefully staged spectacles. After being punished, convicted criminals were often marked by branding or mutilation to make them carry their shame with them for the rest of their lives. Sometimes a person was not physically punished but had to stand on the scaffold with symbols referring to the crime they had committed. The spectacle was deliberately intended to degrade. Such shaming would result in infamy and a person could subsequently be cold-shouldered by others in their community for a long time.[53] This was devastating for a burgher, because having a reputation as a reliable and honourable person and business partner was all-important in burgher society. A burgher would defend his reputation and good name at all cost.

Second, Buijtendag was not handled by his peers or equals in rank and status. The men who were sent to apprehend him were the '*Geweldiger*' and his '*Kaffersche Beuls*'[54] — the henchman of the Fiscal and his sidekicks. This was particularly insulting to a burgher, because he should be summoned only by an official messenger of the court.[55] The *kaffers* were slaves and bandits who assisted the executioner and, under the authority of the Independent Fiscal, acted as the policemen of the town. The association of executioners with crime and punishment earned them disgrace and ill repute, which was mostly because they themselves were originally recruited from among criminals. In practice, their infamy was acknowledged by imposing certain spatial restrictions on them. Executioners often had to live outside the town, had their separate pew located right at the back of the church, and were allowed into only one tavern in town where they had to sit at a designated table. They were regarded as the lowest of the low.[56] The same was true for the *kaffers* in Cape Town who assisted them, according to Boers': '[I]t is true, the *Kaffers* whom one had to use, are bad, yes, very bad and society's

---

53 Ross 1999:18–19; Spierenburg, P. 1984. *The Spectacle of Suffering: Executions and the Evolution of Repression: From a Preindustrial Metropolis to the European Experience.* Cambridge: Cambridge University Press, 42–80.
54 *Nederlandsch Afrika*, 143.
55 *Nederlandsch Afrika*, 92.
56 Spierenburg 1984:13–42.

scum, who almost all are criminals themselves and therefore any familiarity or community with them is not in the least honourable.'[57] According to the burgher protesters, a free burgher like Buijtendag should not even have been touched by unfree people. Buijtendag was not afforded the dignity of being treated as a burgher.

Willem Cornelis Boers justified the way Buijtendag had been handled by stating that there was no other choice, because he had violently resisted arrest and had to be constrained. Boers also argued that he did not have the same extensive enforcement apparatus available to him as prosecutors in towns in the Netherlands had, and so unfortunately he had to make do with the *geweldigers* and *kaffers*.[58] He added a statement from his assistant Jan Jacob Doeksteen who confirmed that burghers like Buijtendag were usually arrested by the Company enforcer, to illustrate that there was nothing unusual about the manner of Buijtendag's arrest.[59]

There is no denying that the spectacle surrounding the banishment of Buijtendag caused some uproar in the small burgher community of the Cape. But for the burgher leaders to claim that this was unprecedented or extraordinary was insincere, because they, of all people, were probably well aware of similar cases. It all adds to the impression that the Buijtendag arrest was merely used as a pretext to whip up burgher emotions by protest leaders who needed to build up a support base and was not a genuine motive for outrage.

Elements of the motives discussed above undoubtedly played a role in the outbreak of the burgher protest movement at the Cape. The burghers had indeed developed into a self-aware group with a strong identity, who could have been susceptible to new theories of people power. And in their never-ending search for new economic opportunities, burghers anyway constantly complained about the confines of Company rule. Some burghers may have perceived the whole Buijtendag incident as a wilful display of power by the VOC government towards a group of residents they regarded as of lower status. But none of these reasons, taken on their own, accounted for the extent of the outburst of burgher activism of 1779 and ensuing years. It was more likely that the situation had been exploited by clever men with an agenda, or, as Willem Cornelis Boers phrased it, the banishment drama was used 'as an infallible means to completely capture the minds of the witless

---

57 Boers 1779:50.
58 Ibid 48–49.
59 Boer 1779 Bylaag (Appendix) no. 20.

mob, to execute a plan which they had begun to forge many years ago.[60] Governor Van Plettenberg, too, referred to this view when he stated: '[O]ur Republic has seen in the past that changes are started off by the rabble, while the matadors are waiting behind the scenes.'[61]

Both Boers and Van Plettenberg were astute political leaders, and when they point us in the direction of powerful and influential men who used feelings of discontent among burghers to further their self-interest, we should consider this seriously. It is understandable that the Cape conflict has been described as an uprising of burghers against Company rulers. After all, we have already identified the main protesters as burghers, and they were indeed unhappy with the way the Cape settlement was being ruled by the VOC. But this view does not sufficiently explain why the people who were accused in the burghers' 1779 petition were not only Company officials, but also burghers who had a cosy connection with the administration. The personal attacks formed an essential part of the petition, and they were put in there deliberately by men who had an intimate knowledge of the Cape ruling elite.

60 Ibid 12.
61 Schutte 1982:121.

CHAPTER 9

The Cape elite: Family and power

Power and rule were a family affair in the Dutch Republic. Julia Adams underscores this in her book *The Familial State*, which distinguishes Dutch regent rule from other types of administration, such as bureaucracy or simple patronage (which could extend to all and sundry), by the undeniable and overwhelming presence of a familial component.[1] Regents built dynasties. They obtained positions for their sons to set them on a career path to leading roles in the city governments. Marriages of daughters were carefully planned to benefit the family aim of extending power. Different families were bound together through common interest. The resulting networks have been defined as factions, which were clusters of political forces in cities in the Dutch Republic.[2]

Regents, most of whom were also merchants, protected their commercial interests by controlling political power. They closed ranks and kept attractive and lucrative political offices within the ruling group. The right to award positions and functions to family members or clients provided them with currency to buy support and extend their influence. The clientele profited from their relations with the principal by being able to advance their careers. The early modern Dutch regarded kinship with a great measure of flexibility, perhaps even more so in the high and middle layers of society. The family was not just the core of parents and siblings, but most definitely also uncles, aunts, cousins and in-laws. When seeking or providing support for employment or some other patronage, many regents recognised family up to six, seven or even eight degrees removed.[3]

Power was thus concentrated in the hands of only a few families and their clientele, who formed the ruling elite. Richard Lachmann defines an elite as: 'a group of rulers with the capacity to appropriate resources from nonelites and who inhabit a distinct organizational apparatus'.[4] I have described above the rulers and the organisational structure they occupied,

---

1 Adams, J. 2005. *The Familial State: Ruling Families and Merchant Capitalism in Early Modern Europe*. Ithaca, NY: Cornell University Press.
2 Roorda 1978:3.
3 De Jong 1987:34–35; 't Hart 1995:79–80; Adams 2005:76–77.
4 Lachmann, R. 2000. *Capitalists in Spite of Themselves. Elite Conflict and Economic Transitions in Early Modern Europe*. Oxford: Oxford University Press, 9.

but it needs to be emphasised that there was a further dimension to the Dutch format. The regents had developed an elaborate system to buttress their ruling structure. The different families had to prevent conflict to avoid their political house of cards tumbling down. Infighting and arguments could cause serious financial and social damage to the regent families. To reduce the potential for conflict, leading families entered into formal written arrangements, also known as 'contracts of correspondence'. These were detailed agreements through which positions were rotated among families and succession matters were decided. The contracts determined exactly the turns each leading family would take in getting positions on city councils and the VOC board of directors, and in other leading functions.[5]

The contracts of correspondence created an inflexible system. There was no room to accept new, rising families because all the available offices were already distributed and no new offices were created. The contracts further made it impossible for families that had lost wealth due to adverse business conditions to sell their offices. And even when a falling birth-rate in regent families in the eighteenth century made it difficult for them to fill all available posts, they still did not add new families to their networks and contracts. This rigidity greatly undermined the political and economic power of the Dutch state.[6] Yet, despite the apparent straitjacket of familial agreements, there were shifts in power. A family which had lost its wealth may not have lost its political offices, but it was almost certainly deprived of its former influence, which left a vacuum for other families to fill. This could lead to a realignment of forces wherein new factions were formed to take control of public offices and their lucrative offshoots.

The VOC and its settlements were not immune to or isolated from the dynamics of Dutch patrimonial rule. The overseas trade was integral to the economic survival of the Dutch ruling elite and the merchant families did their best to ensure they controlled a fair share of it. As a result, members of these families had leading functions in the various chambers of the Company and bestowed offices in overseas settlements to people in their own network. Dutch networks extended their reach far and wide, which resulted in colonial patrimonial networks evolving in each of the Dutch settlements. The networks in the Republic and in overseas settlements were all linked to each other in various ways and to certain degrees. A web of connectedness spread out over the Dutch empire.

5　De Jong 1987:56–61; Adams 2005:146–150.
6　Lachmann 2000:162–165.

The shaping of the ruling elite in the Cape settlement was closely linked to the political system that had developed in the Dutch Republic, and familial networks were just as important there as elsewhere in the Dutch seaborne empire. Its development is well illustrated by the careers and actions of three Cape governors and their families: the Van Riebeecks, the Van der Stels and the Swellengrebels. Each of these represented a different stage of the elite's evolution.

The Van Riebeeck family

The career of Jan van Riebeeck in the service of the Company is split into two periods of employment in East Asia, with his period of governing the Cape settlement wedged in between. The progression of Van Riebeeck's VOC employment in the two phases shows a contrasting course and demonstrates well the benefit of family networks.

Jan van Riebeeck was born in 1619 in the town of Culemborg into a well-off family.[7] His father was a surgeon, and as a young 20-year old he followed in his father's footsteps by becoming an assistant ship's surgeon in the employ of the VOC. Once in the centre of Company power in Asia — Batavia — he became a clerical assistant. But he swiftly rose through the ranks with postings in Aceh, Formosa and Deshima. By 1643 he was posted to Tonkin and promoted to the rank of merchant. Van Riebeeck undoubtedly benefited from the patronage of Governor-General Antonio van Diemen, who was also from Culemborg and was a full cousin of Van Riebeeck's father and maternal grandmother. Van Diemen was known to have actively supported the careers of several family members.

Unfortunately, Antonio van Diemen died in April 1645, and with that Van Riebeeck's protection was gone. Van Diemen's successor, Cornelis van der Lijn, and his associates were not keen on shielding the familial appointees of the previous governor-general. Soon Gerrit van Harn, provisions master in Tonkin and the uncle of Van Riebeeck, was accused of private trading. This was not always easy to prove, but the smear alone was usually sufficient for the Company authorities, who were always fiercely protective of their economic interests, to remove the accused from his position. And if one family member was believed to be a criminal, others were seen with a

---

7   Coolhaas, WPh. 1966. De carriere van Jan van Riebeeck. *Historia* 1: 18–35; Van Ledden, W-P. 2005. *Jan van Riebeeck tussen Wal en Schip. Een Onderzoek naar de Beeldvorming over Jan van Riebeeck in Nederland en Zuid-Afrika omstreeks 1900, 1950 en 2000*. Hilversum: Verloren, 17–27; Ward, K. 2015. Patrimonialism, imperialism, and colonialism at the Cape of Good Hope under Dutch East India Company rule, c. 1652–1795. In M Charrad & J Adams (eds). *Patrimonial Capitalism and Empire. Political Power and Social Theory* Volume 28, 91–113, 95–97.

fair amount of suspicion. Shortly after, tainted by accusations of illegal enrichment, Van Riebeeck was recalled to Batavia and sent back to the Netherlands in January 1648 in disgrace, even though the administration did not manage to make a firm case against him, and he was not formally fired as a merchant.

In Amsterdam, the matter was not taken further, which showed that Van Riebeeck's removal was more a cleaning out of the Van Diemen house than a real attempt to deal with corrupt practices. Van Riebeeck wanted to rehabilitate himself and asked for a new appointment in Asia. The VOC directors declined, and so he decided to find his financial footing in the Netherlands, where he married his first wife, Maria de la Queillerie, in 1649. Shortly after that, his fortunes turned again when his adversaries in Asia were recalled to the Netherlands under investigation for serious misconduct. Governor-General Van der Lijn returned to Amsterdam in 1650. It seemed that an obstruction was removed, and the Heeren XVII resolved to give Jan van Riebeeck another chance and made him the first commander of the Cape of Good Hope.

Van Riebeeck accepted this post, only because he had a keen desire to go back to the East. He was motivated to show his worth in the new settlement, in the hope that he would be rewarded with a high-level and lucrative appointment in Asia. He undoubtedly worked hard at the Cape to make an impression, but his heart was not there, and he constantly nagged the Company directors to send him to Asia. They finally gave in and made him commander of Malacca in 1662. Van Riebeeck made a success of this position, but it did not translate to a promotion to governor or a member of the Council of India, for which he continued to pester the directors. Two years after his arrival in Malacca his wife died, leaving him with four daughters. For their benefit, Van Riebeeck decided to ask for his resignation and return to the Netherlands. While waiting for passage in Batavia, he unexpectedly was offered the position of secretary of the governor-general and of the Council of India, which he accepted. Even though he was then able to take part in meetings of the Council, to his chagrin he never became a fully fledged member, which remained his ambition until his death in January 1677.

Van Riebeeck's second career in Asia was very different from his first period of employment. He had struggled to climb the ladder simply because he did not have the family sponsorship he had enjoyed in his earlier employment. He had to manage under his own steam, which clearly was not as successful. His constant pressure for promotion and a better post became a source of irritation to the Company directors. And above all, though Van

Riebeeck was not without talent, he was also not exceptional. His belief in himself outpaced the appreciation from his superiors. It was his post as the first commander of the Cape of Good Hope that earned him a place in history. Without that he would probably have been forgotten, as many other employees of the Company were.

His son Abraham fared much better. He did have the advantage of family connections and, in 1709, was appointed to the highest and most coveted position in Asia, that of governor-general. Abraham van Riebeeck succeeded his own son-in-law Joan van Hoorn, who was married to Johanna Maria van Riebeeck, the widow of the Governor of Ceylon and Councillor of India, Gerard de Heere. Joan van Hoorn was the son-in-law of his predecessor, Governor-general Willem van Outhoorn. These kinship relations, which his father had missed in later life, made a successful career much easier for Abraham van Riebeeck.

The dynamics of patrimonial networks, or lack thereof, were not evident at the Cape at the time that Jan van Riebeeck was the commander, first, because this settlement was still in its infancy, but second, because he had his eye on a post in Asia. Since he was not planning to stay at the Cape for long, there was no good reason for him to establish a local network of support. This picture started to change dramatically from the turn of the seventeenth century, during the time of the father and son governors, Simon and Willem Adriaan van der Stel. Both men were, by all accounts, prime products of the Dutch regent culture. Whereas Jan van Riebeeck and his immediate successors were of a humbler lineage, the Van der Stels were the cream of the Amsterdam patriciate. They had a built-in sense of entitlement and brought this with them to the Cape settlement.

The Van der Stels

Simon van der Stel was born in the East (1639), where his father Adriaen had just been appointed commander of the island Mauritius.[8] The family later moved to Ceylon, where Adriaen was murdered during a local uprising. Simon was then further raised in Batavia, and at a later age he was sent to the Netherlands for his education. He married Johanna Jacoba Six in 1663, when he was 24 years old. Through that marriage, he became part of a powerful family collective with tentacles reaching deep into all aspects of Dutch political, social and commercial life. The Six family and the closely related Hinlopen family were, at the time, the most influential

---

8 Information on Simon van der Stel: Böeseken 1964; Schoeman 2013 (*Here & Boere*).

patrician families in Amsterdam and surrounds. Simon's marriage into this family complex ensured that he soon became a wealthy and successful entrepreneur and landowner.

How or why Simon van der Stel was appointed as commander of the Cape settlement in 1678 is not exactly clear. He was already 40 years old and well established in the Republic. There was no apparent reason for him to accept the post. He was also not the most obvious choice, because he had never been in Company service and there were other, more suitable, men who had served as administrators in Asian settlements. Whatever the case may have been, his family connections and the influence of the Six and Hinlopen families in leading circles of the Company worked in his favour. Several members of the family network had been or still were VOC directors, and others had served in high positions overseas. Once Simon van der Stel was a candidate for the position of Cape commander, they used their persuasive power to finalise the appointment.[9]

In the Cape settlement around the turn of the seventeenth century, Company officials were still somewhat separate from the rest of the population. They were mostly unmarried and on their way to their next posting. In contrast, the burgher group had become more settled and social distinctions within that group had become more apparent. The wealthiest among the settlers became part of the local administration. A ruling elite of high-ranking VOC officials and prominent burghers began to form and family networks started to consolidate local power through the acquisition of property and the building of a clientele.

The Van der Stels, with their patrician background, must have felt right at home in this group. Towards the end of his tenure at the Cape, Simon van der Stel's position was upgraded from commander to governor. He began to spend more time on the development of his estate, Constantia, and seemed more interested in leading the life of a landed gentleman than that of a Company administrator. In that sense, he fitted right in with some of the wealthiest burgher farmers.

However, the relationship between Simon van der Stel and the Heeren XVII was tense, because they did not agree completely with the way the government of the Cape was handled. In 1696 Van der Stel was relieved of his duties as governor. Yet the Six-Hinlopen collective was still dominant enough to ensure that another member of their network, Willem Adriaan van der Stel (Simon's son), was appointed governor in 1697. Willem Adriaan was also not a career VOC employee. He had spent most of his life until

---

9 Schoeman 2013:25–28 (*Here & Boere*); Ward 2015:99–100.

then in Amsterdam, where he had served as a member of the church administration of the *Zuiderkerk* and a city councillor, and where he had gathered his fortune.

Once he was governor of the Cape, Willem Adriaan continued the trend begun by his father, and expanded the family's land and clientele network. In Chapter 5 I outlined how his actions threatened parts of the leading settler community, who reacted by staging a protest. The VOC management stepped in and removed Van der Stel from his post. This was now an easy step to take, because the tide in the Netherlands had turned against him. Van der Stel no longer enjoyed the protection of most Amsterdam VOC directors. By 1706 they were mostly new appointees without direct links to the patrons who had supported him before. And several influential family members had died. Van der Stel became the dispensable victim of a shift in power in the Amsterdam government. While his rise was due to his close relations with the regent elite in Amsterdam, so his fall came following the lack thereof.[10]

The Heeren XVII effectively stopped the Cape Company elite in its tracks and ended the shaping of a local power base that was outside their sphere of influence. The situation remained like that for a while, and there was still a distinction between (mostly transient) Company officials and burghers. But the lines between these groups began to blur fast. After some generations of settlement, Cape families began to consist of VOC employees and burghers. By the end of the 1730s, a new ruling elite was in the making, which was led by a Cape-born governor with extensive local family ties, and his Company men, who had married into local burgher families. This Cape elite managed to remain at the top until the 1770s.

Cracks at the top

The minutes of the meeting of the Council of Policy held in the Cape Castle on the morning of 20 September 1737 provide a rare glimpse into the prevailing power struggles which belied the perceived united facade of VOC officialdom. Perhaps the minutes were so detailed, because the secretary of the Council, Rijk Tulbagh, who was a supporter of the losing party of that day, *secunde* Hendrik Swellengrebel senior, wanted to expose the bullying of their opponent, Daniel van den Henghel. The described events highlight faction politics in Cape ruling circles.

The day before the meeting, Governor Adriaan van Kervel had died.

---

10 Schutte 1989:307.

His deputy, Hendrik Swellengrebel, convened the members of the Council to determine who would take charge until the Heeren XVII decided on the succession. Swellengrebel had been born at the Cape in 1700 as the son of former Company employee Johannes Balthasar Swellengrebel. Swellengrebel senior had been a member of the Council of Policy until 1716, when he was given the choice to resign or sell his extensive landholdings. He chose to become a burgher and continue with his lucrative farming enterprise. His son Hendrik was sent to the Netherlands for his education and later entered the service of the Company. By 1724 he was a member of the Cape Council of Policy.[11]

The minutes of the Council meeting reflect that Hendrik Swellengrebel held that it had always been Company policy to let the second-in-command take over when a governor passed away. But Independent Fiscal Daniel van den Henghel said that he had occupied the rank of senior merchant longer than Swellengrebel had and was therefore his senior and should become acting governor. Swellengrebel countered that he had been a member of the Council of Policy for longer. As neither man was prepared to give in, the issue was put to a vote, but each had two supporters and the vote was deadlocked. Van den Henghel then tried to exclude Secretary Rijk Tulbagh from the process on the grounds that he was not impartial because he was related to Swellengrebel. Tulbagh took offence and said he always voted according to his conscience. To break the stalemate, it was decided to draw lots. Van den Henghel won and subsequently became acting governor, while Swellengrebel stayed on as *secunde*.[12]

The rise of Swellengrebel

In October and November 1737, the Council of Policy appointed a further two VOC officials as members.[13] One of these was a supporter of Van den Henghel, who then felt confident enough to ask for the Council's recommendation to the Heeren XVII to appoint him governor. He indeed had most of the votes. But Swellengrebel and his supporters announced that they could and would make the same request on behalf of Swellengrebel.[14] Van den Henghel may have had the majority backing of VOC officials at the Cape, but the final decision was going to be made in the Netherlands, and

---

11 Schutte 1982:3.
12 Council of Policy. *Resolutions C 104*, Cape Town: WCARS, 1737.09.20, 34–42.
13 Council of Policy. *Resolutions C 104*, Cape Town: WCARS, 1737.10.01, 43–58;
    1737.11.19, 124–125.
14 Council of Policy. *Resolutions C 106*, Cape Town: WCARS, 1738.02.06, 19–30.

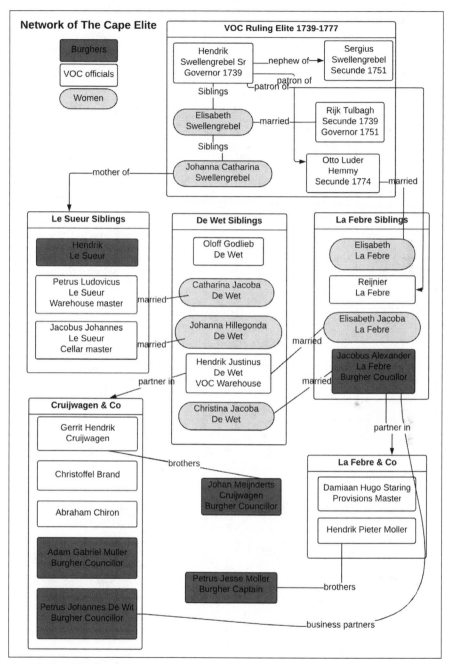

Figure 9.1: Network of the Cape elite
Source: Author

there the opinion had swung in favour of Swellengrebel. The resolution of the VOC directors to officially appoint Hendrik Swellengrebel to governor reached the Cape in April 1739. At the same time Swellengrebel's loyal supporter Rijk Tulbagh was made *secunde*.[15] The always well-informed Otto Mentzel wrote that it was widely rumoured that Swellengrebel's father had distributed 100 000 guilders in the Republic to buy the appointment of his son.[16] The new governor celebrated in lavish style to gain popularity among the general population. Festivities were held for Company personnel as well as burghers, who feasted on an abundance of food, wine, beer and tobacco.

Hendrik Swellengrebel acted as a proper Dutch regent by making sure that his family and friends were given strategic positions within the administration. Whenever a post became vacant, he filled it with one of his kin or an otherwise related party. In the period 1739 to 1749, 10 new posts were created within the top hierarchy of the Cape VOC, and these were filled by men from the Swellengrebel family network. Seven of the posts went to men who had been born at the Cape, like the governor, and they were personally appointed or endorsed by Swellengrebel.[17]

One of these men was Reijnier la Febre, the eldest son of Gijsbert la Febre, who came from the Netherlands. After La Febre senior settled at the Cape he married a local woman and became a butcher. He must have done well for himself, because he rose to prominence to eventually become a burgher councillor. The La Febres were one of the Cape families that had some members in Company service, while others were burgher entrepreneurs. Although his father was a burgher, Reijnier la Febre entered VOC service, and was helped in his career by Hendrik Swellengrebel. The minutes of the Council of Policy of 3 September 1740 reflect that the bookkeeper Reijnier la Febre was appointed to first *commies* (commissioner for trade) on the ship *De Brak* 'on the nomination of the Lord Governor'.[18] It was a critical position, because this ship was used to collect slaves for the Company from Madagascar, and as *commies* La Febre was responsible for the trade negotiations.

After only six months, Reijnier la Febre asked to be relieved of his post. His assistant Otto Luder Hemmy was appointed in his place.[19] Hemmy had arrived at the Cape only the year before, but he had caught the attention of

---

15 Council of Policy. *Resolutions C 110*, Cape Town: WCARS 1739.04.04, 27–32.
16 Mentzel, OF. 2006. *Life at the Cape in the Mid-Eighteenth Century: The Biography of Rudolph Siegfried Allemann*. Cape Town: The Van Riebeeck Society, 110–111.
17 Ibid 128; Ross & Schrikker 2012:34.
18 Council of Policy. *Resolutions C 115*, Cape Town: WCARS, 1740.09.03, 74–78.
19 Council of Policy. *Resolutions C 117*, Cape Town: WCARS, 1741.03.21, 2–60.

Governor Swellengrebel, who made sure he was promoted from sergeant to assistant, the first rung on the ladder of the higher VOC personnel, the so-called *gekwalificeerden*. As *commies* on the ship *De Brak*, Hemmy did a sterling job and 'thanks to his demonstrated diligence and vigilance in the service of the [slave] trade' he was promoted to bookkeeper in January 1742.[20] A year later he married Elisabeth la Febre, a sister of Reijnier, which linked him to one of the most influential Cape families.[21] Hemmy continued to rise through the ranks. He became acting independent fiscal and member of the Council of Policy in 1766, and in 1774 he was appointed as *secunde*. He spent his entire VOC career at the Cape, almost four decades, and was a vital part of the web of connectivity that grew around the Swellengrebel family.

Governor Hendrik Swellengrebel decided to retire in 1751. Although he was not from the Netherlands, he moved there and settled in the province of Utrecht. The Council of Policy asked the Heeren XVII that he be succeeded by the *secunde* Rijk Tulbagh, who by then had spent almost 30 years in Company service at the Cape, and was married to Swellengrebel's sister Elisabeth. The Company directors followed the recommendation of the Cape government and appointed Tulbagh as governor. Sergius Swellengrebel, an uncle of Hendrik, became *secunde*. The Swellengrebels clearly were still well supported by people within the ruling circles of the VOC in the Netherlands.

The tight web of family patronage

In the period during which governors Swellengrebel and Tulbagh ruled the Cape (1740–1771) Cape society became progressively dominated by increasing levels of family patronage and networks. This development was especially clear during the 1760s and 1770s.

A sister of Governor Swellengrebel, Johanna Catharina, was married to Francois le Sueur, the minister of the influential Dutch Reformed church. Two of their sons, nephews of both Swellengrebel and Tulbagh, had outstanding careers in the service of the Company.[22] Petrus Ludovicus le Sueur became a junior merchant and warehouse master in 1765. Two years later he was admitted as a member of the Council of Justice.[23] His

---

20 Council of Policy. *Resolutions C 120*, Cape Town: WCARS, 1742.01.23, 40–41.
21 De Villiers & Pama 1981:301.
22 See the Le Sueur genealogy in: De Villiers & Pama 1981:945–946.
23 Council of Policy. *Resolutions C 143*, Cape Town: WCARS, 1765.03.05, 208; *C 145*, 1767.06.30, 209–216.

brother, Jacobus Johannes le Sueur, studied law in the Netherlands and, after his return to the Cape, was appointed landdrost of the Stellenbosch and Drakenstein District, in 1763. By 1769 Jacobus was back in Cape Town and was promoted to merchant and cashier of the Company. He then became a member of the Council of Policy and in 1778 took the position of cellar master.[24] Jacobus Johannes le Sueur was criticised by the burgher protesters of 1779, who alleged that he forced wine farmers to sell wine to the Company at much lower prices than they would get from foreign ships. And if the farmers were unwilling to sell their wine to the Company at these low prices, he threatened to cut them off altogether and not buy any wine from them.[25] In his correspondence with Hendrik Swellengrebel junior, Le Sueur complained bitterly about the burgher opposition.[26]

The two Le Sueur brothers were married to siblings from the De Wet family. These sisters had two brothers in the top hierarchy of the Cape administration. One was Olof Godlieb de Wet, who had the rank of junior merchant and became secretary of the Orphan Chamber in 1772. He was married to Magdalena Böttiger, which made him the son-in-law of burgher councillor Jan Fredrik Willem Böttiger.[27] The second brother was Hendrik Justinus de Wet, who had an extensive network of links to VOC officials and burgher councillors. Through his first wife, Sophia Brink, he was a son-in-law of burgher councillor Andries Brink senior. His second wife was a niece of burgher councillor Jacobus Alexander la Febre, the youngest brother of the earlier mentioned Reijnier.[28] Hendrik Justinus de Wet was bookkeeper in the VOC warehouse where Petrus Ludovicus le Sueur was master.

Perhaps more important were Hendrik Justinus de Wet's entrepreneurial links. He was one of six partners in the firm Cruijwagen & Co. The other partners were the burgher councillors Adam Gabriel Muller and Petrus Johannes de Wit, the VOC junior merchant Christoffel Brand, the bookkeeper Abraham Chiron and lastly the name partner, Gerrit Hendrik Cruijwagen, the superintendent of the VOC timber store and the slave lodge and brother of burgher councillor Johan Meijnderts Cruijwagen.[29]

---

24 Council of Policy. *Resolutions C 147*, Cape Town: WCARS, 1769.06.06, 189; Schutte 1982:20, 48.

25 Beyers 1967:40–41.

26 See for example his letter in Schutte 1982:83–86.

27 De Villiers & Pama 1981:1127; Schutte 1982:48.

28 De Villiers & Pama 1981:1127, 218; Heese, JA & Lombard, RTJ. 1992. *Suid-Afrikaanse Geslagregisters / South African Genealogies*. Vol 16. Pretoria and Stellenbosch: GSSA, 250.

29 Council of Policy. *Cape Disputes C 2689*, Cape Town: WCARS, 1779.10.09, 49–50; *C 2695*, 377; Council of Policy. *Resolutions C 151*, Cape Town: WCARS, 1773.09.07, 311.

The Cruijwagens were a wealthy family of burghers and VOC officials, and played a leading role in Cape society for many decades.[30]

Gerrit Hendrik Cruijwagen and his firm were the target of several attacks in the burgher protest *Memorie* of 1779. The partnership was accused of monopolising 'the local as well as the foreign trade'. Because so many VOC officials were involved in the firm, it acted against VOC regulations and it competed unfairly with the burghers. Christoffel Brand, for instance, used his position as postholder in False Bay to buy the best and most profitable goods from passing ships and then transport them to Cape Town on Company carts. Cruijwagen himself openly kept a warehouse with all kinds of goods, which he sold in retail.

Another statement by several burghers claimed that Cruijwagen owned a market garden from which he sold vegetables and fruit, and that he hired out slaves to work as tradesmen in competition with the burghers. They further claimed that he was the biggest and richest trader in Cape Town.[31] Cruijwagen did not deny that he was financially well-off and owned real estate, but according to him this was not as a result of his trading activities, but because he had inherited money and had married well. On becoming an adult, he had inherited the princely sum of 25 000 guilders from his parents.[32]

The earlier-mentioned Jacobus Alexander la Febre was the youngest member of the La Febre family, but probably the most important. He was at the forefront of the burgher community and over a period of two decades (1757–1777) he held several positions. In 1754 he had married Christina Jacoba de Wet. This link to both the De Wet and Le Sueur families would have assisted him greatly.[33] He rose through the ranks of the burgher militia to become captain, he was a deacon and elder of the Dutch Reformed Church, and he alternated between being Commissioner of Civil and Marriage Affairs, Orphan Master and a burgher councillor.

In 1774 La Febre formed a trading company with the VOC provisions master, Damiaan Hugo Staring, and the provisions bookkeeper, Hendrik Pieter Moller. The company was called La Febre & Co and its principal business was the buying and selling of wood. In the burgher *Memorie* of 1779 it was stated that, as provisions master, Staring was the only one who was allowed on board ships within the first three days of their arrival in the

---

30 See for this family: Cruywagen, WA. 2007. *Die Cruywagens van Suid-Afrika 1690–1806*. Vanderbijlpark: Kleio.
31 Council of Policy. *Cape Disputes C 2691*, Cape Town: WCARS, 1780.12, 254–255.
32 Cruywagen 2007:339, 359–361.
33 Heese & Lombard 1992:250.

harbour of Cape Town, because he had to check if there were any contagious diseases. The statement claimed that during this quarantine period Staring and his bookkeeper had the time and opportunity to buy all kinds of goods from which they thought they could make a profit for their company. La Febre & Co would subsequently be the only source of goods that were in demand and could set the prices as they pleased. On top of this, the burghers stated, Staring could transport and store his goods free because he made use of Company boats, Company men and the Company provisions wharf.

In his response to the *Memorie,* Staring naturally denied all the charges. He did not know of one provisions master in any of the VOC stations who did not do any trading on the side to supplement his income. He claimed that he spent only about 20 minutes on the ships and would not have had time to scavenge for goods. He said that the trading of La Febre & Co was minimal and could never be labelled as a monopoly, even less so because there was heavy competition from burghers who swarmed around the arriving ships in their own boats.[34] It is likely that La Febre was the money man of the company and that Staring and Moller enabled the use of the VOC facilities. It was even rumoured that Independent Fiscal Willem Cornelis Boers was somehow involved in the business, which meant that it had an influential protector.[35]

Some of the men mentioned above did not only share various familial and entrepreneurial connections, they also were part of other networking forums. One of these was the Freemason Lodge, the Lodge de Goede Hoop, which was formed in Cape Town in 1772. Abraham Chiron was the first Grand Master of the Lodge, Jacobus Alexander la Febre was the Senior Warden and Christoffel Brand the Treasurer. Other freemasons were Petrus Johannes de Wit and Olof Godlieb de Wet.[36]

There was another curious link between many of the families mentioned above: they were owners or part-owners of property in Block B in Cape Town, which was bordered by Adderley Street, Strand Street, St George's Street and Castle Street (as they are now named). It was a prestigious piece of real estate, situated across the road from major VOC buildings, among which were the timber store (where Gerrit Hendrik Cruijwagen was superintendent) and the provisions wharf where Damiaan Hugo Staring

---

34 Council of Policy. *Cape Disputes C 2689*, Cape Town: WCARS, 1779.10.09, 52; Staring 1948:178–181.
35 Statement by Hermanus van Wielligh and Daniel Wieser — Council of Policy. *Burgher Complaints C 2673*, Cape Town: WCARS, 1779.04.27, 20.
36 Non-public records, *Lodge De Goede Hoop A 731 — 8/1*, Cape Town: WCARS, 1772–1778.

lived. Block B was the first block on the Heerengracht, on which many VOC and burgher notables resided and where the Dutch Reformed Church and the VOC hospital were situated. During the 1750s and 1760s Reijnier and his sister Elisabeth la Febre acquired several plots and houses in Block B. In 1767 Elisabeth's husband Otto Luder Hemmy bought a further property on the block, where he and his family lived until his appointment as *secunde*. He then sold the house to Willem Cornelis Boers. After the death of Elisabeth la Febre, a large part of Block B was bought by Cruijwagen in 1779. A section of Block B on the corner of Strand Street and Heerengracht was bought in 1777 by Abraham Chiron, who sold it the next year to Hendrik Justinus de Wet.[37] The property transactions in this one piece of prime real estate in Cape Town reflect the connections between the people who were part of the ruling elite at the time.

Swellengrebel returns

After the conflict at the Cape broke out in 1779, one member of the Swellengrebel family became involved in it in a remarkable manner. Hendrik Swellengrebel junior and some of his siblings had been sent to the Republic to further their education and did not return to the Cape permanently. He eventually settled on the family estate Schoonoord in Utrecht and led the life of a member of the landed gentry and a regent. His position on the Board of Chapters of the Utrecht cathedral was bought for him by his father in 1752. He visited the Cape during 1776/77 and it was then that he was reacquainted with some of the prominent members of Cape society, among whom was the wealthy farmer Hendrik Cloete, which would result in a lively correspondence between the two men.[38] Swellengrebel's subsequent meddling in Cape affairs from the Netherlands illustrates the constant interactions between members of networks in the Republic and overseas settlements.

Once Swellengrebel and some senior Company administrators found out that the Cape burgher delegates planned to submit a petition which contained personal attacks on several prominent Cape officials, they became concerned. They maintained that submitting a petition with these kinds of '*personaliteiten*' would greatly harm the burgher efforts and set them on a path to failure, because they would surely antagonise the Company directors. They wanted to mediate and achieve a more favourable outcome. The group

---

37 Cairns, M. 1974. *Cradle of Commerce. The Story of Block B*. Cape Town: Woolworths, 34, 49–52.
38 Schutte 1982:3–6.

of mediators was sympathetic to the plight of the Cape burghers and did not want their mission to be put at risk unnecessarily. They tried to convince the Cape representatives to tone down the petition to suggest 'a general plan of redress for the Colony'.[39] This was in line with established practice: petitions 'usually included proposals to remedy particular problems',[40] and because this was generally accepted it would be something the opposing parties would be more inclined to negotiate.

But first, Swellengrebel had to persuade the Company, and above all its main representative in the Netherlands, First Advocate Frederik Willem Boers, to accept the petition, and that was a hurdle he could not overcome. The First Advocate, who was 'the pivot around which the entire Company turns',[41] and Swellengrebel had a tremendous disagreement about the amount of freedom that should be given to the burghers. Swellengrebel maintained that burghers should have the guarantee that their person and their property could not be touched unless the right court process was followed, and that this procedure would have to involve burgher participation. He acknowledged that banishment was a power given to city governments but stated that it should be used only in extreme circumstances, and that burghers should still have the right of appeal to higher authorities. First Advocate Boers was vehemently opposed to this view, perhaps motivated by his desire to defend the actions of his cousin at the Cape, Willem Cornelis Boers.

The two men did not manage to solve their differences. The only thing they agreed on was that Swellengrebel would continue to try to persuade the Cape delegates to tone down their petition. But without anything forthcoming from the side of the Company, the men possibly became distrustful of Swellengrebel's efforts and opted to continue to set out their *Memorie* in the way they had originally planned. Once VOC director Cornelis van der Oudermeulen got word that the Cape burghers were on the verge of submitting their petition, he made a last-ditch effort to stop them. He requested a conference between First Advocate Boers, Swellengrebel, himself and the Cape delegation 'to see if they could put the matters back on the road that was set out by them before'.[42] At first it seemed that the leader of the burgher delegates, Jacobus van Reenen, was willing to discuss the matter. But he was being deceptive, because he himself needed the personal accusations to be in the petition for his own purposes (as will be confirmed in the next chapter). He later informed Van der Oudermeulen

---

39 Schutte 1982:89.
40 Prak 2008:61.
41 Schutte 1982:90.
42 Ibid 87.

144

that the delegates had decided to submit their petition unchanged to the Heeren XVII. On the day of the submission, 16 October 1779, a clearly disappointed Van der Oudermeulen wrote to Swellengrebel that he 'should not trouble himself anymore' and that all they could do now was to stand on the side and watch events unfold of which 'the consequences can only end in misery'.[43]

However, Swellengrebel's interest in Cape matters continued and he compiled a document containing arguments and proposals to improve the condition for the burghers at the Cape. It did not differ substantially from what the burghers had stated before. It set out the favourable conditions of the Cape climate and soil and that as a result the settlement had become a victim of its own success, with overproduction and a limited market. The remedy was that farmers should be allowed to sell their produce freely. As a practised negotiator, Swellengrebel wrote in diplomatic and respectful terms which spelled out the position of the wealthy farmers clearly, but at the same time left the way open for the VOC directors to consider the petition positively. He sent this 'draft of arguments' to Hendrik Cloete in July 1783 and proposed that Cloete should use it to set up a request to the governor and Council of Policy. Swellengrebel politely, but resolutely, suggested to Cloete that he should ask a small number of prominent settlers, who were not involved in the political troubles but were known to be knowledgeable and informed, to co-sign the request with him. He further advised Cloete to submit the request before the return fleet left, so that it reached the Republic well before the beginning of the autumn meeting of the Heeren XVII. To ensure that his document would reach Cloete, Swellengrebel sent two versions of his draft to the Cape.[44]

Cloete did exactly what Swellengrebel advised him, and in February 1784, 14 members of the 'wealthiest, oldest and most illustrious Families within the Cape burgher group' presented a petition to the Council of Policy. The Council of Policy remarked that the signatories to this petition 'had always loathed the behaviour and actions of another section of the Residents', by which they obviously meant the Cape protesters.[45] The members of the Cape government seemed to hold the supplicants in higher esteem than the members of the protest movement. Even though the VOC officials did not necessarily agree with this group of eminent burghers, they were described with respect and not with contempt as were the protesters of 1779. The

---

43 Schutte 1982:87.
44 Schutte 1982:196–201.
45 Council of Policy. *Resolutions C 171*, Cape Town: WCARS, 1786.04.19, 138.

exchange about the request of February 1784 was one between gentlemen who clearly regarded each other as equals, which is not surprising because these top-ranking burghers were, either by marriage or other kinship bonds, connected to members of the administration.[46]

The Council of Policy decided to send the request to the VOC directors in the Republic. But the directors still could not bring themselves to let go of their protectionist views. The only concession they were prepared to make was that the Company would buy all the surplus of the farmers at previously negotiated prices, and would then sell it overseas on behalf of the farmers.[47] This decision was not satisfactory for a wealthy farmer entrepreneur like Hendrik Cloete. He set out to get what he wanted and that was the right to be able to sell his wines freely. It was to be a battle that lasted for many years and in which Cloete found himself blocked at every turn by the unyielding position of the VOC.[48]

Hendrik Swellengrebel directed the events surrounding the submission of the request by Cloete and associates on 17 February 1784. Since his visit to the Cape, he had harboured an ambition to have a leading role in the Cape and was thus manoeuvring to put himself in the line of sight of the VOC directors to become governor like his father and uncle before him. This would have pleased several people at the Cape. Hendrik Cloete wrote to Swellengrebel in 1780, and again in 1784, that he and many 'old friends had a longing for that family'. They would be delighted if he were to be appointed as governor to restore peace and order at the Cape.[49] Swellengrebel made sure to remain on call during the early 1780s in case the Heeren XVII needed his advice on Cape matters. He used his connections to make clear that he was ready to be of service. He was disappointed, however, and had to admit that 'as long as the First Minister Advocate will direct matters, nothing can be done'. He stated that First Advocate Frederik Willem Boers, his longstanding adversary, dominated the meetings of the directors and 'the Colony will be sacrificed to the honour of his cousin'.[50] Swellengrebel was no match for the manipulative Boers. In the end, he could not muster enough support among the VOC elite to secure the position he wanted. In his best efforts to play a role of significance in Cape politics, Swellengrebel

---

46 Schutte 1982:17–18.
47 Beyers 1967:104.
48 See for this: Schutte, GJ. 2003. *Hendrik Cloete, Groot Constantia and the VOC*. Cape Town: Van Riebeeck Society.
49 Schutte 1982:95, 203.
50 Ibid 10.

did not realise that the Cape network, of which he was a last remnant, no longer had the same gravitas it used to have.

Hendrik Swellengrebel junior had considered himself to be a Dutch outpost of the ruling network, which for decades had dominated Cape society. His family was among those connected through an intricate web of familial, entrepreneurial, social and political relationships. In this network of power certain names kept recurring: Swellengrebel, De Wet, Cruijwagen, Le Sueur and La Febre. The families had a substantial urban base, which found its origin in the kind of business most of them were involved in. They controlled the incoming and outgoing trade routes, and in so doing they dominated economic life. This control was possible only with assistance and backing from the Company and its officials. It is especially remarkable that by the second half of the eighteenth century, the ruling elite consisted of VOC officials and prominent burghers, and that these men supported and protected each other. In leading circles, the traditional divide between burghers and officials had been bridged by common interest.

CHAPTER 10

A challenge from within

Governor Rijk Tulbagh died in August 1771. His death marked the beginning of the end of the ruling collective and energised a movement among a group of wealthy farmers who were looking to reshuffle the members of the ruling elite.

The VOC directors decided that Tulbagh should be succeeded by Baron Pieter van Reede van Oudtshoorn, who had extensive connections within the Cape settlement, where he had previously served as Independent Fiscal and *secunde*. He had resigned in 1766 and returned to Europe to make use of his inheritance from a wealthy English family member. Van Reede van Oudtshoorn would likely have continued the tradition of his governor predecessors, because he and his family were closely linked to the Cape elite. But we will never know because he died on his way to the Cape. Following his death, the Council of Policy asked the directors to give *secunde* and Acting Governor Joachim van Plettenberg the permanent appointment, to which they agreed.

Van Plettenberg was a descendant of an aristocratic family from the northeast of the Netherlands and the product of Dutch regent culture. As a 25-year-old, he had entered Company service and almost immediately became a member of the Council of Justice in Batavia. His noble lineage, as well as his family connections with Company officials in the East, ensured his quick promotion. Within two years he was transferred to the Cape to take up the post of Independent Fiscal. From 1770 he combined that function with the position of *secunde* and, after Tulbagh's death, with that of acting governor. He wielded a great deal of power in the settlement. Besides that, he had considerable financial resources, because just before he left Batavia, he had married the wealthy widow Cornelia Charlotte Feith. Her late husband, Louis Taillefert, had been commander of Bengal, which was known to be a lucrative post with many possibilities to make good money.[1]

Although Van Plettenberg may have had a title, position and money, at the Cape he was an outsider. He had been a VOC employee for only a few years, and he was young. In fact, he was the youngest member of the Council of Policy. His colleagues had considerably more experience. Many

---

1 Schoeman 2016:12–16.

of his immediate subordinates had spent several decades at the Cape or were born there and were therefore well versed in the dynamics of local networks. Van Plettenberg did not have a Cape wife and did not have any other family connections in the Cape community. As a new governor he differed from his predecessors in that he did not have the same wide support and clientele base as they had had. The converse was that the Cape's ruling collective could no longer count on the automatic protection of the governor, because the new man on the job was a stranger to them.

The distance between Van Plettenberg and the rest of the ruling elite was noticed by the protesters of 1779. While they heavily criticised members of the administration and several prominent burghers, in none of the documents produced during the unrest was the governor accused of any wrongdoing. This could be attributed to the fact that the burghers thought rather positively about him. In the letter that was distributed in May 1778 he was referred to 'as a gentleman who is known to be polite and friendly and who will surely do his duty and give us satisfaction'.[2] But it could also very well have been a smart attempt to isolate the governor further from his colleagues, who must have wondered why he seemed to remain unscathed in the turmoil.

With Van Plettenberg unable to exercise strict control over his VOC officials, who in turn were unsure if they had his support, cracks began to appear within the ruling elite. Things did not fall apart immediately, because when Van Plettenberg was appointed permanently to governor, Otto Luder Hemmy was made *secunde*. An old hand, he must have inspired some confidence among members of the establishment. However, the relief did not last long, because he died in January 1777, and with him one of the last remaining bastions of the ruling elite disappeared.

At the same time, a prominent burgher fell ill and could no longer fill his leading role. Jacobus Alexander la Febre, described in the previous chapter, was a member of three leading networks — the companies of La Febre & Co and Cruijwagen & Co, and the Le Sueur/De Wet family node — and was therefore a central figure in the web of relations of burgher councillors and VOC officials. He had contracted a lung disease and his condition deteriorated fast. His partner in La Febre & Co, Damiaan Hugo Staring, wrote that by the beginning of 1779 La Febre had been sick for quite some time and all indications were that he would die soon. They decided to wind down the company and eventually closed the business altogether. La Febre died in April 1779.

---

2 Council of Policy. *Cape Disputes C 2689*, Cape Town: WCARS, 18.

Things were not looking good for the leading network in the 1770s, and powerful men were ready to step into the void. Apart from internal factors, there were external reasons that prompted burghers with vested commercial interests to flex their muscles. The American War of Independence (1775–1783) had left the VOC in deep debt. The Company's share price declined from 786 guilders in 1733 to 120 guilders by 1794. To be able to extend its mandate it had to allow the Dutch government greater control over its affairs and had to ask several times for a financial bailout. Just as residents in the Dutch Republic did, the Cape burghers became aware that all was not well with the Company. Many feared that its demise was inevitable, and they had to do something to ensure they would not be dragged down with it.[3]

Many of the concerned burghers were wealthy grain and wine farmers operating in the areas surrounding Cape Town, whose families had benefited most from the expanding agricultural economy of the eighteenth century.[4] That serious money had been made in these two sectors was evident from the farmers' investments. They acquired large tracts of land, raw materials and equipment. Most importantly, they had the finances to pay for a steady stream of imported labour in the form of slaves. Their wealth increased progressively throughout the eighteenth century. In the 1730s the average net value of the farmers' estates was about 9 300 guilders, but by the 1770s this had risen to 24 330 guilders.[5] This wealth came to be concentrated in the hands of fewer families. In 1731 there were 53 families who had at least one member who owned a minimum of 10 000 vines in the District of Stellenbosch and Drakenstein. By 1782 there were 22 families to whom this applied. These families together owned almost half the total number of vines in the district.[6] This development points to a high degree of continuity within the agricultural sector of the south-western Cape. The farming families had accumulated their wealth over several generations — and it was the position and role of the women in these families that had made this possible.

3 Gaastra 1991:164–170.
4 The information in the following section is based on: Guelke, L & Shell, R. 1983. An early colonial landed gentry: Land and wealth in the Cape colony, 1682–1731. *Journal of Historical Geography* 9: 265–286; Ross 1983:193–217; Dooling, W. 2005. The making of a colonial elite: Property, family and landed stability in the Cape colony, c. 1750–1834. *Journal of Southern African Studies* 31(1): 147–162.
5 Ross 1983:205.
6 Ibid 207.

Women holding it together

Roman-Dutch succession law stipulates that deceased estates are to be divided between the surviving spouse and children. This meant that land and property would be split up into increasingly smaller portions, which would not assist the accrual of wealth. But at the Cape the land on which a farm building and other property stood belonged to the VOC. It was given on loan and therefore division was not possible. The consequence was that farms were sold in their entirety to be able to give each heir the share they were entitled to. A study of the names of titleholders reveals that landed property changed hands regularly — there was a succession of different owners. But these owners were not incoming farmers. They were historically connected to the rural areas of the Cape and often already owned other farms and estates. Therefore, the ownership of property stayed essentially in the hands of the same group of wine- and grain-farming families.

The women in these families played a crucial role in this process. Most women were much younger than their husbands when they first married and were therefore more likely to be the surviving spouse. These widows then controlled considerable wealth in the form of land and slaves, and because of that they were actively courted by bachelors. In most cases the widow married again and, following Roman-Dutch marriage law, the new husband effectively became the owner of his wife's property. It could happen that the same farm was transferred from the first husband to the second husband and from him again to a son of the first husband or to a brother-in-law. Different names made it seem that the farm had many different owners, but in fact they were all members of the same family revolving around the widow.[7]

The Cape's landed gentry

Martin Hall has made a detailed study of the titleholders of 41 Cape farms during the eighteenth century.[8] He concludes that 'all the names of title-holders … can be connected to seven families.'[9] These families were: De Villiers, Van der Merwe, Groenewald, Grové, Retief, Van Breda and Louw. Yet only a quarter of the titleholders had the name of one of the seven families, which indicated that the others came to own the farms through their marriage to a woman who was directly descended from the families.

---

7 For a more detailed explanation of the processes described here, see: Dooling 2005.
8 Hall, M. 1994. The secret lives of houses: Women and gables in the eighteenth-century Cape. *Social Dynamics* 20(1): 1–48.
9 Ibid 7.

Women were essential in binding together the rural elite. What is also apparent is that the seven families were all connected to each other through intermarriage. Hall estimates that 'almost 40% of the male title-holders either married cousins, or had parents who were married cousins.'[10]

One man who stood out in this group of farmers was Johannes Albertus Meijburgh, who married a great-granddaughter of the founder of the Van der Merwe family, Sophia Margaretha Morkel, in 1747. Meijburgh became the owner of the Meerlust farm in 1756.[11] By the 1770s, this estate was by far the most substantial in the Cape, with 80 000 vines, 150 head of cattle, 2 500 sheep and 54 slaves. In 1776 Meijburgh celebrated his success by renovating his farmhouse extensively and building on to its facade an elaborate gable. He thereby transformed an example of European country architecture into something far more stately. It was a clear signal to society that here was a man of high social standing. Meijburgh's wealth translated into political prominence when he became one of the influential *heemraden* in the Stellenbosch District. Hall writes, 'Therefore, in terms of generational seniority, economic position and "symbolic capital", Johannes Albertus Myburgh emerges as the likely hub of the Van der Merwe social landscape in the late eighteenth century.'[12] The Meijburgh name features among the forerunners of the burgher protest movement: father Johannes Albertus (former *heemraad*), son Philippus Albertus (*heemraad*), and nephews Albertus Johannes (lieutenant burgher militia) and Albertus Petrus, were signatories of the 1779 petition.

Capital and economic power kept circulating within the small farming elite. This created an underlying stability, which ensured that the same families controlled and expanded their ownership of land and slaves (ie, wealth) for several generations. It was inevitable that they would turn their economic strength into political and social power in the rural districts close to Cape Town. Members of these leading families, apart from being involved in their own agricultural enterprises, often played a prominent role in the administration of the Cape and Stellenbosch districts. It was from these families that the *heemraden*, highest burgher militia officers, church elders and deacons were recruited. Over time these prominent farming families gained considerable influence over local administration, justice and access to the means to expand their economic interests, for example through the distribution of land. The VOC administration and its representative in these

---

10 Hall 1994:7.
11 Interestingly the first owner of this property was Henning Hüsing.
12 Hall 1994:14.

rural districts, the *landdrost*, realised that they would be more successful in maintaining Company power if they managed to strike a balance between the interests of the Company and those of farmers.[13] They did so by granting the elite farmers substantial local control over land and labour, while the farmers in turn were happy to accept that the political administration remained in Company hands as long as they and their families were looked after.

But towards the end of the eighteenth century this began to change. Many farmers seeking to expand their economic reach realised that they were too dependent on the VOC and too restricted by Company rules and regulations. Several of the farmers supported the 1779 protest petition with statements detailing how they were forced to accept lower prices for their wine than originally agreed to by the Company, and that if they objected, they were threatened they would not be allowed to sell their wine at all. They also could not export any wine without the permission of the Company. Even Hendrik Cloete, although no supporter of the protest movement, complained bitterly that he was not allowed 'to provide his good friends in Europe with a small amount of wine.'[14]

Many of the economic demands and proposals of the 1779 *Memorie* favoured the farmers of the Cape and Stellenbosch districts. They suggested that control over the buying of wine and grain and other agricultural produce, for export and supply to the Company, should be transferred directly to burghers without the interference of VOC officials. Another proposal was that the farmers should be able to take occupation of open land between farms if it could be shown that it was not viable to fit another farm there, which meant that they could increase the size of their existing landholdings.[15] The plans put forward in the *Memorie* included allowing free trade with the Asian territories and the Netherlands, which would benefit the farmers, who could then export agricultural produce and import slave labour. The petition attacked monopolistic firms like Cruijwagen & Co and La Febre & Co, because the farmers felt that their trade practices drove up the prices for imported goods. Trade should be free and in the hands of burghers.

The *Memorie* of 1779 was to a considerable extent set up to assist and benefit the farmers. It was therefore unsurprising to find many of them among the protesters. Members of the leading farmer families — Meijburgh,

13 Ross 1983:196–197, 208.
14 Schutte 1982:59.
15 Beyers 1967:54–57.

De Waal, Van Breda, Verweij, Olivier, De Villiers, Van Brakel — supported the protest movement. Yet it is remarkable that, apart from making it publicly known that they backed the protests, none of them openly took a leading role. It was they who truly were the 'matadors behind the scenes', as Governor Van Plettenberg described them. Influential and powerful as they were, they chose two people to act as their proxies.

The first of these was Jacobus van Reenen, the leader of the burgher delegation to the Republic. Van Reenen was born at the Cape in 1727, the son of the German immigrant Jacob van Reenen, who had become a wealthy man and had extensive business interests in farming, wine trading and property dealing.[16] Being born into a prosperous family, nothing stood in the way of Jacobus van Reenen's ascendance in Cape public society. He was promoted from cornet to lieutenant in the burgher militia in 1763.[17] During 1768 and 1769 he was an orphan master and in 1769 and 1770 he was a burgher councillor. He was again appointed in that position for the years 1776 and 1777. Jacobus van Reenen was an enterprising burgher, like his father, and he owned many properties and farms. These caused him to request the Council of Policy in August 1770 to release him from all his burgher duties and positions, because 'the management of his farms and loan farms, some of which were situated far into the interior, keeps him increasingly busy'.[18] Jacobus van Reenen had close kinship ties to the farming community in the Cape District. His wife, Maria Franke, was a full cousin of Cornelis, Johannes, Gijsbert and Daniel Verweij, all four of them signatories of the 1779 protest petition.[19] Some of his 14 children had also married into prominent farming families.

The meat *pacht*

Notwithstanding his other business interests, it was without a doubt Van Reenen's position as meat *pachter* that formed the basis for his prosperity. This warrants some elaboration on the meat *pacht* and the men involved in this enterprise. In the early years of the Cape settlement the Company kept its own cattle farms to supply the meat needed for Cape Town and passing ships, but soon the holding and maintenance of the cattle farms proved to be too expensive. It was also too costly to send out employees to buy cattle from the burgher farmers and transport them to the Cape. And it was not

---

16 Wagenaar, G. 1976. Johannes Gysbertus van Reenen — Sy Aandeel in die Kaapse Geskiedenis tot 1806. MA dissertation, University of Pretoria, 1–2.
17 Council of Policy. *Resolutions C 141*, Cape Town: WCARS, 1763.11.15, 320.
18 Council of Policy. *Resolutions C 148*, Cape Town: WCARS, 1770.08.14, 241–243.
19 De Villiers & Pama 1981:1021–1022.

at all practical for the farmers to deliver the necessary cattle and meat to the Cape themselves. If every farmer brought their own cattle to town, it would result in chaos and situations that might be difficult to control. The cheaper and more convenient solution to the problem was to outsource the supply of fresh meat to contractors, the so-called meat *pachters*.

The Company negotiated to pay a set price for meat, to keep control of its expenses. Moreover, they sold the contract to supply meat and this income was a form of revenue for the Company, albeit not a major one. The meat *pacht*, or the contract for the delivery of meat to the Company, was usually sold in four parts and bought by a group of burghers operating in partnership. It was necessary for the contractors to work as a syndicate, because enough funds had to be available to buy cattle from the suppliers. In addition, each contractor had to have two wealthy and reputable burghers who would stand surety for him. This was not without risk, because the Company would hold the sureties liable should the contractor not be able to fulfil his financial obligations in terms of the contract.[20]

The meat *pacht* was granted by the VOC for a period of five years. Among its conditions were that the contractors had to sell healthy and fresh meat and that it would always be available. To make sure there was a steady supply of fresh meat the contractors could make use of VOC holding farms situated close to Cape Town, like Groene Kloof. They also had the benefit of access to the Company shambles for slaughtering the cattle and did not have to invest money for this.[21]

During the eighteenth century, the Cape experienced a considerable growth in the production of cattle and meat and in the size of the meat market. The consumption of meat by the Company quadrupled between the 1720s and the 1790s. The population of the Cape settlement increased steadily throughout the eighteenth century which grew the size of the internal market. The meat *pacht* gave the contractors a monopoly on the sale of meat to foreign vessels visiting the Cape and after 1770 the number of ships increased enormously. Lastly, the export of meat products, which had begun during the 1750s, rose.[22] The result was that the meat *pachters* made good money and became very wealthy burghers.

The same could not be said about the actual producers, the cattle farmers. The price of meat was set in Cape Town and because of the meat *pacht* system they had to sell their meat through middlemen. The contractors

---

20 Wagenaar 1976:37–41.
21 Mentzel, Vol. II, 55–56; Ross, 'Die Kaap die Goeie Hoop', 253–254; Wagenaar 1976: 36–37.
22 Van Duin & Ross 1987:58–80; Worden 2012:50–51.

tended to deal mostly with the larger farmers, from whom they could get a constant supply of cattle. The farmers did have some negotiation tools at their disposal. They could, for instance, withhold their cattle from the market or collude to fix prices. But their bargaining power was not strong, because they had to sell their stock if they wanted to make a living, and they therefore were often forced to accept low prices.

The cattle farmers regularly complained about this situation. And yet the 1779 *Memorie* made no mention of the meat *pacht*. Given the importance of cattle farming and meat consumption for the Cape economy this was a rather glaring omission. It is hard to believe that the writers of the protest document simply forgot to deal with the meat *pacht*. It had to have been a deliberate oversight by the main author of the petition, Jacobus van Reenen, who also happened to be a beneficiary of the meat *pacht* system. He first became a meat contractor in 1747 and he was one of the *pachters* from then until 1773 without interruption. After a short break between 1773 and 1778, the meat contract reverted to the Van Reenen family and they held it until the 1790s. The contract had made the Van Reenens rich and there was therefore no reason for them to to change the system. Jacobus Van Reenen preferred to let sleeping dogs lie and chose not to mention it. The omission is especially significant because it is a firm indication that the protest leaders were more interested in protecting their own interests than those of the entire burgher community, as they purported to do.

The alcohol *pacht*

The Van Reenen name became synonymous with the meat trade and supply. But that was not the only enterprise in which the family was involved, and for the most part of the eighteenth century they were 'the most diversified, enterprising and successful entrepreneurs'[23] and one of the most influential and wealthiest families in Cape society.[24] This made them particularly vulnerable to international economic conditions. Amsterdam experienced a severe monetary crisis in 1763. The Seven Years War (1756–1763) had brought about changes in Europe's economy, increasing economic activity in Prussia and shifting the financial centre to Hamburg. Merchant bankers were betting on an economic boom in Prussia after the war and increased their trading investments there. However, the economic growth in Eastern Europe did not materialise, the merchants defaulted on their loans and

---

23 Ross 1989:256 (The Cape of Good Hope and the world economy).
24 See also: Havemann, R & Fourie, J. 2015. The Cape of Perfect Storms: Colonial Africa's first financial crash, 1788–1793. ERSA *Working Paper 511*.

their assets were frozen. The entire Amsterdam market for bills of exchange collapsed.[25] From 1772 to 1775, Jacobus van Reenen made an overseas business trip, during which he visited several European countries. The reason for this could well have been to see if he could collect on outstanding French bills of exchange.[26]

The wealthy farmer collective knew that they needed to set up a larger support base. They started using their networks of business and family relations in urban Cape Town, which had created an increasingly complex mutual dependency between farmers and urban entrepreneurs, to advance their interests. They linked up with the influential alcohol licensees and traders, with bakers and smiths and other urban tradesmen.[27] The alliance with the alcohol *pachters* was particularly useful to the cause of the farming families, because it was a strong link between the Cape Settlement and the VOC. And it is here that Jacobus van Reenen also played a key role.

The liquor trade at the Cape was very profitable. To regulate it and create a stable source of revenue, the Company implemented a system that was imported from the Dutch Republic. Certain privileges, such as the right to sell liquor, were leased. From the late 1670s, the rights to sell different kinds of alcohol were auctioned to the highest bidder annually, and this arrangement remained one of the cornerstones of the Cape economy for more than 100 years. The successful bidders and buyers of the alcohol licences were known as the alcohol *pachters*.[28] The income from the sale of these licences was the single most important source of revenue for the Cape government throughout the eighteenth century. From 1730 to 1739 almost 31 per cent of the total net income of the Cape settlement came from the sale of the alcohol *pachten*. And by the last decade of VOC rule this percentage was 38 per cent.[29]

The yearly auction of the alcohol licences happened on 31 August (unless this fell on a Sunday) and was a big event on the business and social calendar of the Cape. Many residents gathered in the Castle as spectators or

---

25 Havemann & Fourie 2015:7.
26 Wagenaar 1976:5–7; Schutte 1982:84.
27 See for more details on this process: Baartman 2011:161–168, 172–180.
28 For a detailed description of the evolution and working of the alcohol *pacht* system see Groenewald, G. 2009. *Kinship, Entrepreneurship and Social Capital: The Making of a Free-Burgher Community in Eighteenth-Century Cape Town*. Cape Town: Unpublished paper, 15–47. See also Groenewald, G. 2007. A Cape bourgeoisie?: Alcohol, entrepreneurs and the evolution of an urban free-burgher society in VOC Cape Town. In N Worden (ed.). *Contingent Lives. Social Identity and Material Culture in the VOC World*. Cape Town: UCT Press, 278–304, 279.
29 Groenewald 2009:45–46; Van Duin & Ross 1987:51.

to take part in the auction and there was a steady supply of tobacco, wine, beer, cakes and pastries. Otto Mentzel provided an entertaining description of the auction day and process:

> It is amusing to study the demeanour of the various competitors for the purchase of the lease. To the casual onlooker most of them seem indifferent to, even disinterested about, what is going on. Yet their careless air is a mask; in reality each is highly strung, each watches with palpitating heart for the moment the auctioneer will call out the figure he had decided to pay for the lease. The triumphant shout of 'Mine!' is ready on his lips. The discomfiture and chagrin of those who are disappointed when the auctioneer's hammer has fallen is all too noticeable; the countenance that turns pale and red in turn tells its own tale.[30]

There were two striking and closely related elements that were ingrained in the alcohol *pacht* system: vast sums of money had to be paid (and could of course be earned) and one needed the right relations to get a firm footing in the liquor trade. Most *pachten*, and especially the more lucrative ones, were sold at several thousands of guilders; the general *pacht* to sell Cape wines was auctioned for tens of thousands of guilders. Clearly this was not meant for people who could not afford it. And that leads to the second element. As with the meat *pacht*, each alcohol licensee had to provide two burghers to stand surety for the payment of the *pacht* monies and who would sign the contract together with him.[31]

These two aspects of the alcohol *pacht* are very significant. A *pachter* either had to be wealthy himself or have sufficient and reliable financial backing. Therefore, relationships both with financiers and with sureties were of utmost importance in this business. Because trust was a key aspect in these bonds, the backers were usually family members or close friends. It was essential for alcohol *pachters* to build a tight social network. These networks came to play a vital role during the political troubles of the late 1770s.[32]

An examination of the data regarding the alcohol *pachters* and their sureties for the period 1775–1779 reveals valuable information. The six

---

30 Mentzel, Vol. II, 52.
31 Groenewald 2009:34–35; Groenewald 2007:284–285.
32 The relationships of the alcohol *pachters* and the importance of social capital for economic success and the shaping of burgher identity and society at the Cape during the VOC period is the subject of the ground-breaking thesis of Gerald Groenewald, *Kinship, Entrepreneurship and Social Capital*, 2009.

most profitable and expensive *pachten* were: the rights to sell brandy (which was sold in four parts), the licence to sell wine to foreign ships, and the most lucrative one — the general *pacht* to sell Cape wine. Between 1775 and 1779 five burghers pursued these *pachten*. It so happened that these men were five of the six alcohol *pachters* who dominated the liquor retail trade in Cape Town during the 1770s.[33] The five *pachters* formed two distinctive groups.

The Johannes Roep and Johan Jacob Schreuder group included Johan Casper Holtman, Johan Christoffel Luster, Jan Andries Bam and Johannes Smook. These men were all active at the *pacht* auctions but only Roep and Schreuder managed to acquire some of the most important *pachten*. More significant is that all these men were standing surety for Roep and Schreuder, while these two also backed each other. Johannes Roep and Johan Jacob Schreuder and their sureties evidently formed a syndicate.

The second group was formed by Maarten Baatman, Martin Melk and Willem de Kruger who used another set of sureties. They seemed to be able to call on a wider and more varied collection of backers. Only Holtman appears in both groups but he was used just once by the latter.

The most striking difference between the two groups is that all the men in the Roep-Schreuder group, except for one, were among the 404 signatories of the May 1779 protest petition, while most of the second network of *pachters* and their sureties did not sign it.

This can be explained by looking at a specific family dynasty which, from the 1730s, started to develop around the control of the brewing and selling of malt beer. Aletta de Nijs and her second husband, Hans Jurgen Honk, established a prosperous business as brewers of malt beer on their farm De Papenboom. For four decades, the malt beer *pacht* was in the hands of burghers linked to De Nijs: her sons-in-law, grandsons-in-law and close associates. This network of *pachters* included Johan Jacob Schreuder and Johannes Roep.

Roep was a German immigrant, who became a burgher in 1760. The following year he married Johanna Elisabeth Staf, a granddaughter of Aletta de Nijs. It is likely that Roep entered the alcohol *pacht* world because of this marriage. He bought his first *pacht* in 1767, and not surprisingly, that was the licence to sell malt beer. From then until the late 1770s he remained involved in the alcohol trade and bought a substantial number of *pachten*.

Schreuder was also a German immigrant and became a burgher in 1754. He was a carpenter by trade, but in 1761 he invested in his first alcohol licence and during the following 29 years he owned 39 *pachten*,

---

33 Groenewald 2009:132.

among which was the malt beer *pacht*. It was in his garden that the first protest meetings of the burghers were organised by Barend Hendrik Taute and Johannes Henricus Redelinghuijs in 1778.

Schreuder was not directly related to the De Nijs dynasty, but he was supported regularly by sureties with strong links to the family. One of these was Jan Willem Hurter. Like Roep and Schreuder, Hurter was a German immigrant. He became a burgher in 1762. In 1755 he married Barbara Honk, the daughter of Aletta de Nijs and Hans Jurgen Honk, and he inherited the malt beer brewery at De Papenboom after Honk's death. Hurter bought the malt beer *pacht* only seven times over 20 years, but because he owned the brewery he was the sole provider of beer to all the malt beer *pachters*. He also contracted as *bijtapper* (assistant tavern keeper) for the *pachters* of the brandy licence for Rondebosch and False Bay, one of whom was Johannes Roep and the other Johannes Casper Holtman, a regular Schreuder surety.[34]

The similarities between the three men are evident: they were all Germans and arrived at the Cape in the same period; Roep and Hurter both married into the family of malt beer brewers; and all three belonged to a network of men who regularly supported each other as sureties. It could be argued that the most important of the three men was Jan Willem Hurter. He expanded the successful enterprise built by Aletta de Nijs and Hans Jurgen Honk and brought his family to prominence in Cape society. He was appointed Commissioner of Civil and Marriage Affairs in 1775 and 1776.[35] Another sign of his high status was that in 1775 his eldest daughter, Aletta Catharina, married a son of Jacobus van Reenen, Dirk Gijsbertus. This bond was strengthened further in 1779 when Hurter stood surety for his son-in-law when the latter ventured into the meat *pacht*.

The alliance between the Hurters and the Van Reenens marked the beginning of a shift for the Roep-Schreuder group of alcohol *pachters*. In the early 1770s there was more fluidity between the two groups of alcohol *pachters* described above. Baatman used Schreuder as surety and vice versa. Roep was used once as surety by Melk. Yet after 1775 a clear divide appeared between the two groups, and it is not unlikely that Jacobus van Reenen brought these *pachters* and their associates into the political camp he had formed with the wealthy Western Cape farmers.

Jacobus van Reenen, the prominent entrepreneur with a wide network of partners and dependants, was used by the farmers to establish connections with the Cape urban business world. He also had international

---

34 Groenewald 2009:137–144.
35 Council of Policy. *Resolutions C 152*, Cape Town: WCARS, 1774.12.06, 400–403.

connections and undoubtedly was familiar with people in the highest circles of the VOC. This was why he was the man picked to represent the protesters in the Republic, where he spearheaded the campaign to discredit members of the ruling clique via the 1779 *Memorie*.

Van der Poel

The second proxy of the farmers behind the petition was given a different task. He was supposed to mobilise and lead the local forces. His name was Cornelis van der Poel, the burgher councillor we first met in Chapter 6. Van der Poel was born on 16 November 1736 and took his burgher oath in October 1753 when he was 18 years old.[36] After that, he joined the ranks of the burgher infantry. So far there was nothing remarkable about this man, although it must be noted that he was born into a privileged family. Both his grandfather and father were farmers and entrepreneurs who had filled various high-ranking positions within Cape society. But Cornelis van der Poel's ascendancy in the ranks of the militia and burgher administration was anything but ordinary. He was promoted from *vaanjonker* (standard-bearer) to *vaandrig* (ensign) in February 1766. He therefore skipped the two ranks of corporal and sergeant to join the officer corps and become a member of the Burgher Military Council.[37]

This Council recorded the resignations, changes, appointments and promotions within the burgher militia and dealt with disciplinary matters. It also handled all appointments below the rank of officer, although these decisions needed the final approval of the Council of Policy. Officers were appointed by the local government. According to Clause 1 of the instructions for the burgher militia of 1768, the Burgher Military Council had to consist of the captains, lieutenants and ensigns of the burgher companies.[38] There were six companies — two cavalries and four infantries — and each of these companies had one captain (or *ritmeester*, in the cavalry), one lieutenant and one ensign (titled *vaandrig* in the infantry and *cornet* in the cavalry). This meant that 18 burgher officers were members of the Burgher Military Council.[39] It was therefore a select body with a high authority within the burgher community.

---

36 Council of Policy. *Oath Book C 2663*, Cape Town: WCARS, 1753.10, 69.
37 Council of Policy. *Resolutions C 144*, Cape Town: WCARS, 1766.02.11, 87.
38 Council of Policy. *Burgher Military Council BKR 8*, Cape Town: WCARS, 1–2.
39 Besides the six companies mentioned, there were a Compagnie de Reserves and a Compagnie d'Invalides, which were meant for retired, invalid and infirm burghers. In April 1781, it was announced by the governor, who made a special and unique appearance in the meeting of the Burgher Military Council, that from then on, the

Cornelis van der Poel became a lieutenant in September 1772, and when his older brother Albertus resigned as captain of the burgher infantry due to ill health, Cornelis was appointed in his place in April 1776.[40]

In December 1777, Van der Poel became a burgher councillor — a function he would fulfil until the end of 1780.[41] Unlike all other burgher councillors, Van der Poel was never an orphan master or a commissioner of Marriage Affairs. He did not even serve on the church council. After his three-year stint as burgher councillor, he was never appointed to any other public function. His career in public administration was thus quite out of the ordinary and suspicions arose that his ascent to the highest burgher position was deliberately accelerated. In an anonymous pamphlet which appeared in the Cape at the end of 1780 (*Nieuw-Jaars Gift aan de Caabse burgerije*), the author pointed out that this did not go unnoticed in the small Cape settlement. He wrote that Van der Poel was not regarded as a suitable candidate for burgher office, because of his 'high-flying schemes' and 'ambitious nature'. But then 'through conniving and underhanded tricks he managed to get the support of men of distinction and cleared the road to be appointed as burgher councillor'.[42]

These 'men of distinction' were the group controlled by Jacobus van Reenen and the Meijburgh family. The connection between the Van der Poels and the Meijburghs was particularly close. The father of Cornelis, Jonas van der Poel, was the first to marry into the Meijburgh family. Then four of his five sons followed suit by marrying a Meijburgh bride.[43] In 1751, older brother Albertus took as his wife Hendrina Aletta, a sister of Johannes Albertus Meijburgh, and in 1768 Cornelis married Elsie Elisabeth, a daughter of Meijburgh.

The strength of the link between Jacobus van Reenen, Meijburgh, and Van der Poel was evident when in 1774 Van Reenen could not acquire the meat licence, because he was overseas. The men who became meat *pachters* between 1774 and 1778 were Cornelis van der Poel, Johannes Albertus Meijburgh and Philippus Albertus Meijburgh. In January 1775, the Council of Policy recorded that Meijburgh senior had transferred his portion of the

---

Council would consist of the captains and first lieutenants of the six active companies as well as the two reserve companies. Thus before 1781 that was not the case — Council of Policy. *Burgher Military Council BKR 2*, Cape Town: WCARS.

40 Council of Policy. *Resolutions C 150*, Cape Town: WCARS, 1772.09.01, 368 / C 154, 1776.08.20, 263.

41 Council of Policy. *Resolutions C 155*, Cape Town: WCARS, 1777.12.09, 386.

42 Verbatim Copies, *VC 161, Nieuw-Jaars Gift aan de Caabse burgerije*, Cape Town: WCARS, 18.

43 De Villiers & Pama 1981:713–715.

meat *pacht* to his brother-in-law Albertus van der Poel.[44] By 1779 the meat contract was back with the Van Reenens. One cannot escape the impression that these entrepreneurs had prearranged it all behind closed doors, to keep the lucrative contract from falling into the hands of outsiders or another faction.

Cornelis van der Poel was manoeuvred into a leading position from the middle of the 1770s. As burgher councillor he was the highest placed in the burgher community and the one who negotiated directly with the Company administration. Therefore, immediately after the Buijtendag arrest, he and his two colleagues went to the governor to confront him. He was also the first burgher to sign the May 1779 petition. He furthermore was a senior figure within the Burgher Military Council, where 12 of the 18 officers were known to be dissidents.[45] It gave him, and his associates, control over a substantial force which did not hesitate to flex its muscles in October 1779. Van der Poel was the face of the protest movement. The author of the *Nieuw-Jaars Gift* was in no doubt about the foremost agitator behind the burgher protests: 'Cornelis van der Poel! that arrogant, audacious, self-important and stuck-up creature.'[46] He consistently referred to Van der Poel as '*den Hooftman*' (the Chief). Governor Van Plettenberg also saw Van der Poel as a main 'instigator of the discord' and singled him out as one who particularly tried to turn the opinion of the burghers against him.[47]

Van der Poel's shrewdness was confirmed by witness statements in a court case held in 1802. He sued burgher councillor Oloff Martinus Bergh for insulting his honour. Van der Poel had visited a recently widowed woman and had discussed her financial situation with her. The widow was about to sell a property and Van der Poel had told her that she should invest the proceeds with him, and that he would pay her interest. But the widow had already approached Bergh about the matter. In a clever, but rather manipulative move, Van der Poel told her that he was happy that she was sorted out, but he also let drop that he did not know Bergh very well, although he had heard somewhere that Bergh was not as financially stable as he claimed to be. The widow then changed her mind and invested her money with Van der Poel. Bergh was extremely upset and accused Van der Poel of defaming him. He challenged Van der Poel to a duel and insulted him in the process. The case went to mediation and Bergh was forced to offer his

---

44 Council of Policy. *Resolutions C 153*, Cape Town: WCARS, 1775.01.10, 58–60.
45 Baartman 2011:190.
46 Verbatim Copies, *VC 161, Nieuw-Jaars Gift aan de Caabse burgerije*, Cape Town: WCARS, 18.
47 Council of Policy. *Cape Disputes C 2692*, Cape Town: WCARS, 1781.03.20, 23.

apologies to Van der Poel and state that he was indeed an honourable man. Van der Poel had discredited Bergh, but he flipped matters around and in the end it was Bergh who was made to apologise.[48]

It is obvious that Cornelis Van der Poel had the ability to cajole his fellow burghers into joining the opposition to the VOC government. His talents as agitator were recognised by other influential burghers, like the Meijburghs and their associates, and put to effective use in their lobby to gain more power.

The most remarkable aspect of the men who were in the forefront of the burgher protests is that they were just as much part of the ruling elite as the men they targeted in their attacks. The Meijburghs, Van Reenens, Van der Poels and many of their fellow dissenters were all outstanding entrepreneurs and farmers, some of whom held high positions in government structures. There were even family connections. Burgher councillor Gerrit Hendrik Meijer was a full cousin of the Cruijwagens. The third wife of the father of his colleague Christaan George Maasdorp was a sister of Jacobus Alexander la Febre. And after his first wife, Elsie Elisabeth Meijburgh, passed away, Cornelis van der Poel married Susanna Smuts in 1773, thereby becoming the brother-in-law of burgher councillors Johannes van Sittert senior and Johannes Smuts, who both were firmly in the anti-protester camp. These men were not outsiders, nor were they poor burghers.

The political conflict that started in 1779 was not one in which burghers set out to try to bring down the VOC government. It was a skirmish between members of the elite. The Cape administration and their burgher associates were challenged from within by men who backed up their action by forming a coalition of groups of burghers, who joined for various reasons. The leaders wanted just one thing for themselves: a seat at the main table. They wanted access to the centre of power where the trade routes were controlled. The current members of the ruling elite were standing in the way of their advancement. Petitioning alone was not enough, and therefore the challengers decided to use direct personal attacks on members of the ruling group in the hope that the way would be cleared for them.

---

48 Council of Justice, *Civil Cases, Original Rolls and Minutes CJ 910*, 768–769, 872–873, 986–987, Cape Town: WCARS; *General Series CJ 1329*, 102–103; *CJ 1336*, 370–403, Cape Town: WCARS.

CHAPTER 11

Protests continued ... and betrayed

A t first the challengers of the ruling elite seemed to be successful in breaking up the opposing faction: some of the high-placed VOC officials decided that their position had become untenable, or that it was just not worth all the trouble to remain at the Cape, and left.

One of the first to offer his resignation was Governor Joachim van Plettenberg. As the head of government, he accepted responsibility for the unrest that had broken out on his watch and he wrote to the VOC directors that 'the current division among the country's residents, sooner and better will be stopped and abated by another governor than the undersigned'.[1] His resignation was not immediately accepted, because the Company directors were reluctant to change governors during the uncertainties of the Fourth Anglo-Dutch War (1780–1784). Van Plettenberg was asked to stay on for the time being and he remained at the Cape until 1785. In November of that year and back in the Netherlands, a relieved, and perhaps also slightly bitter Van Plettenberg wrote to Hendrik Swellengrebel: '[T]hank God that I am far away now, because it would be difficult for me to serve a Company, of which the manner of acting nauseates me so much that I almost regret having served it as an honourable man'.[2] Van Plettenberg was one of the few local Company employees who had wanted a more reasonable and accommodating response to the burgher demands for the benefit of the Cape settlement as a whole. He may also have been annoyed that none of the officials, despite their open transgressions of Company rules, of which he especially must have been very aware, were found guilty. Van Plettenberg had been a loyal servant of the VOC, even during the stressful times of the Cape conflict, but the flagrant disregard by the VOC directors of the needs and wishes of a large part of the population disgusted him.

Out with the old

One man who had been harshly criticised by the protesting burghers was Provisions Master Damiaan Hugo Staring. His official response to the complaints about him showed that he was infuriated and felt nothing but

---

1 Council of Policy. *Cape Disputes C 2692*, Cape Town: WCARS, 1781.04.20, 84.
2 Schutte 1982:218.

contempt for the burghers, which was typical of most of the VOC officials who came to the Cape from Europe. He wrote that it was hard for him as 'a respectable man, who is a member of government and in the fatherland known as an honourable soldier, to have to account to such commoners, who want to interfere with my administration, even though I owe them no explanation'.[3] It was no surprise that Staring was not going to put up with the burghers' censure. During 1781, he informed his family in the Republic that he intended to come home, but he certainly did not want to give the impression that he was running away. At the earliest opportunity, he requested the Council of Policy to release him from his duties and gave as the reason that he felt his place was in the Netherlands now that the country was at war with England. Staring had been on loan from the Amsterdam Admiralty as a temporary employee of the VOC. He left the Cape in February 1782. However, once back in the Republic he did not re-enter the service of the Admiralty as expected but focused on his role as landlord of the estate Wildenborch in the province of Gelderland. In the late summer of 1783 he died of dysentery.[4]

Another principal adversary of the burghers was of course Independent Fiscal Willem Cornelis Boers. It was widely speculated, even by supporters of Boers, that he had been encouraged by the Company directors to offer his resignation because he had become so unpopular in many parts of Cape society. The reason given for his return to the Republic was, however, ill-health. Boers had already exchanged public life in the Cape for a rural existence by late 1782. In March 1783 there was a ship that could take him to Europe. He left the Cape in haste the following month.[5]

In the Netherlands Boers heard that his good friend Staring had died, and it was then that he began to court Staring's widow, Sophia Weinanda VerHuell. Boers married her in 1785 and became the new landlord of Wildenborch. He was offered the post of legal adviser and council secretary of Leiden in 1787. It was a rehabilitation for him after his less than honourable retreat from the Cape, which without doubt had become public knowledge in the Netherlands. But Cape events kept haunting Boers, especially because Barend Jacob Artoijs had settled in Leiden, where he became a successful and influential advocate. Artoijs had been one of the representatives of the burghers in their protest against the VOC. Boers was again accused of

---

3   Staring 1948:190.
4   Ibid 102–111.
5   Council of Policy. *Resolutions C 164*, Cape Town: WCARS, 1783.04.09, 364; Staring 1948:113–114.

having an arrogant and domineering attitude. By the beginning of 1789 he gave up his post and returned to Gelderland.[6]

For the Cape-born VOC officials targeted by the burgher protesters, it was often not an option to go to the Netherlands. Their roots were in the Cape settlement and they were members of families who had been there for generations. Hendrik Justinus De Wet decided to leave the VOC service and become a burgher. He even became a burgher councillor in 1786. Gerrit Hendrik Cruijwagen focused on his Company duties but died in 1788 from various ailments.[7] Jacobus Johannes le Sueur, the staunch opponent of the burghers, eventually became a lawyer in Cape Town, but does not seem to have been particularly successful, judging by his complaint to his son that things were not going well financially.[8]

Things stay the same

Although the main members of the erstwhile ruling faction in the Cape had moved from the centre of power and were no longer able to stand in the way of the economic advancement of the wealthy farmers and entrepreneurs, the Company was still in charge. And the Heeren XVII had made it clear that they continued to have the final say over how the Cape settlement was to be ruled. There was to be no economic reform as the burgher protesters had argued and hoped for. The true state of economic affairs was camouflaged by the economic upturn that followed the Anglo-Dutch war, which brought more ships, trade and the business of several foreign garrisons to the Cape. But the prominent farmers knew very well that this was only temporary and that longer-term restructuring (like tax reforms, free trade with the East and promoting other industries) was needed to make the settlement economically sustainable.

The Company doubled down on their adverse decisions about the burghers' demands, by appointing in place of those who had resigned officials whom they expected to continue implementing VOC policies. In December 1783 the chief director of the VOC, *Stadholder* Willem V, announced that he had chosen Colonel Cornelis Jacob van de Graaff to take over from Joachim van Plettenberg as governor of the Cape. It was widely known that First Advocate of the VOC, Frederik Willem Boers, had actively supported this appointment. Van de Graaff was beholden to his patrons and

---

6   Staring 1948:115–119.
7   Schutte 1982:265.
8   Barend-Van Haeften, M. 2003. *De Kaap: Goede Hoop halverwege Indie. Bloemlezing van Kaapteksten uit de Compagniestijd.* Hilversum: Verloren, 180–181.

would faithfully carry out their agenda and that of the Company in general, which was to look after the commercial interests of the VOC only. The new governor was nothing more than a director's pet, and was seen as such by many Cape burghers.[9]

A further unpleasant surprise was the appointment of Jan Jacob Serrurier as Independent Fiscal. This was first because he was young: Serrurier was 25 years old at the time and therefore barely a legal adult. Should it happen that the governor and *secunde* died, Serrurier would take over the reins of the settlement and many burghers thought that he was too inexperienced for this. There were older and more qualified officials at the Cape who should rather have been considered for the function of prosecutor. Besides, and it seems that this was the main reason for much of the burghers' unhappiness, Serrurier had earned a bad reputation among them. His judicial actions resulting in the banishment of the burgher Anthony Krijnauw[10] had shown that he was 'more hateful, malicious, and more loathsome of the protesting burgher group, than his predecessor Fiscal Boers had ever been'.[11] Some burghers felt that their rights had come under threat by the appointment of this man as Independent Fiscal, because he was exceptionally prejudiced towards them.

The 1784 proposal

After the decisions of the VOC directors to largely dismiss the burghers' complaints, a strong feeling of disappointment spread at the Cape, and it was then that Johannes Henricus Redelinghuijs returned as protest leader. He began his later account of what happened at the Cape in 1784 and the years immediately thereafter by articulating the spirit of discontent:

> *In the year 1784 the protesting and redress-demanding burghers of the Cape of Good Hope were deeply concerned about a decision taken in Amsterdam on the third of December of the previous year by the directors of the Dutch East-India Company in response to two memoranda presented to them already in 1779; this decision, instead of putting an end to the oppression under which the burghers*

---

9   Schutte 1982:10–11; Schoeman 2016:121–125.
10 In July 1783 Anthony Krijnauw was found guilty of writing a defamatory pamphlet about the landdrost of Stellenbosch and Drakenstein and banished from the Cape forever — South African Law Reports. *Appelate Division: Decisions of the Supreme Court of South Africa, Apellate Division* (Cape Town 1923), 334.
11 Beyers 1967:319.

had suffered for a long time, opened the door wide to the exercise of the most arbitrary power.[12]

Even though the burgher complaints of 1779 had been fair and properly founded, according to a group of 'distinguished residents',[13] it became clear that nothing would change. The Cape administration would be even more tyrannical than it had ever been before. Some burghers maintained that to accept this treatment could lead to only one thing: 'a slavery which was shameful and unworthy of human nature'.[14]

Meetings were held, and on 28 August 1784 a proposal to 'all honourable Patriots, supporters of justice and righteousness, and freedom loving burghers' was published by 76 prominent burghers.[15] The proposal assumed that the burghers did not want to place themselves in a position of slavery but would try all possible means to prevent this from happening. It therefore proposed that the burghers should organise themselves to choose two or three competent people to travel to the Dutch Republic to present their case to 'our high and lawful sovereign, the honourable lords of the States-General of the United Netherlands'.[16]

The proposal was followed in November 1784 by an act of appointment (*Acte van qualificatie*), which was passed and supported by 413 burghers. They confirmed the election of a body of 'representatives of the protesting and redress-demanding burghers' which would be tasked with championing the burgher cause and the co-ordination of the activities of the protesting burghers. The elected representatives were: Marthinus Adrianus Bergh, Christiaan George Maasdorp, Gerrit Hendrik Meijer, Hendrik Pieter Warnecke, Johannes Albertus Meijburgh, Johannes de Villiers, Jan Pietersz, Hendrik Louw, Philippus Albertus Meijburgh, Daniel Verweij, Johannes Casparus Groenewald and Johannes Roos.[17] Johannes Henricus Redelinghuijs and Johannes Augustus Bresler would share the roles of bookkeeper and secretary.

Only 3 of the 11 representatives (Bergh, Warnecke and Groenewald) had not been among the 404 protesters of 1779. The others — for instance, Maasdorp, Meijer, De Villiers and the two Meijburghs — had been leaders

---

12 Redelinghuijs 1792:5–6.
13 Ibid 10.
14 Council of Policy. *Burgher Complaints C 2675*, Cape Town: WCARS, 1786.04.04, 114.
15 Council of Policy. *Burgher Complaints C 2675*, Cape Town: WCARS, 111–124; Beyers 1967:313–315.
16 Redelinghuijs 1792:104.
17 Council of Policy. *Meetings of Burgher representatives: Resolutions C 2687*, Cape Town: WCARS, 32–33.

of the original protest movement and belonged to the burgher elite at the Cape. And as with the protest movement of 1779, the leadership of the 1784 protest was again clearly formed from among wealthy farmers of the Cape country areas and their close entrepreneurial allies. Their support came from the same kind of people as before: burghers from the middle and higher social strata of the Cape. This was spelt out in an official protest document dated 8 March 1785, which was issued in the name of 'the former complainants, as well as current ones, the former participants, as well as the ones now participating.'[18] In a footnote, Redelinghuijs made sure that his readers understood that the original protesters of 1779 were being joined by the current dissenters. The protest campaign of 1784 was a continuance of the earlier movements of 1779 and not a different movement, but it was being given new life. The protests should thus be seen in the same context as before: an expression of burgher discontent with Company restrictions, led by several members of the burgher elite, who were primarily looking after their own interests.

Nevertheless, there were some important new aspects. First, it seemed that the protest leaders had abandoned all expectation that the Company would act in the interests of the Cape settlement and its burgher residents. This time round, the protesters were opposed to any further administration of the Cape settlement by officials of the VOC. They were seeking a change of government. According to Redelinghuijs, they declared that the Cape should withdraw from governance by the VOC and seek to place itself under the authority of the Dutch States-General in the Republic. It would then be like one of the generality territories (*generaliteits-landen*). These areas (parts of Brabant, Flanders and Limburg), had been won by the United Netherlands from the Spanish and did not have any say in the government of the seven United Provinces. They were governed directly by the States-General. The 1784 protesters believed that under the Dutch government they would be treated more favourably. Redelinghuijs furthermore wrote that in 1784 many people expected the Company to collapse soon and therefore it would be better to seek refuge under the protection of the highest government of the Republic, because the alternative could be that the Cape would fall into the hands of its (British) enemies.[19]

A second new aspect was that the leaders of the protest movement were clearly identified according to the district they represented. It was recorded that Bergh, Maasdorp, Meijer, Warnecke and Verweij were the

18 Redelinghuijs 1792:116.
19 Ibid 10–12.

representatives of the Cape District; Johannes Albertus Meijburgh, De Villiers and Groenewald those of the Stellenbosch District; and Louw, Philippus Albertus Meijburgh and Roos represented the Drakenstein District. The minutes of the first meeting of the representatives in November 1784 documented the seating arrangements in detail. At the head of the table was the chairman, Marthinus Adrianus Bergh. To his right were seated the Cape representatives, to his left the Stellenbosch men and opposite him were the men from Drakenstein. Behind the chairman sat the two secretaries.[20] The Cape District had two more representatives than the others, and one of the Cape District men was also chairman. This district was clearly perceived to be the most important part of the settlement. This arrangement also indicated that the members of the Cape burgher group had now begun to define themselves by the district in which they resided and not by a connection to the Cape settlement in general. The sense of identity among Cape residents was maturing further.

The inclusion of Marthinus Adrianus Bergh among the representatives was curious. He was a descendant of a prominent Cape family. His father, Olof Martini Bergh, was the secretary of the Council of Policy. Marthinus Adrianus Bergh had made a career in the service of the VOC and had held several positions at the Cape, such as landdrost of the District of Stellenbosch and Drakenstein. The 1779 *Memorie* had contained complaints against both father and son Bergh. About Bergh junior it stated that while he was landdrost he had not shown any respect for the burghers, but had labelled them with the contemptuous term 'canalje' (riff-raff).[21] Governor Van Plettenberg noted that Bergh was rather self-obsessed and that his arrogance had not made him any friends among the burghers. Another Company official stated that Bergh 'was disliked, because of his unpredictable behaviour'.[22] But the governor had not taken any action against Bergh out of respect for his father. This changed in 1778, after Van Plettenberg received copies of letters that Bergh junior had written to people in the Republic in which he described the governor and his administration as oppressive and prejudicial against the burghers. Van Plettenberg was furious, but his friend and colleague Bergh senior implored him not to punish Martinus Adrianus publicly. Instead, Bergh junior was strongly advised to hand in his resignation as landdrost, which he did on 14 December 1778. His reason was that his 'hearing problem' no longer allowed him to perform his duties

---

20 Council of Policy. *Meetings of Burgher representatives: Resolutions C 2687,* Cape Town: WCARS, 36–37.
21 Beyers 1967:43.
22 Schutte 1982:85.

properly.[23] But as usual, the residents of the small Cape settlement knew better. Hendrik Cloete commented that 'the order to present his request was long overdue'.[24]

His forced resignation had left Marthinus Adrianus Bergh embittered against the VOC government and he submitted two petitions to the Heeren XVII in which he complained about the way he had been treated by the governor.[25] He apparently saw the 1779 burgher protests as a good opportunity to spite the administration and those who had supported his fall from grace. There was a strong suspicion among his former colleagues in the Company that Bergh 'went out of his way to fan the fires of dissatisfaction' among the burghers.[26]

In 1779 Bergh had met with and been consulted by the protesters, even though the *Memorie* contained complaints about him and his father, and relations between him and the burgher population were strained. But it was only in October 1784 that Bergh was formally requested to join forces with them.[27] Not only did he become an ally of the burghers, but he was also appointed chairman of the body of burgher representatives, which was elected in November. It would prove to be a bad mistake.

The next wave of petitions

In rapid succession, the Committee of Representatives drew up several petitions to present to the Dutch States-General, which indicated that they planned not to approach the Company authorities any longer. The first petition was produced on 14 December 1784.[28] The beginning of this document was reminiscent of the protest pamphlets that had been dropped on the streets of Cape Town in May 1778. It invoked the law of nature that members of every nation had the right to defend themselves against any threat to their person and possessions, especially if that threat came from the very government that was supposed to protect them. It is not surprising that one of the main compilers of this petition was the same Johannes Henricus Redelinghuijs who had been responsible for the pamphlets of 1778. The representatives continued to describe the burghers' disappointment and

---

23 Council of Policy. *Resolutions C 156*, Cape Town: WCARS, 1778.12.15, 438–441; Beyers 1967:128–130.
24 Schutte 1982:56.
25 Council of Policy. *Cape Disputes C 2690*, Cape Town: WCARS, 1779.03.01, 1779.05.10, 2–30.
26 Schutte 1982:85.
27 Council of Policy. *Meetings of Burgher representatives: Resolutions C 2687,*Cape Town: WCARS, 1784.10.01, 3–17.
28 Beyers 1967:316–322.

anger about the unfavourable response of the VOC directors to the 1779 complaints. And they stated that they expected the newly appointed Company administrators to have little or no regard for their rights, which was why they were appealing directly to their sovereigns, the members of the Dutch States-General, to protect them and restore law and order at the Cape.

A week later this petition was followed by a second one, in which the burgher representatives described how their worst fears had been realised. The homes of Marthinus Adrianus Bergh and the burghers Jan Smith Jurriaansz and Daniel Verweij had been searched by Company soldiers without any rightful reason. The protesting burghers felt that this was a clear case of intimidation by the Company administration and called on the States-General to save them from harm. A third petition dated 29 December 1784 reiterated the previous two and argued that the burghers should be allowed to have their meetings and draw up petitions because they had no intention of undertaking anything that would threaten the Dutch Republic. This document also asked that a direct line of communication be opened between the States-General and the protesters without interference from the Company.[29]

Knowing that their requests were unlikely to be met by the VOC while it was in charge of the Cape, the burghers needed to take matters in their own hands. They decided to send a delegation to the Dutch Republic to present their case directly to the members of the States-General. On 13 February 1785 four delegates were elected: Marthinus Adrianus Bergh as leader, Johannes Roos (an elder brother of Tieleman Roos), Johannes Henricus Redelinghuijs and Johannes Augustus Bresler.[30] On 22 February 1785, the Council of Policy dealt with a request from Marthinus Adrianus Bergh asking for permission to go to the Dutch Republic. He stated that the administration of his investments and other business in the Netherlands required his presence in person. He also wanted to take two of his children to arrange for their education and study.[31] The requests of the other three delegates came before the Council of Policy on 15 March 1785. Each of them wrote that they needed to take care of family and other affairs in the Netherlands. Johannes Roos wanted to take his wife and four or five children

---

29 Beyers 1967:89–90.
30 Council of Policy. *Meetings of Burgher representatives: Resolutions C 2687,* Cape Town: WCARS, 1785.02.13, 80–90.
31 Council of Policy. *Resolutions C 168,* Cape Town: WCARS, 1785.02.22, 208–214.

with him and Johannes Henricus Redelinghuijs asked for permission to travel with his wife. The government granted the requests.[32]

The betrayal

Soon after the four Cape burgher delegates arrived in the Republic, cracks began to appear in their united front. Redelinghuijs wrote that with hindsight it had never been the intention of Marthinus Adrianus Bergh to co-operate with the burgher delegation. Bergh 'had most likely already before his departure from the Cape plotted to outright hoodwink and deceive his fellow delegates'.[33] Bergh's treacherous attitude seemingly became known when on 26 December 1785 an advertisement appeared in the *Leydse Courant*.[34] This was Bergh's attempt to distance himself from *Nederlandsch Afrika*, the pamphlet that had been published in 1783. Bergh stated that he had discovered that many people in the Dutch Republic thought he was the writer. This concerned him because, according to him, it contained many untruths and misconceptions about the Cape settlement. He denied being the author or that he had in any way contributed to the pamphlet. Redelinghuijs and his fellow delegates were highly upset. In their view Bergh had labelled the burgher protests and complaints illegal, and with that he had broken his solemn oath to defend and present the burgher cause to his best ability. To make matters worse, he had called the VOC government officials 'honourable' (*braaf*). In short, Bergh had committed 'perjury and unholy treason'.[35]

Even though Bergh's advertisement can be considered unwise and unfortunate in the light of his role as appointed leader of the Cape burgher protesters, it really was just a notice stating that he had not been involved in the production of *Nederlandsch Afrika* and not much more than that. But perhaps, being a former Company official, he was never fully trusted and his actions had finally confirmed the suspicions of his fellow delegates. With Redelinghuijs in the forefront, they did not hesitate to sideline Bergh. They immediately drafted a contra-advertisement which was published in the *Zuid-Hollandsche Courant* on 2 January 1786.[36] They publicly condemned Bergh's actions as 'surreptitious, treasonous and indiscreet'. Redelinghuijs accused Bergh of publishing his advertisement to gain favour with the decision-makers within the Company, because he wanted to be appointed

---

32 Council of Policy. *Resolutions C 168*, Cape Town: WCARS, 1785.03.15, 248–258.
33 Redelinghuijs 1792:26.
34 Ibid 123–124.
35 Ibid 26–27.
36 Ibid 125–131.

to the important and powerful post of Independent Fiscal of the Cape settlement, which had become vacant after the death of Jan Jacob Serrurier in May 1785.[37] Attempts by Bergh to apologise were futile. His fellow delegates had made up their minds and decided to remove Bergh as their leader. The Committee of Representatives at the Cape was informed accordingly and was told to ratify this decision, otherwise the delegates would resign their commission.[38] And thus the involvement of Marthinus Adrianus Bergh in the burgher protests ended.

The remaining delegates continued the work they were supposed to do on behalf of the burghers of the Cape settlement. In May 1785, the Dutch States-General received the three petitions that had been prepared by the protesters during December 1784. With the help of legal advisers, the delegates then prepared a further petition to the Dutch States-General, which was submitted on 4 April 1786.[39] In this document the familiar burgher complaints were once more described. But it also made a very clear appeal to the States-General to remove control of the Cape settlement from the VOC. The burghers further requested that the States-General undertake a thorough investigation of the oppressive conditions under which they were forced to live.

The members of the States-General passed the request on to their fellow regents in the VOC and asked for an explanation. But the VOC directors were not keen to comply. They had taken a final decision about the Cape burgher complaints, which was officially confirmed at their meeting of the first week of July 1785. There was to be no major change from the earlier position of December 1783. The only concession they made was that the Cape burghers would be permitted to sell as much of their produce to passing ships as they could and what remained would be bought by the Company at prices determined annually by a committee consisting of three VOC officials and three burghers. This was as much free trade as the Company would allow. With this the VOC directors felt that they had dealt with the burgher complaints extensively and sufficiently. A decision having been made, certain policies had been implemented which needed time to come to fruition. The directors simply refused to revisit the issue.[40]

The Cape burgher cause was dealt a further blow in 1786. In March of that year the VOC directors implemented a decision to make up

---

37 Ibid 27–31; Council of Policy. *Resolutions C 168*, Cape Town: WCARS, 1785.06.17, 494.
38 Redelinghuijs 1792:36–37.
39 Council of Policy. *Burgher Complaints C 2678*, Cape Town: WCARS, 10–38;
   Redelinghuijs 1792:133–150.
40 Redelinghuijs 1792:151–152; Beyers 1967:105–106.

the Council of Justice with six VOC officials and six burghers.[41] Among the six permanently appointed burgher councillors were Christiaan George Maasdorp and Gerrit Hendrik Meijer, protest leaders of 1779 and members of the Committee of Representatives elected in November 1784. Johannes Henricus Redelinghuijs could not understand why these burghers, who had committed themselves to the burgher cause repeatedly and had opposed the 'wicked' Company regime, had chosen to voluntarily become associated with that very government and accept these positions. According to him, they were hypocrites and traitors, who had now entered their names on the 'roll of rogues'.[42] That leaders of the burgher malcontents had crossed over to the other side had to have a negative effect on the protest movement, in Redelinghuijs' opinion. It would not take long, he argued, before their 'patriotic zeal had cooled down'.[43]

Redelinghuijs was right. With the appointment of some of their own as permanent burgher councillors, the 'matadors behind the scenes' had accomplished, at least in part, what they had set out to do in the 1770s: to have a presence in the administration and a firm foot in the door to power. For them it was no longer necessary to continue with the protests. They immediately ensured that further action came to a grinding halt.

In a letter to the delegates dated 29 June 1786, the Committee of Representatives withdrew the delegates' authority to represent the Cape protesters. They were instructed to cease their actions and to hand over their documents to the attorneys. The delegates felt as if they had been stabbed in the back. They were infuriated but had no intention of ending their mission.[44]

The protest leaders may have had an inkling that this would be the reaction, but they had an ace up their sleeves. They cut off all financial support to the delegates. Before the elected delegates left the Cape, firm financial arrangements had been made. It was decided to pay them an annual stipend as well as the costs of passage and other expenses. The protesting burghers had pledged to raise a sum of 50 000 guilders for this, which was to be administered by the Committee of Representatives. This undertaking was subsequently firmly and solemnly sworn to in two statements in March and April 1785.[45] The promise to 'honestly and soundly' ensure that this financial agreement was adhered to was 'ratified in triplicate' by 94 wealthy

41 Council of Policy. *Resolutions C 171*, Cape Town: WCARS, 1786.03.05, 28–29.
42 Redelinghuijs 1792:42–44.
43 Ibid 49.
44 Ibid 49–57.
45 Ibid 113–117.

and prominent burghers.[46] Redelinghuijs and his colleagues thus left the Cape in complete confidence that they would be financially secure while they were lobbying for the burgher cause in the Republic. It never entered their minds that the honourable burghers would 'stain with indelible disgrace' their solemn oath.[47] Yet that is exactly what happened: all financial support was ceased immediately. The final accounts were made up on 8 May 1788.[48] The Cape delegates were forced to use up their own capital for their living expenses and finally were reduced to begging from friends.

The Committee of Representatives acted ruthlessly and rejected requests even from their relatives. Redelinghuijs' wife, Maria Elisabeth de Villiers, wrote a heartrending personal letter to her uncles, who were members of the Committee, in which she sketched the terrible conditions in which she and her husband had to live because of the betrayal of the Representatives, and she asked them with 'bleeding heart' to step in and resume the payments.[49] It was all to no avail.

It was hard for Johannes Henricus Redelinghuijs to accept that by 1787 the Cape burgher protests had run their course. The movement so enthusiastically revived in 1784 had failed to achieve anything significant, unlike the powerful men behind it. They really did not care about the burgher complaints, but only their personal gain. They had no qualms about letting the protest movement implode. All Redelinghuijs could do was to publish his feelings of frustration and utter betrayal in his book *De Eerloosheid Ontmaskerd*.

---

46 Ibid 114–115.
47 Redelinghuijs 1792:19–20.
48 Council of Policy. *Burgher Complaints C 2678*, Cape Town: WCARS, 97–102.
49 Redelinghuijs 1792:196–198.

CHAPTER 12

Not Cape Patriots

The term 'Cape Patriots', as a reference to the protesters of 1779 and beyond, was highlighted by South African historian Coenraad Beyers in his two studies of the protest movement. The first was published in 1929.[1] Almost 40 years later, he wrote the second and extended edition of this work.[2] The opening lines of both books read:

> *The researcher of the history of the origins of the Afrikaner nation will find his attention particularly captivated by the ongoing agitation and turmoil which is detected among a considerable portion of the colonists of South Africa during the last quarter of the 18th century; namely, predominantly among the burghers who generally called themselves Patriots.*[3]

Since the publication of Beyers' studies, the political conflict in the Cape settlement during the 1770s and 1780s has consistently been referred to as the uprising of the Patriot movement, while it also has been described as a struggle between dissatisfied burghers and an oppressive VOC administration. This book has shown that the latter description is inaccurate. In this closing chapter I argue that the portrayal of the protests as a Patriot movement is erroneous, too.

The Dutch Patriots

The Dutch 'Patriot movement' was the manifestation of a phenomenon which occurred in many cities in the Dutch Republic in the 1780s. There, it was essentially a protest by Dutch burghers against the position and centralist rule of the *stadholder*, the Prince of Orange, and the oligarchy of regents. The movement pleaded for political reforms, more rights for the burghers, and for a restoration of the local autonomy of the cities.[4]

---

1 Beyers 1929.
2 Beyers 1967.
3 Beyers 1929:xvi; 1967:19.
4 The literature on the Dutch Patriot movement is extensive: De Wit, CHE. 1974. *De Nederlandse Revolutie van de Achttiende Eeuw 1780–1787*. Oirsbeek: H.J.J. Lindelauf; Schama, S. 1977. *Patriots and Liberators: Revolution in the Netherlands 1780–1813*. New York/Amsterdam: Harper Perennial; Te Brake, WP. 1985. Popular politics and the Dutch

In the Dutch Republic, popular discontent with the growing influence of the Orange *stadholder* in local and provincial politics had been festering for several decades. But the position of the *stadholder* seemed untouchable because, through a well-developed patronage system, he had obtained extensive powers and authority throughout the Republic and he could count on a network of support among local regents. Then, in 1780 the Republic was drawn into a war with England. Dutch smugglers in the Caribbean were supporting American rebels against the British, and the accusation by the English that Dutch representatives were negotiating with American colonists set the sparks flying.

The Fourth Anglo-Dutch War turned out to be a major political and economic debacle for an already struggling Republic. Somebody had to be held responsible and the natural focus of the blame became *Stadholder* Willem V, who was also Captain-General of the army and Admiral-General of the navy. In September 1781, a minor member of the gentry in the province Overijssel, Joan Derk van der Capellen, distributed his *Letter aan het volk van Nederland* (Letter to the people of the Netherlands). This passionate and inflammatory pamphlet was severely critical of the *stadholder* and argued that the many domestic problems of the Republic were the consequences of the uncontrolled lust for power of the Prince of Orange and his regent cronies. Van der Capellen called on the people of the Netherlands to liberate themselves from this yoke in a peaceful manner by means of freely elected burgher committees supported by free militias.

The pamphlet resonated with the Dutch people and after 'a period of politicization and initial mobilization primarily in opposition to the Prince of Orange (1782–1784), the Patriots only gradually radicalized their demands and challenged the old-regime oligarchy ... (1784–1786)'.[5] From 1782 the *stadholder* began to lose his grip over local politics in the important province of Holland. His control over the military garrison in The Hague was removed, after which he retreated to his estates in the east of

---

Patriot revolution. In *Theory and Society* 14(2): 199–222; Prak, M. Citizen radicalism and democracy in the Dutch Republic: The Patriot movement of the 1780s. In *Theory and Society* 20(1): 73–102; Jacob, MC & Mijnhardt WW (eds). 1992. *The Dutch Republic in the Eighteenth Century. Decline, Enlightenment and Revolution.* Ithaca, NY: Cornell University Press; Klein, SRE. 1995. *Patriots Republikanisme: Politieke Cultuur in Nederland (1766–1787).* Amsterdam: Amsterdam University Press; Wilschut, A. 2000. *Goejanverwellesluis: De Strijd tussen Patriotten en Prinsgezinden, 1780–1787.* Hilversum: Verloren. A compelling biography of the life and times of one of the main Patriots, Joan Derk van der Capellen tot den Pol is: Hella S. Haasse. 1989. *Schaduwbeeld of Het Geheim van Appeltern. Kroniek van Een Leven.* Amsterdam: Querido.

5   Te Brake 1985:202.

the Netherlands. He was finally stripped of his titles of Captain-General and Admiral-General in 1786. The regents who supported the *stadholder* found themselves powerless against the Patriots and their burgher militia. They were either replaced or forced to give in to the burghers' demands.

In June 1787, the Patriots overplayed their hand by briefly detaining the wife of Willem V, Wilhelmina of Prussia, at Goejanverwellesluis. She was on her way to the province of Holland to garner support for her husband. After being stopped in her tracks and being forced to return to Nijmegen, she informed her brother, the king of Prussia, of her humiliating experience. Soon after, Prussian forces invaded the Republic and ensured that the *stadholder* and his Orangist supporters were restored to power. This effectively meant the end of Patriot resistance.

A Cape parallel?

When one reads Beyers' book, there can be no doubt that he views the Cape protesters as the same as those in the Netherlands. He quotes Dutch historian Nicolas Japikse, who commented on his work: 'The Cape also had its Patriot movement'.[6] And later he writes that 'Patriotic ideas had reached distant South Africa and there had worked powerfully in the consciousness of the Cape burghers' to move them to take up their fight against a system of Company maladministration'.[7] The problem with this statement is that there is simply not sufficient proof that the Dutch Patriot ideals indeed were prevalent among Cape burghers (see Chapter 8). Documents such as the 1779 *Memorie* produced by the movement do not support this. The Cape protests were lacklustre in comparison to similar events in the towns and cities in the Dutch Republic, where petitions had thousands of signatures, the protests were huge, and there were threats to change the regent administrations with the support of military force.

One of Beyers' arguments to bolster his claim that the Cape Patriots were associated with the Dutch Patriots was that the leaders of the Cape protesters linked up with prominent Patriots in the Netherlands and sought their support.[8] But he mixed up the various stages of the protest. All the material he used to support his argument referred to the second delegation of Cape burghers, which was sent to the Dutch Republic in 1785 as a response to the decision of the VOC directors in 1783, and not to the first one of 1779. The first burgher delegation never tried to connect with Dutch

---

6 Beyers 1967:21.
7 Ibid 213.
8 Ibid 211–213; see also Schutte 1974:69.

Patriots, and the documents they produced never contained a stance against the *stadholder* and regents. If anything, they were seeking their support rather than risking the success of their mission by opposing them.

By the time the second group of Cape burgher emissaries arrived in the Netherlands the situation there had changed considerably. The Dutch Patriot unrest was well and truly under way, and the leaders of this movement began to pay some attention to the turmoil in the Cape settlement. But this was more a case of circumstance than kindred spirits. The VOC was in severe financial trouble in 1783 and the directors were forced to ask the States-General for a bail-out, reasoning that the Company was of enormous benefit to the economic well-being of the Republic. The news that the VOC had asked for financial assistance unleashed a flood of reaction in the Netherlands. Many there agreed that perhaps some form of financial help would be appropriate, but also pointed out that the Company directors had brought their misfortunes upon themselves. They had been greedy and had failed to put proper measures in place, both in patria and in the overseas settlements, which could have saved the Company from the situation it found itself in. Some even went as far as demanding that the Company be put under the supervision of the Dutch state. This measure was partly implemented in 1786 with the establishment of a *Vijfde Departement* (Fifth Department), which was added to the Amsterdam Chamber and which had six directors appointed by the States-General. It was supposed to seek a solution to the troubles of the VOC, which could include austerity measures.[9] The criticism of the VOC by the Dutch Patriots was part of their overall strategy of opposition to the *stadholder*. As chief director, he was easily identified with the Company, which was condemned for its incompetent management of finances and of overseas settlements.[10]

The above set of circumstances drew the attention of the Dutch Patriots to the overseas Company settlements, including the Cape. In 1783, the first references to the problems of the burghers in the Cape settlement appeared in Dutch pamphlets and newspapers. The 1779 *Memorie* was made public in the Republic and *Nederlandsch Afrika* appeared. Naturally the information about the ineptitude of Company officials, and by association that of the Dutch regents, was a welcome source of information to the Patriots. It was used to support the argument that, if the States-General did not step in and make sure that the Company respected the rights of the burghers, there would be a revolution like the one in America, and the Cape would be lost

---

9 Schutte 1974:41–54; Gaastra 1991:164–168.
10 Schutte 1974:76–77; Gaastra 1991:164.

to the Republic. This would have major adverse economic consequences for the Netherlands and its overseas empire. There was sympathy for the Cape burgher protests among the Dutch Patriots, but it seemed that the Patriots mainly drew on the complaints of the Cape burghers for their own purposes and used them as a tool with which to lash out at the VOC directors, regents and ultimately the *stadholder*.[11] The scope of the involvement of Dutch Patriots with the Cape malcontents did not go much further, and there were no attempts to equate the Cape conflict with the Patriot struggle in the Republic. The Patriot discourse about the burghers of the Cape was one-sided and produced only in the Netherlands. There were no signs that anything came from, or even resonated in, the Cape settlement itself.

This was certainly not because of a lack of effort on the part of the one Cape delegate possessed with revolutionary passion: Johannes Henricus Redelinghuijs. After booting out Marthinus Adrianus Bergh in December 1785, he took over leadership of the burgher delegation to the Netherlands and reached out to Patriot leaders. In February 1786 the Cape delegates wrote a letter to Robert Jasper van der Capellen, a cousin of Joan Derk van der Capellen, who had died in 1784, and leader of the Dutch Patriots in the eastern Dutch provinces. In this letter they implored him to also 'have an eye for the well-being of the thousands of Burghers in the settlements' and asked him to speak for the Cape burghers when burgher matters were discussed by the provincial States.[12]

Redelinghuijs took inspiration from the enlightened pamphlets appearing in the Netherlands in the documents and petitions he wrote on behalf of the Cape burgher protesters. He may have wanted to establish a sense of affiliation to the Dutch Patriots, but he was working on his own. Redelinghuijs was almost solely responsible for the 1778 pamphlet and the documents which were produced during the Cape protests in 1785. He may have invoked the Patriot ideals, but these found no fertile ground among Cape burghers. There simply was no 'powerful working of Patriotic ideas' among Cape burghers, as Coenraad Beyers would have us believe.

The difference between a Patriot and a patriot

One could forgive Beyers for naming the Cape protesters 'Patriots', because this label was used in various documents relating to the troubles, only not with his preferred meaning. What is confusing is that both supporters and opponents of the protest movement in the Cape claimed to be patriots,

---

11 Schutte 1974:76–86.
12 Council of Policy. *Burgher Complaints C 2678*, Cape Town: WCARS, 1786.02.28, 7–8.

which gives rise to the question of who the real patriots were and what they understood the term to mean.

The Cape protesters regularly held collections of money with which they supported their efforts and which paid for the delegation that was sent to the Netherlands to represent them. Above one of the collection lists, dated January 1781, the wording 'every true patriot' appeared.[13] And in March 1781, Governor Van Plettenberg wrote in his official response to the burgher complaints: '[T]hose residents of this settlement, who have shown their dissatisfaction for a while now, for that reason appropriated for themselves the honourable name of Patriots.'[14] Van Plettenberg implied that he did not agree with this epithet.

The meaning of the word 'patriot' went through several changes in the Dutch Republic during the seventeenth and eighteenth centuries. At first, patriots were considered to be supporters of the Prince of Orange against the Spanish king and his oppressive rule. But after the Dutch Republic was established, dissatisfaction with the consecutive *stadholders* of the Orange family grew as people realised that they and the regent rulers might not have the best intentions for the residents of the country. By the middle of the eighteenth century a shift had taken place and opponents of the *stadholder* were called patriots. By that time the word also had an apparent and undeniable moral connotation. The earlier, more neutral, meaning of 'patriot', to imply a 'fellow countryman' or 'townsman', had changed to describe a person who loved his fatherland and who championed the rights and liberties of its residents. A person like that became a 'good patriot'. Over time the word 'good' fell away, because the appellation 'patriot' alone had become enough to denote the righteous and noble understanding of the word.[15]

The burgher protesters of the Cape settlement certainly saw themselves as this respectable kind of patriot. This is evident in their 1779 petition in which they went to great lengths to make it clear that they had no intention to change or challenge the VOC government as such. They were, however, very concerned about the general state of decay and the abuse of power by some officials and wanted to bring this to the attention of the Company directors. They claimed to be motivated by a love for their country, which they would not see go to wreck and ruin.

That the supporters of the Cape protest movement believed this

---

13 Council of Policy. *Burgher Complaints C 2674*, Cape Town: WCARS, 84.
14 Council of Policy. *Cape Disputes C 2692*, Cape Town: WCARS, 10.
15 De Jong, EH. 2014. *Weldenkende Burgers en Oranjeliefhebbers. Patriotten en Prinsgezinden in Leiden, 1775–1795*. Hilversum: Verloren, 26–31.

virtuous description applied to themselves is evident from an incident that occurred in 1780 and about which burgher militia member Jan Willem Lutsche complained to the Council of Justice.[16] Lutsche had tried to persuade other burghers to recant their decision to sign the protest petition against the government. His activities in this regard were not appreciated, as he discovered while on Burgher Watch duty on 21 September 1780. Corporal Hendrik Hermanus Bos entered the Burgher Watch House and called out 'Mameluk' and then 'Mameluk Koning'. Lutsche had explained in his statement to the Council that 'a Mameluk according to divine scripture is a liar, a traitor, and a denouncer of God'. Clearly this serious insult was directed at Lutsche, because his nickname was Koning.[17] And when he told Bos that a Mameluk was a rogue, Bos replied: 'Koning, you are double that.' Shortly after this exchange, Bos said to everyone present: '[A]ll worthy burghers must come to the back to hear what I will announce.' He then started to read the statement of the daughter of Carel Hendrik Buijtendag about the events that had befallen her father in January 1779, but he was stopped by the officer in charge, Lieutenant Dirk Gijsbert van Reenen. That same evening Bos sent his slave to the Burgher Watch House with two bottles of wine to 'drink to the health of all worthy Burghers'. The Dutch term used by Bos was 'brave', which in the eighteenth century meant 'being honourable'. What this episode illustrated is that only burghers who truly supported the burgher cause could be regarded as worthy and valuable members of the community.

But not everybody agreed with this, as is clear from the 1780 pamphlet *Nieuw-Jaars Gift*.[18] In the first paragraph the author explained that he had long been silent and observed what had happened, but that he now 'as a pure and real Patriot also had to appear on stage'. He went on to describe the blessed and prosperous state of the Cape settlement, of which he was undeniably an extremely proud resident. He even agreed that the treatment meted out to Carel Hendrik Buijtendag was detestable and deserved to be challenged. But then he utterly condemned the methods used by the protesters and blamed them for the terrible divisions that had appeared in the Cape community. The author launched into a vicious personal attack on burgher leaders like Cornelis van der Poel. He called them rebels and described them as 'those who so inappropriately dared to call themselves patriots'. The author signed off as 'den Welmeenende Patriot' (the true Patriot). He asked the readers of his pamphlet to pass it on, especially to those who had remained loyal to

---

16 Council of Policy. *Burgher Complaints C 2674*, Cape Town: WCARS, 55–69.
17 Council of Policy. *Cape Disputes C 2691*, Cape Town: WCARS, 241–242.
18 Verbatim Copies, *VC 161*, *Nieuw-Jaars Gift aan de Caabse burgerije*, Cape Town: WCARS.

their lawful government. This opponent of the burgher protest movement was adamant that those burghers who followed the protest leaders had forgotten their oath to respect and obey their rightful government and were therefore not worthy of being called patriots. That term was reserved only for 'honour and oath loving residents'. In his pamphlet the term 'patriot' was also associated with being a respectable resident who loved his country and would not deliberately cause any harm to it. For the author of *Nieuw-Jaars Gift* this meant that he should not join the burgher cause and oppose the Cape government.

From the discourse that took place in the early 1780s it becomes evident that the term 'patriot', as used by both supporters and opponents of the burgher protest movement, meant nothing more than 'a person who strongly loves and supports his country'. And both sides felt that they were more sincere than the other in this sentiment. The protesters did not associate themselves with Dutch Patriots in any shape or form. The only connection between the Cape protest movement and the Dutch Patriot movement was that they were contemporaneous. The use of the 'Cape Patriot' label, in the meaning that Beyers intended, therefore, leads to unnecessary confusion about the motives of the burghers who opposed the administration. The group of disgruntled burghers were not Patriots but should more appropriately and simply be called protesters.

A rebuttal to Coenraad Beyers

So why was Coenraad Beyers so determined to prove that the burghers were Patriots? Paging through his book *Die Kaapse Patriotte*, one comes across the photo of Paul Kruger, who was president of the Zuid-Afrikaansche Republiek from 1883 to 1900. It seems out of place in a book about a late eighteenth-century Cape conflict, but it makes sense when reading Beyers' conclusion, in which he states that from among the ranks of the Patriots emerged the noble figures of Piet Retief and Paul Kruger.[19] In his book, Beyers demonstrated a deep admiration for the Afrikaner *volk* who had dared to stand up to the British oppressors, even though all odds were stacked against them. Beyers published two versions of his book: the first (1929) in the midst of a growing Afrikaner nationalism; the second (1967) when this nationalism had been established.

In Beyers' view, the protesters of the eighteenth-century Dutch settlement fitted perfectly into the nineteenth-century Afrikaner struggle

---

19 Beyers 1967:291.

narrative. And in a highly politicised and troubled twentieth-century South Africa, the Cape protests were regarded by some, mostly Afrikaner, historians as the first awakening of Afrikaner nationalism. André du Toit and Hermann Giliomee, for example, wrote: 'From the 1780s on, however, there is an unbroken sequence of Afrikaner political thinking on a variety of themes and issues.'[20] The story of the downtrodden Cape burghers who were brave enough to stand up against an unsympathetic and autocratic VOC government, in their view, was a perfect focal point in the history of the Afrikaner people and the struggle with their foes, the British colonial rulers.

In the second version of *Die Kaapse Patriotte*, Coenraad Beyers added a chapter on the political protests of Afrikaners in Graaff-Reinet and Swellendam against the British authorities, after 1795. He claimed that the farmers of the frontier felt threatened by encroaching Xhosas and Khoikhoi. (In fact, it was the other way around.) According to Beyers, the farmers were standing up for their right to defend themselves, and in doing so were continuing where the burgher protesters of the southwestern Cape had left off. He then stated that the Patriot ideals of the eighteenth-century protesters lived on in all Afrikaner protests and struggles that happened in the nineteenth and early twentieth century.

But in comparing the burgher protests and political dynamics in Dutch Africa with the struggle of an Afrikaner nation in British Africa, Beyers and others were trying to connect two different worlds. They were seeking to backdate nineteenth-century history to the eighteenth century, which has resulted in a gross distortion of the historical narrative. The Little Tradition of Dutch popular politics, in which groups of people tried to persuade authorities that they had justifiable complaints that should be resolved, had very little in common with a nationalist group standing against colonial oppressors from another country. In the Little Tradition, the disgruntled protestors did not try to liberate themselves or be independent. They were attempting to negotiate within the existing system to bring about change. Beyers was determined to show something that was not there, and unfortunately this exercise has obscured what really happened during the Cape burgher protests.

One facet of the conflict that Beyers correctly emphasises is the persistent attempts by Cape burghers to have their rights recognised. There was a basic disagreement between VOC and burghers about the status of the burghers. The Company directors argued that the group was subject to

---

20 Du Toit, A & Giliomee, H. 1983. *Afrikaner Political Thought: Analysis & Documents. Volume One: 1780–1850*. Johannesburg & Cape Town: David Philip, xxx.

the commercial needs of the VOC, while the burghers felt that they should have the same rights and position as their Dutch counterparts. Undoubtedly this disagreement was a source of constant tension. It remained below the surface in times of prosperity, but the moment burghers began to feel the pinch of straitened circumstances, their call for an appreciation of their rights became stronger and they began to push against the boundaries dictated by the Company administration. But their discontent did not cause any significant disturbance until leading members of the burgher community wanted to wrest economic and political control from the ruling faction. They saw the arrest of Carel Hendrik Buijtendag as a wonderful opportunity to exploit the strained relations between VOC officials and the burgher group, and years of conflict followed. As a contemporary observer described it: 'some people among us have managed to use this incident to pretend concern about the violation of burgher freedom while wanting to achieve far different private and hidden agendas.'[21]

There was no need to be more specific about the men behind the scenes, because they were well known in the small settlement. They were prominent notables and businessmen. But what is more, they and their adversaries were members of the same group: the ruling elite. The structure of government was inhabited by members of two separate groups — Company officials and burghers — who were bound together by a common interest in the economic progress of the settlement, which they achieved by extracting the labour and skills of non-elites. In the Cape situation these were mostly slaves, who had no rights whatsoever and were not a political force that needed to be reckoned with. But there was also a group of VOC employees and burghers who were at the bottom of the social and economic ladder. And then there was the middle class, which mostly supported the elite, who could be expected to safeguard their financial security and from whom they gained commercial benefits. It was not difficult for the farmers and entrepreneurs at the top to secure the support of burghers directly below them on the social ladder. The members of the elite did not have much to fear from non-elites. This lack of pressure from below left space and opportunity for ruling factions to challenge each other. And that happened at the Cape on at least two major occasions. The first big upset was the uprising against Governor Willem Adriaan van der Stel, who, blinded by hubris, had managed to antagonise some influential burghers. The second

---

21 Verbatim Copies, *VC 161, Nieuw-Jaars Gift aan de Caabse burgerije*, Cape Town: WCARS, 5.

time that the stability of the elite was threatened was of course during the conflict of the 1770s and 1780s.

The Cape conflict was rooted in a Dutch social and political system where self-serving regents lived in a world of privilege and presumption. It also resulted from the structurally unsound economic conditions dominated by a short-sighted trading company which did little to control its corrupt officials and their burgher clientele. The Cape conflict was a fight between leading members of the ruling elite for access to the centre of power, not a heroic struggle of burgher underdogs against oppressive Company rulers. The conflict can only be explained within the context of the historic world of the United Netherlands as it had developed over centuries, and as such it mirrored the past and was not a window on the future.

BIBLIOGRAPHY
Primary sources

Western Cape Archives and Record Service, Cape Town (WCARS)

C — Council of Policy

C 1:	Resolutions, 1657
C 27:	Resolutions, 1709
C 49:	Resolutions, 1719
C 104:	Resolutions, 1737
C 106:	Resolutions, 1738
C 110:	Resolutions, 1739
C 115:	Resolutions, 1740
C 117:	Resolutions, 1741
C 120:	Resolutions, 1742
C 123:	Resolutions, 1745
C 125:	Resolutions, 1747
C 130:	Resolutions, 1752
C 132:	Resolutions, 1754
C 141:	Resolutions, 1763
C 143:	Resolutions, 1765
C 144:	Resolutions, 1766
C 145:	Resolutions, 1767
C 147:	Resolutions, 1769
C 148:	Resolutions, 1770
C 150:	Resolutions, 1772
C 151:	Resolutions, 1773
C 152:	Resolutions, 1774
C 153:	Resolutions, 1775
C 154:	Resolutions, 1776
C 155:	Resolutions, 1777
C 156:	Resolutions, 1778
C 157:	Resolutions, 1779
C 158:	Resolutions, 1780
C 159–160:	Resolutions, 1781
C 164:	Resolutions, 1783
C 165:	Resolutions, 1783
C 166:	Resolutions, 1784
C 168:	Resolutions, 1785
C 171:	Resolutions, 1786
C 174:	Resolutions, 1787
C 177:	Resolutions, 1788
C 184:	Resolutions, 1789
C 190:	Resolutions, 1790
C 197:	Resolutions, 1791
C 222:	Resolutions, 1794
C 274:	Incoming Correspondence, 1640

C 1101:	Petitions and Nominations, 1739–40
C 1118:	Petitions and Nominations, 1751
C 1151:	Petitions and Nominations, 1769–70
C 1166:	Petitions and Nominations, 1776
C 1171–1172:	Petitions and Nominations, 1778
C 1173:	Petitions and Nominations, 1779
C 2057:	Journals, 1779
C 2282:	Proclamation (Placaat) Books, 1745–53
C 2283:	Proclamation (Placaat) Books, 1754–60
C 2285:	Proclamation (Placaat) Books, 1766–75
C 2661:	Oath Book, 1692–1748
C 2662–2664:	Oath Book, 1748–95
C 2665:	Burgher Complaints, 1716–82
C 2673:	Burgher Complaints, 1777–79
C 2674:	Burgher Complaints, 1779–84
C 2675:	Burgher Complaints, 1785–88
C 2678:	Burgher Complaints, 1786–88
C 2687:	Meetings of Burgher representatives: Resolutions, 1784–85
C 2689–2696:	Cape Disputes (Kaapsche Geschillen) I–IV, 1779–85

CJ — Council of Justice, Civil Section

CJ 876:	Original Rolls and Minutes, 1782
CJ 883:	Original Rolls and Minutes, 1789
CJ 910:	Original Rolls and Minutes, 1802
CJ 1125:	General Series, 1782
CJ 1163:	General Series, 1789
CJ 1221:	General Series, 1794–95
CJ 1329:	General Series, 1802
CJ 1336:	General Series, 1802

BKR — Burgher Military Council

| BKR 2: | Minute Book, 1767–93 |
| BKR 8: | Diverse Papers, 1768–95 |

BRD — Burgher Council

BRD 1:	Minute Book, 1769–85
BRD 24:	Tax lists, 1773, 1783
BRD 25:	Tax lists, 1787–95

M — Miscellaneous documents

| M 41: | Funeral Notices, 1760 |

MOOC — Master of the Supreme Court

MOOC 14/62, vol. 13,20: Liquidation and Distribution Accounts, 1784–85

MOOC 14/66, vol. 14,10: Liquidation and Distribution Accounts
MOOC 37/1/39:   Wills General Series, 1764

Non-public records

A 583:   FS Malan 1795–1941
A 731–8/1:   Lodge de Goede Hoop, 1772–78

VC — Verbatim copies

VC 161   Nieuw-Jaars Gift aan de Caabse burgerije

Secondary sources

Adams, J. 2005. *The Familial State: Ruling Families and Merchant Capitalism in Early Modern Europe*. Ithaca, NY: Cornell University Press.

Adhikari, M. 2010. *The Anatomy of a South African Genocide: The Extermination of the Cape San Peoples*. Cape Town: UCT Press.

Armstrong, JC & Worden, NA. 1989. The slaves, 1652–1834. In R Elphick & H Giliomee (eds). *The Shaping of South African Society, 1652–1840*. 2nd ed. Cape Town: Maskew Miller Longman, 109–183.

Baartman, T. 2011. Fighting for the Spoils. Cape Burgerschap and Faction Disputes in Cape Town in the 1770s. PhD thesis, University of Cape Town.

Baartman, T. 2012. Protest and Dutch burgher identity. In N Worden (ed.). *Cape Town between East and West. Social Identities in a Dutch Colonial Town*. Cape Town: Jacana, 65–83.

Baartman, T. 2012. *The most precious possession: Honour, reputation and the Cape Council of Justice*. Unpublished paper, Cape Town.

Baartman, T. 2015. Dutch contexts of Cape burgher protests. *New Contree* 73: 40–60.

Barend-Van Haeften, M. 2003. *De Kaap: Goede Hoop halverwege Indie. Bloemlezing van Kaapteksten uit de Compagniestijd*. Hilversum: Verloren.

Bernard, F. 1783. *Nederlandsch Afrika; of Historisch en Staatkundig Tafereel van den Oorsprongelyken Staat der Volkplantinge aan de Kaap de Goede Hoop, Vergeleeken met den Tegenwoordigen Staat dier Volkplantinge, In't licht Gegeeven naar het Handschrift van een wel onderricht Opmerker*.

Beyers, C. 1967. *Die Kaapse Patriotte gedurende die Laaste Kwart van die Agtiende Eeu en die Voortlewing van hul Denkbeelde*. 2nd ed. Pretoria: Van Schaik.

Biewenga, A. 1999. *De Kaap de Goede Hoop. Een Nederlandse Vestigingskolonie, 1680–1730*. Amsterdam: B Bakker.

Biewenga, AW 2002. Kerk in een volksplanting: de Kaap de Goede Hoop. In GJ Schutte (ed). *Het Indisch Sion. De Gereformeerde Kerk onder de Verenigde Oost-Indische Compagnie*. Hilversum: Verloren, 201–218.

Blockmans, WP. 1988. Alternatives to monarchical centralisation: The great tradition of revolt in Flanders and Brabant. In HG Koenigsberger (ed.). *Republiken und Republikanismus im Europa der Frühen Neuzeit*. Munich: Oldenbourg Wissenschaftsverlag, 145–154.

Blussé, L. 1985. An insane administration and insanitary town: The Dutch East India Company and Batavia (1619–1799). In R Ross & GJ Telkamp (eds). *Colonial Cities: Essays on Urbanism in a Colonial Context.* Dordrecht: Martinus Nijhoff Publishers, 65–85.

Blussé, L. 1997. *Bitters Bruid. Een Koloniaal Huwelijksdrama in de Gouden Eeuw.* Amsterdam: Uitgeverij Balans.

Blussé, L. 2008. *Visible Cities. Canton, Nagasaki, and Batavia and the Coming of the Americans.* Cambridge, Massachusetts: Harvard University Press.

Boers, WC. 1779. *Verantwoording Gedaan Maken, ende aan de Wel-Edele Hoog Achtbare Heeren Bewindhebberen der Generale Geoctroyeerde Oost-Indische Compagnie der Vereenigde Nederlanden.* Cabo de Goede Hoop.

Böeseken, AJ. 1964. *Simon van der Stel en sy Kinders.* Cape Town: Nasou.

Böeseken, AJ. 1977. *Slaves and Free Blacks at the Cape, 1658–1700.* Cape Town: Tafelberg.

Böeseken, AJ. 1981. The arrival of Van Riebeeck at the Cape. In CFJ Muller (ed.). *Five Hundred Years. A History of South Africa.* 3rd ed. Pretoria/Cape Town/ Johannesburg: H&R Academica, 18–35.

Böeseken, AJ. 1981. The Company and its subjects. In CFJ Muller (ed.). *Five Hundred Years. A History of South Africa.* 3rd ed. Pretoria/Cape Town/Johannesburg: H&R Academica, 63–79.

Böeseken, AJ. 1981. The settlement under the Van der Stels. In CFJ Muller (ed.). *Five Hundred Years. A History of South Africa.* 3rd ed. Pretoria/Cape Town/ Johannesburg: H&R Academica, 35–50.

Boone, M & Prak, M. 1995. Rulers, patricians and burghers: The great and little traditions of urban revolt in the Low Countries. In K Davids & J Lucassen (eds). *A Miracle Mirrored: The Dutch Republic in European Perspective.* Cambridge: Cambridge University Press, 99–134.

Borschberg, P. 2010. Ethnicity, language and culture in Melaka after the transition from Portuguese to Dutch rule (seventeenth century). *Journal of the Malaysian Branch of the Royal Asiatic Society* 83(2): 93–117.

Boshoff, WH & Fourie, J. 2008. Explaining ship traffic fluctuations in the early Cape settlement: 1652–1793. *Stellenbosch Economic Working Papers 01/08.*

Boshoff, WH & Fourie, J. 2008. The significance of the Cape trade route to economic activity in the Cape colony: A medium-term business cycle analysis. *Stellenbosch Economic Working Papers 23/08.*

Bosma, U & Raben, R. 2008. *Being 'Dutch' in the Indies: A History of Creolisation and Empire, 1500–1920.* Singapore: NUS Press.

Bosman, DB & Thom, HB (eds). 1955. *Daghregister Gehouden by den Oppercoopman Jan Anthonisz Van Riebeeck, Deel II, 1665–1658.* Kaapstad: Van Riebeeck Vereniging .

Boxer, CR. 1973. *The Dutch Seaborne Empire, 1600–1800.* Harmondsworth: Penguin Books.

Broers, EJ. 1996. Vrij onbeschaamt en zeer oneerbiedig. De civiele rechtspraak in Brabantse beledigingszaken in de zeventiende en achttiende eeuw. *Leidschrift* 12(1): 55–72.

Brouwer, J. 2014. *Levenstekens: Gekaapte Brieven uit het Rampjaar 1672.* Hilversum: Verloren.

Bruijn, I. 2009. *Ship's Surgeons of the Dutch East India Company. Commerce and the Progress of Medicine in the Eighteenth Century.* Leiden: Leiden University Press.

Bruijn, JS, Gaastra, FS & Schöffer, I. 1987. *Dutch-Asiatic Shipping in the 17th and 18th Centuries.* Vol. I. The Hague: Rijks Geschiedkundige Publicatien.

Cairns, M. 1974. *Cradle of Commerce. The Story of Block B.* Cape Town: Woolworths.

Cantwell, A-M. 2008. Landscapes and other objects: Creating Dutch New Netherland. *New York History* Fall: 315–345.

Coetzee, L-M. 2015. Fashion and the world of the women of the VOC official elite. *New Contree* 73: 61–87.

Coolhaas, WPh. 1966. De carriere van Jan van Riebeeck. *Historia* 1: 18–35.

Cruywagen, WA. 2007. *Die Cruywagens van Suid-Afrika 1690–1806.* Vanderbijlpark: Kleio.

Dash, M. 2002. *De Ondergang van de Batavia. Het Ware Verhaal.* Amsterdam/ Antwerpen: de Arbeiderspers.

De Bont, F. 2014. *Op het Vorige is Genoeg Gewoekerd. Een Vergelijkende Studie naar Voedseloproeren in Holland, 1690–1770.* Nijmegen: Radboud Universiteit.

De Jong, EH. 2014. *Weldenkende Burgers en Oranjeliefhebbers. Patriotten en Prinsgezinden in Leiden, 1775–1795.* Hilversum: Verloren.

De Jong, J. 1987. *Een Deftig Bestaan. Het Dagelijks Leven van Regenten in de 17de en 18de Eeuw.* Utrecht/Antwerpen: Kosmos.

De Villiers, CC & Pama, C. 1981. *Geslagsregisters van die Ou Kaapse Families.* 2 vols. Cape Town and Rotterdam: AA Balkema.

De Wet, GC. 1981. *Die Vryliede en Vryswartes in die Kaapse Nedersetting, 1657–1707.* Kaapstad: Historiese Publikasie-Vereniging.

De Zwart, P. 2013. Real wages at the Cape of Good Hope: A long-term perspective, 1652–1912. *Tijdschrift for Sociale en Economische Geschiedenis / The Low Countries Journal of Social and Economic History* 10(2): 28–58.

Dekker, R. 1982. *Holland in Beroering. Oproeren in de 17e and 18e Eeuw.* Baarn: Ambo.

Den Heijer, HJ. 2005. *De Geoctroieerde Compagnie: De VOC and de WIC als Voorlopers van de Naamloze Vennootschap.* Deventer: Kluwer.

Dick, AL. (n.d.) Gewone lesers aan die Kaap, c. 1680 tot 1850. *LitNet Akademies* 9(2): 21.

Dooling, W. 2005. The making of a colonial elite: Property, family and landed stability in the Cape colony, c. 1750–1834. *Journal of Southern African Studies* 31(1): 147–162.

Douma, J. 1999. Slavernij in het Nederlandse koloniale tijdperk: Waarom een zwarte bladzijde? *Transparant* 10(3): 4–12.

Du Toit, A & Giliomee, H. 1983. *Afrikaner Political Thought: Analysis & Documents. Volume One: 1780–1850.* Johannesburg & Cape Town: David Philip.

Du Toit, PS. 1937. *Onderwys aan die Kaap onder die Kompanjie 1652–1795.* Cape Town and Johannesburg: Juta.

Elphick, R. 1985. *Khoikhoi and the Founding of White South Africa.* 2nd ed. Johannesburg: Ravan Press.

Elphick, R. & Giliomee, H. 1989. (eds). *The Shaping of South African Society, 1652–1840*, 2nd ed. Cape Town: Maskew Miller Longman.

Elphick, R & Giliomee, H. 1989. The origins and entrenchment of European dominance at the Cape, 1652–c. 1840. In H Giliomee & R Elphick (eds). *The Shaping of South African Society, 1652–1840*. Cape Town: Maskew Miller Longman, 521–566.

Elphick, R & Shell, R. 1989. Intergroup relations: Khoikhoi, settlers, slaves and free blacks, 1652–1795. In H Giliomee & R Elphick (eds). *The Shaping of South African Society, 1652–1840*. Cape Town: Maskew Miller Longman.

Emmer, P & Gommans, J. 2012. *Rijk aan de Rand van de Wereld. De Geschiedenis van Nederland Overzee 1600–1800*. Amsterdam: Bert Bakker.

Fourie, J. November 2012. New estimates of settler life span and other demographic trends in South Africa, 1652–1948. *Stellenbosch Economic Working Papers 20/12* (November 2012).

Fourie, J. 2013. The remarkable wealth of the Dutch Cape Colony: Measurements from eighteenth-century probate inventories. *Economic History Review* 66(2): 419–448.

Fourie, J. 2014. Subverting the standard view of the Cape economy: Robert Ross's cliometric contribution and the work it inspired. *Stellenbosch Economic Working Papers 16*.

Fourie, J. 4 April 2016. *Three hundred years of firm myopia*. https://johanfourie.com/2016/04/12/three-hundred-years-of-firm-myopia-2/ (Accessed 13 April 2019).

Fourie, J & Cilliers, J. 2014. Die huwelikspatrone van Europese setlaars aan die Kaap, 1652–1910. *New Contree* 69: 45–70.

Fourie, J & Green, E. March 2013. The missing people: Accounting for indigenous populations in Cape colonial history. *Economic Research Foundation Southern Africa (ERSA) Working Paper 425*.

Fourie, J & Von Fintel, D. 2010. The dynamics of inequality in a newly settled, pre-industrial society. *Cliometrica* 4(3): 229–267.

Fourie, J & Von Fintel, D. 2011. A history with evidence: Income inequality in the Dutch Cape Colony. *Economic History of Developing Regions* 26: 16–48.

Frijhoff, W. 2008. Was the Dutch Republic a Calvinist community? The state, the confessions, and culture in the early modern Netherlands. In A Holenstein, T Maissen & M Prak (eds). *The Republican Alternative. The Netherlands and Switzerland Compared*. Amsterdam: Amsterdam University Press, 99–122.

Gaastra, FS. 1991. *De Geschiedenis van de VOC*. Zutphen: Walburg Pers.

Gaastra, FS & Bruijn, JR. 1993. The Dutch East India Company's shipping, 1602–1795, in a comparative perspective. In FS Gaastra & JR Bruijn (eds). *Ships, Sailors and Spices. East India Companies and Their Shipping in the 16th, 17th and 18th Centuries*. Amsterdam: NEHA, 177–182.

Giliomee, H. 2003. *The Afrikaners. Biography of a People*. Charlottesville/Cape Town: Tafelberg/University of Virginia Press.

Groeneboer, K. 1998. *Gateway to the West. The Dutch Language in Colonial Indonesia 1600–1950. A History of Language Policy*. Amsterdam: Amsterdam University Press.

Groenewald, G. 2007. A Cape bourgeoisie?: Alcohol, entrepreneurs and the evolution of an urban free-burgher society in VOC Cape Town. In N Worden (ed.).

Contingent Lives. Social Identity and Material Culture in the VOC World. Cape Town: University of Cape Town Press, 278–304, 279.

Groenewald, G. 2009. An early modern entrepreneur: Hendrik Oostwald Eksteen and the creation of wealth in Dutch colonial Cape Town, 1702–1741. *Kronos* 35(1): 7–31.

Groenewald, G. 2009. *Kinship, Entrepreneurship and Social Capital: The Making of a Free-Burgher Community in Eighteenth-Century Cape Town.* Cape Town: Unpublished paper.

Groenewald, G. 2010. Slaves and Free blacks in VOC Cape Town, 1652–1795. *History Compass* 8/9: 964–983.

Groenewald, G. 2012. More comfort, better prosperity, and greater advantage: Free burghers, alcohol retail and the VOC authorities at the Cape of Good Hope, 1652–1680. *Historia* 57(1): 1–21.

Groenveld, S et al. 1979. *De Kogel door de Kerk? De Opstand in de Nederlanden en de Rol van de Unie van Utrecht 1559–1609.* Zutphen: Walburg Pers.

Guelke, L. 1989. Freehold farmers and frontier settlers, 1657–1780. In R Elphick & H Giliomee (eds). *The Shaping of South African Society, 1652–1840.* 2nd ed. Cape Town: Maskew Miller Longman, 66–108.

Guelke, L & Shell, R. 1983. An early colonial landed gentry: Land and wealth in the Cape colony, 1682–1731. *Journal of Historical Geography* 9: 265–286.

Hall, M. 1994. The secret lives of houses: Women and gables in the eighteenth-century Cape. *Social Dynamics* 20(1): 1–48.

Havemann, R & Fourie, J. 2015. The Cape of Perfect Storms: Colonial Africa's first financial crash, 1788–1793. *ERSA Working Paper 511.*

Heese, HF. 2005. *Groep sonder grense: Die rol en status van die gemengde bevolking aan die Kaap, 1652–1795.* Cape Town: Protea Boekhuis.

Heese, JA 1971. *Die Herkoms van die Afrikaner 1657–1867.* Cape Town: AA Balkema.

Heese, JA & Lombard, RTJ. 1986–2007. *Suid-Afrikaanse Geslagregisters / South African Genealogies.* Pretoria and Stellenbosch: GSSA.

Hirschman, AO. 1970. *Exit, Voice, and Loyalty: Responses to Decline in Firms, Organizations, and States.* Cambridge MA: Harvard University Press.

Hoonhout, B. 2018. Vrije grond onbereikbaar voor slaven. In M 't Hart et al (eds). *Wereldgeschiedenis van Nederland.* Amsterdam: Ambo Anthos, 323–328.

Huigen, S. 2009. *Knowledge and Colonialism: Eighteenth-century Travellers in South Africa.* Leiden: Brill.

Hulshof, A. 1941. H.A. van Reede tot Drakenstein, journaal van zijn verblijf aan de Kaap. *Bijdragen en Mededeelingen van het Historisch Genootschap* Utrecht, 62.

Huygen van Linschoten, J. 1596. *Itinerario, Voyage ofte Schipvaert van Jan Huygen van Linschoten naar Oost ofte Portugaeis Indien.* Amsterdam: Cornelis Claesz.

Iliffe, J. 1987. *The African Poor. A History.* Cambridge, NY: Cambridge University Press.

Israel, JI. 1995. *The Dutch Republic. Its Rise, Greatness and Fall 1477–1806.* New York: Oxford University Press.

Keegan, TJ. 1996. *Colonial South Africa and the Origins of the Racial Order.* Charlottesville, VA: University of Virginia Press.

Kuijpers, E & Prak, M. 2002. Burger, ingezetene, vreemdeling: Burgerschap in Amsterdam in de 17e en 18e Eeuw. In J Kloek & K Tilmans (eds). *Burger. Een Geschiedenis van het Begrip 'Burger' in de Nederlanden van de Middeleeuwen tot de 21ste Eeuw*. Amsterdam: Amsterdam University Press, 113–132.

Lachmann, R. 2000. *Capitalists in Spite of Themselves. Elite Conflict and Economic Transitions in Early Modern Europe*. Oxford: Oxford University Press.

Leupen, P. 2002. Burger, stad en zegel: Een verkenning door de Noordelijke Nederlanden. In J Kloek & K Tilmans (eds). *Burger. Een Geschiedenis van het Begrip 'Burger' in de Nederlanden van de Middeleeuwen tot de 21ste Eeuw*. Amsterdam: Amsterdam University Press, 19–31.

Lurvink, K. 2019. Underwriting slavery: Insurance and slavery in the Dutch Republic (1718–1778). *Slavery & Abolition* 40(2).

Malan, A. 2012. The cultural landscape. In N Worden (ed.). *Cape Town between East and West. Social Identities in a Dutch Colonial Town*. Cape Town: Jacana, 1–25.

Malherbe, VC. 2006. Illegitimacy and family formation in colonial Cape Town, to c. 1850. *Journal of Social History* 19(4): 1153–1176.

Mentzel, OF. 1921. *A Geographical-Topographical Description of the Cape of Good Hope*. Vol. I. Cape Town: The Van Riebeeck Society.

Mentzel, OF. 1925. *A Geographical-Topographical Description of the Cape of Good Hope*. Vol. II. Cape Town: The Van Riebeeck Society.

Mentzel, OF. 2006. *Life at the Cape in the Mid-Eighteenth Century: The Biography of Rudolph Siegfried Allemann*. Cape Town: The Van Riebeeck Society.

Mijnhardt, WW. 1998. The Dutch Republic as a town. *Eighteenth-Century Studies* 31(3): 345–348.

Morris, M. 2004. *Every Step of the Way: The Journey to Freedom in South Africa*. Cape Town: HSRC Press.

Nas, PJM. 1990. The origin and development of the urban municipality in Indonesia. *Sojourn* 5(1): 86–112.

Newton-King, S. 2012. Family, friendship and survival among freed slaves. In N Worden (ed.). *Cape Town between East and West. Social Identities in a Dutch Colonial Town*. Cape Town: Jacana, 153–175.

Oosterhoff, JL. 1985. Zeelandia, a Dutch colonial city on Formosa (1624–1662). In J Ross & GJ Telkamp (eds). *Colonial Cities: Essays on Urbanism in a Colonial Context*. Dordrecht: Martinus Nijhoff Publishers, 51–63.

Oostindie, G. 2008. Migration and its legacies in the Dutch colonial world. In G Oostindie (ed). *Dutch Colonialism, Migration and Cultural Heritage*. Leiden: Brill, 1–22.

Oostindie, G. & Roitman, JV. 2014. Introduction. In G Oostindie & JV Roitman (eds.). *Dutch Atlantic Connections, 1680–1800: Linking Empires, Bridging Borders*. Leiden: Brill, 1–21.

Panhuysen, L. 2011. *Een Nederlander in de Wildernis. De Ontdekkingreizen van Robert Jacob Gordon (1743–1795) in Zuid-Afrika*. Amsterdam: Nieuw Amsterdam/ Rijksmuseum.

Penn, N. 1999. *Rogues, Rebels and Runaways: Eighteenth-Century Cape Characters*. Cape Town: David Philip.

Prak, M. 1997. Burghers into citizens: Urban and national citizenship in the Netherlands during the revolutionary era (c. 1800). *Theory and Society* 26(4): 403–420.

Prak, M. 1997. Burghers, citizens and popular politics in the Dutch Republic. *Eighteenth-Century Studies* 30(4): 443–448.

Prak, M. 1999. *Republikeinse Veelheid, Democratisch Enkelvoud. Social Verandering in het Revolutietijdvak, 's-Hertogenbosch 1770–1820*. Nijmegen: SUN.

Prak, M. 2000. The Dutch Republic's city-state culture (17th–18th centuries). In MH Hansen (ed). *A Comparative Study of Thirty City-State Cultures. An Investigation Conducted by the Copenhagen Polis Centre* Copenhagen: Kongelige Danske Videnskabernes Selskab, 343–358.

Prak, M. 2005. *The Dutch Republic in the Seventeenth Century: The Golden Age*. Cambridge: Cambridge University Press.

Prak, M. 2008. Challenges for the Republic: Coordination and loyalty in the Dutch Republic. In A Holenstein, T Maissen & M Prak (eds). *The Republican Alternative. The Netherlands and Switzerland Compared*. Amsterdam: Amsterdam University Press, 51–74.

Raben, R. 1993. Klein Holland in Azie. Ideologie en pragmatisme in de Nederlandse koloniale stedebouw, 1600–1800. *Leidschrift* 9(2): 45–63.

Raben, R. 2013. A new Dutch imperial history? Perambulations in a prospective field. *BMGN – Low Countries Historical Review* 128(1): 5–30.

Ramerini, M. (n.d.) *Africa. List of Dutch colonial forts and possessions*. https://www.colonialvoyage.com/africa-list-dutch-colonial-forts-possessions (Accessed 12 April 2019).

Redelinghuijs, JH. 1792. *De Eerloosheid Ontmaskerd*. Amsterdam: JA Crajenschot.

Redelinghuijs, JH. 1795. *Memorie Overgegeeven aan de Provisioneele Representanten des Volks van Holland*. Amsterdam: PE Briet.

Redelinghuijs, JH. 1796. *Verzameling van Authentieke en Andere Stukken, Betreffende de Zaak tusschen Johannes Henricus Redelinghuijs aan de Eene, en Pieter Paulus en Reinier Leendert Bouwens aan de Andere Zijde; Voorzien van Ophelderende Aanmerkingen*. Amsterdam: PE Briet.

Roorda, DJ. 1978. *Partij en Factie. De Oproeren van 1672 in de Steden van Holland en Zeeland, een Krachtmeting tussen Partijen en Facties*. Groningen: Wolters-Noordhoff.

Ross, R. 1983. The rise of the Cape gentry. *Journal of Southern African Studies* 9(2): 193–217.

Ross, R. 1985. Cape Town (1750–1850): Synthesis in the dialectic of continents. In RF Betts, R Ross & GJ Telkamp (eds). *Colonial Cities. Essays on Urbanism in a Colonial Context*. Dordrecht: Martinus Nijhoff Publishers, 105–121.

Ross, R. 1989. Structure and culture in pre-industrial Cape Town: A survey of knowledge and ignorance. In WG James & M Simons (eds). *The Angry Divide. Social & Economic History of the Western Cape*. Cape Town: David Philip, 40–46.

Ross, R. 1989. The Cape of Good Hope and the world economy, 1652–1835. In R Elphick & H Giliomee (eds). *The Shaping of South African Society, 1652–1840*. 2nd ed. Cape Town: Maskew Miller Longman, 243–280.

Ross, R. 1993. *Beyond the Pale. Essays on the History of Colonial South Africa*. Hanover and London: Wesleyan University Press.

Ross, R. 1993. The 'white' population of South Africa in the eighteenth century. In R Ross. *Beyond the Pale. Essays on the History of Colonial South Africa*. Hanover and London: Wesleyan University Press, 125–137.

Ross, R. 1999. *Status and Respectability in the Cape Colony, 1750–1870: A Tragedy of Manners*. Cambridge: Cambridge University Press.

Ross, R. 2007. Sumptuary laws in Europe, the Netherlands and the Dutch colonies. In N Worden (ed). *Contingent Lives. Social Identity and Material Culture in the VOC World*. Cape Town: UCT Press, 382–390.

Ross, R & Schrikker, A. 2012. The VOC official elite. In N Worden (ed). *Cape Town between East and West. Social Identities in a Dutch Colonial Town*. Cape Town: Jacana, 26–44.

Ross, R & Telkamp, GJ (eds). 1985. *Colonial Cities: Essays on Urbanism in a Colonial Context*. Dordrecht: Martinus Nijhoff Publishers.

Saldanha, A. 2010. The Itineraries of Geography: Jan Huygen van Linschoten's *Itinerario* and Dutch expeditions to the Indian Ocean, 1594–1602. *Annals of the Association of American Geographers* 101(1): 149–177.

Schama, S. 1987. *The Embarrassment of Riches: An Interpretation of Dutch Culture in the Golden Age*. New York: Vintage.

Schoeman, K. 2001. *Armosyn van die Kaap: Die Wêreld van 'n Slavin 1652–1733*. Cape Town: Human & Rousseau.

Schoeman, K. 2004. *'n Duitser aan die Kaap, 1724–1765. Die Lewe en Loopbaan van Hendrik Schoeman*. Pretoria: Protea Book House.

Schoeman, K. 2007. *Early Slavery at the Cape of Good Hope 1652–1717*. Pretoria: Protea Book House.

Schoeman, K. 2013. *Here & Boere. Die Kolonie aan die Kaap onder die Van der Stels, 1679–1712*. Pretoria: Protea Boekhuis.

Schoeman, K. 2013. *Twee Kaapse Lewens. Henricus & Aletta Beck en die Samelewing van hul Tyd, 1702–1755*. Pretoria: Protea Boekhuis.

Schoeman, K. 2016. *Swanesang. Die Einde van die Kompanjiestyd aan die Kaap, 1771–1795*. Pretoria: Protea Boekhuis.

Schutte, G. 2008. What was Pieter Cloete doing in Utrecht? *Quarterly Bulletin of the National Library of South Africa* 62(1): 36–43.

Schutte, GJ. 1974. *De Nederlandse Patriotten en de Koloniën. Een Onderzoek naar hun Denkbeelden en Optreden, 1770–1800*. Groningen: HD Tjeenk Willink.

Schutte, GJ. 1982. *Briefwisseling van Hendrik Swellengrebel jr oor Kaapse Sake 1778–1792*. Cape Town: Van Riebeeck-Vereniging.

Schutte, GJ. 1989. Company and colonists at the Cape, 1652–1795. In R Elphick & H Giliomee (eds). *The Shaping of South African Society, 1652–1840*. 2nd ed. Cape Town: Maskew Miller Longman, 283–323.

Schutte, GJ. 2002. De kerk onder de Compagnie. In GJ Schutte (ed.). *Het Indisch Sion. De Gereformeerde Kerk onder de Verenigde Oost-Indische Compagnie*. Hilversum: Verloren, 43–64.

Schutte, GJ. 2002. *Het Calvinistisch Nederland. Mythe en Werkelijkheid*. Hilversum: Verloren.

Schutte, GJ. 2003. *Hendrik Cloete, Groot Constantia and the VOC*. Cape Town: Van Riebeeck Society.

Shell, R. 1994. *Children of Bondage. A Social History of the Slave Society at the Cape of Good Hope, 1652–1838*. Johannesburg: Witwatersrand University Press.

Shell, R. & Dick, A. 2012. Jan Smiesing, Slave Lodge schoolmaster and healer, 1697–1734. In N Worden (ed.). *Cape Town between East and West. Social Identities in a Dutch Colonial Town*. Cape Town: Jacana. 128–152.

Singh, A. 2007. Fort Kochin in Kerala 1750–1830. The Social Condition of a Dutch Community in an Indian Milieu. PhD thesis, Leiden University.

Spierenburg, P. 1984. *The Spectacle of Suffering: Executions and the Evolution of Repression: From a Preindustrial Metropolis to the European Experience*. Cambridge: Cambridge University Press.

Staring, A. 1948. *Damiaan Hugo Staring. Een Zeeman uit de Achttiende Eeuw. 1736–1783*. Zutphen: Thiem.

Stavorinus, JS. 1798. *Voyages to the East Indies*. Trans. SH Wilcocke. Vol. III. London: GG & J Robinson.

Stell, G. 2013. Cape Malay Dutch: The missing link between Cape Dutch pidgin and Afrikaans? *Revue Belge de Philologie et d'Histoire* 91(3).

Stell, G. 'Dutch and colonial expansion: Different contact settings, different linguistic outcomes. Introduction. In: *Revue belge de philologie et d'histoire*, tome 91, fasc 3, (2013), 689–694.

Streng, JC. 1997. *Stemme in Staat: De bestuurlijke Elite in de Stadsrepubliek Zwolle 1579–1795*. Hilversum: Verloren.

Swanepoel, C. 2017. The Private Credit Market of the Cape Colony, 1673–1834: Wealth, Property Rights, and Social Networks. PhD thesis, Stellenbosch University.

't Hart, M. 1995. The Dutch Republic: The Urban Impact upon Politics. In K Davids & JA Lucassen. *A Miracle Mirrored: The Dutch Republic in European Perspective*. Cambridge: Cambridge University Press, 57–98.

Taylor, JG. 1983. *The Social World of Batavia. European and Eurasian in Dutch Asia*. Madison: University of Wisconsin Press.

TEPC Transcription Team. 2007. The inventories of the Orphan Chamber of the Cape of Good Hope. In N Worden (ed.). *Contingent Lives. Social Identity and Material Culture in the VOC World*. Cape Town: UCT Press, 3–22.

Trotter, HM. 2001. Sailors as scribes: Travel discourse and the (con)textualization of the Khoikhoi at the Cape of Good Hope, 1649–90. *The Journal of African Travel-Writing* Vols 8 & 9: 30–44.

Ulrich, N. 2015. Cape of storms: Surveying and rethinking popular resistance in the eighteenth-century Cape colony. *New Contree* 73: 16–39.

Ulrich, N. 2016. Rethinking citizenship and subjecthood in Southern Africa: Khoesan, labor relations, and the colonial state in the Cape of Good Hope (c. 1652–1815). In E Hunter (ed.). *Citizenship, Belonging and Political Community in Africa: Dialogues between Past and Present*. Athens, Ohio: Ohio University Press, 43–73.

Van den Heuvel, C. 2011. Multi-layered grids and Dutch town planning. Flexibility and temporality in the design of settlements in the Low Countries and Overseas. In P Lombaerde & C van den Heuvel (eds). *Early Modern*

Urbanism and the Grid. Town Planning in the Low Countries in International Context. Exchanges in Theory and Practice 1550–1800, Architectura Moderna 10. Turnhout: Brepols. 27–44.

Van den Tol J. 2016. *Petitions and the duality of structure: Lobbying in the seventeenth-century Dutch Atlantic* in *The Many-Headed Monster.* https://manyheadedmonster.wordpress.com/2016/11/21/petitions-and-the-duality-of-structure-lobbying-in-the-seventeenth-century-dutch-atlantic/ (Accessed 30 July 2019).

Van der Heijden, M et al (eds). 2009. *Serving the Urban Community. The Rise of Public Facilities in the Low Countries.* Amsterdam: Amsterdam University Press.

Van der Walt, T. 2004. The German contribution to South African librarianship. *Innovation* 28: 41–51.

Van Deursen, AT. 2006. The Dutch Republic, 1588–1780. In JCH Blom & E Lamberts (eds). *History of the Low Countries.* Oxford, New York: Berghahn Books. 143–218.

Van Duin, PC & Ross, R. 1987. The economy of the Cape Colony in the eighteenth century. *Intercontinenta.* Leiden: Centre for the History of European Expansion.

Van Gelder, R. 1997. *Het Oost-Indisch Avontuur. Duitsers in Dienst van de VOC (1600–1800).* Nijmegen: SUN.

Van Gelder, R. Letters, journals and seeds: Forgotten Dutch mail in the National Archives in London. In N Worden (ed). 2007. *Contingent Lives. Social Identity and Material Culture in the VOC World.* Cape Town: UCT Press. 538–545.

Van Gelder, R. 2012. *Zeepost. Nooit Bezorgde Brieven uit de 17de en 18de Eeuw.* Amsterdam: Olympus.

Van Ledden, W-P. 2005. *Jan van Riebeeck tussen Wal en Schip. Een Onderzoek naar de Beeldvorming over Jan van Riebeeck in Nederland en Zuid-Afrika omstreeks 1900, 1950 en 2000.* Hilversum: Verloren.

Van Meeteren, A. 2006. *Op Hoop van Akkoord. Instrumenteel Forumgebruik bij Geschilbeslechting in Leiden in de Zeventiende Eeuw.* Hilversum: Verloren.

Van Nierop, HFK. 2000. Private interests, public policies: Petitions in the Dutch Repubic. In AK Wheelock & A Seeff (eds). *The Public and Private in Dutch Culture of the Golden Age.* London: Associated University Presses. 33–39.

Van Oers, R. 2000. *Dutch Town Planning Overseas during VOC and WIC Rule (1600–1880).* Zutphen: Walburg Pers.

Van Oers, R. 2012. *Landscape as guiding element in the design and planning of Dutch colonial settlements (1600–1800).* http://www.projetsdepaysage.fr/fr/landscape_as_guiding_element_in_the_design_and_planning_of_dutch_colonial_settlements_1600_1800_ (Accessed 14 April 2019).

Velema, WE. 2007. *Republicans: Essays on Eighteenth-Century Dutch Political Thought.* Leiden: Brill.

Velema, WRE. 1993. *Enlightenment and Conservatism in the Dutch Republic. The Political Thought of Elie Luzac (1721–1796).* Assen/Maastricht: Van Gorcum.

Vink, M. 2003. The world's oldest trade: Dutch slavery and slave trade in the Indian Ocean in the seventeenth century. *Journal of World History* 14(2): 131–177.

Wagenaar, G. 1976. Johannes Gysbertus van Reenen — Sy Aandeel in die Kaapse Geskiedenis tot 1806. MA dissertation, University of Pretoria.

Ward, K. 2009. *Networks of Empire: Forced Migration in the Dutch East India Company.* Cambridge: Cambridge University Press.

Ward, K. 2012. Southeast Asian migrants. In N Worden (ed.). *Cape Town between East and West. Social Identities in a Dutch Colonial Town.* Cape Town: Jacana. 84–100.

Ward, K. 2015. Patrimonialism, imperialism, and colonialism at the Cape of Good Hope under Dutch East India Company rule, c. 1652-1795. In M Charrad & J Adams (eds). *Patrimonial Capitalism and Empire. Political Power and Social Theory* Volume 28, 91–113.

Westra, PE. 2011. Boeke en boekversamelings tydens die Kompanjiesbewind aan die Kaap. *Quarterly Bulletin of the National Library of South Africa* 65(1&2): 42–50.

Weststeijn, A. 2019. Colonies of concord: Religious escapism and experimentation in Dutch overseas expansion, ca. 1650-1700. In J Spaans & J Touber (eds). *Enlightened Religion. From Confessional Churches to Polite Piety in the Dutch Republic.* Leiden: Brill. 104–130.

Wijsenbeek, T. 2007. Identity lost: Huguenot refugees in the Dutch Republic and its former colonies in North America and South Africa, 1650 to 1750: a comparison. In N Worden (ed.). *Contingent Lives. Social Identity and Material Culture in the VOC World.* Cape Town: UCT Press. 91–109.

Worden, N. 1998/1999. Space and identity in VOC Cape Town. *Kronos* 25: 72–87.

Worden, N. 2007. New approaches to VOC history in South Africa. *South African Historical Journal* 59(1): 3–18.

Worden, N. (ed). 2007. *Contingent Lives. Social Identity and Material Culture in the VOC World.* Cape Town: UCT Press.

Worden, N. (ed.). 2012. *Cape Town between East and West. Social Identities in a Dutch Colonial Town.* Cape Town: Jacana.

Worden, N. 2012. Introduction. In N Worden (ed). *Cape Town between East and West. Social Identities in a Dutch Colonial Town.* Cape Town: Jacana, ix–xxii.

Worden, N. November 2014. Cape slaves in the paper empire of the VOC. *Kronos* 40: 23–44.

Worden, N, Van Heyningen, E & Bickford-Smith, V. 1998. *Cape Town. The Making of a City.* Cape Town: David Philip Publishers.

INDEX

Page numbers in italics refer to illustrations